# The Ulysses Syndrome

## A Psychological Approach to Basque Migrations

**Current Research Series No. 14**

# The Ulysses Syndrome

A Pyschological Approach to Basque Migrations

**Edited by Joseba Atxotegi**

This book was published with generous financial support from the Basque Government.

Center for Basque Studies
University of Nevada, Reno
1664 North Virginia St.
Reno, Nevada 89557 USA
http://basque.unr.edu

Copyright © 2020 by the Center for Basque Studies and the University of Nevada, Reno
Series: Current Research Series, No. 14
Series Editor: Xabier Irujo
ISBN-13: 978-1-949805-13-0
All rights reserved.

Cover design by Matt Strelecki

LIBRARY OF CONGRESS CATALOGING-IN-PUBLICATION DATA:
Names: Atxotegi, Joseba, editor.
Title: The Ulysses syndrome : a psychological approach to Basque migrations / edited by Joseba Atxotegi.
Other titles: Psychological approach to Basque migrations
Description: Reno, Nevada : Center for Basque Studies, University of Nevada, Reno, 2019. | Series: Current Research Series ; no. 14 | Summary: "A book on the psychological condition of Ulysses syndrome, which ails immigrants. This is a condition which ails the Basque country as it accepts many immigrants and refugees"-- Provided by publisher.
Identifiers: LCCN 2019044093 | ISBN 9781949805130 (paperback)
Subjects: LCSH: Basques--Migrations. | Basque diaspora. | País Vasco (Spain)--Emigration and immigration--Psychological aspects. | Pays Basque (France)--Emigration and immigration--Psychological aspects. | Immigrants--France--Pays Basque--Psychology. | Immigrants--Spain--País Vasco--Psychology.
Classification: LCC DP302.B55 U49 2019 | DDC 305.899/92--dc23
LC record available at https://lccn.loc.gov/2019044093

Printed in the United States of America

# Contents

# PART I

# Foreword

This book has a double purpose. On the one hand, it aims to make known to scholars and to all those interested in Basque culture and society, the reality of Basque migrations from a psychological perspective. But, on the other hand, it also constitutes an attempt by the authors of the book, Basque researchers, professionals, and academics, to better understand the scope of the enormous importance that migrations have had in the cultural and social structuring of the Basque Country.

The book fundamentally collects the presentations made at a conference on this topic held on May 10, 2019 in the Aula Magna of the Faculty of Psychology of the University of the Basque Country. The conference was organized jointly with the Center for Basque Studies at the University of Nevada, Reno.

In the book, three great perspectives in relation to Basque migrations are addressed. First, the study of the experiences of the Basques and their descendants who have emigrated, especially in migration to America. Second, the study of the experiences of immigrants who have arrived in the Basque Country and who have experienced the process of social and cultural integration in the Basque Country. And third, the study of the current Basque migrations of the 21st century that have very different characteristics compared to those of previous times. As a whole, the book thus offers a complete vision of Basque migrations, taking the psychological and psychosocial perspective as the axis of the study. In addition, the book integrates contributions from different theoretical perspectives in the field of mental health (psychosocial, cognitive-behavioral, psychoanalytic, community, systemic), adding greater richness and plurality to the content addressed. It is interesting to see how the sense of belonging to a community can be a factor that favors dialogue and collaboration, not always easy, between professionals and academics.

It is important to note that the Basque Country has experienced intense emigraton and immigration movements simultaneously for more than a century, a phenomenon that occurs in very few societies. Thus, the United States has received millions of immigrants but has hardly experienced phenomena of emigration, human groups that have left the country in large numbers. Italy, to take another example, has experienced intense emigration, especially to the United States, but has received comparatively few immigrants. In the Basque case, the influence that this double experience of emigration and immigration has had on the psychological dynamics of society, being also a small country, deserves to be studied in depth. This book serves as an attempt to move in that direction.

The psychological study of migrations is a fairly recent area of research in psychiatry and psychology. Less than a century ago, the first studies on mental disorders in immigrants were published by a pioneer, the Norwegian psychiatrist, who emigrated to the United States, O. Odegård, who in the 1930s investigated the mental disorders stemming from the migrations of his compatriots to the US. In recent years, especially, there has been a great development of what we could call the new specialty within the area of psychology and mental health: the psychology and psychiatry of migration. To this specialty, Basque psychiatry has contributed the concept of the Ulysses Syndrome, used in the mental health work of immigrants in many countries.

The increase in social sensitivity for human rights has led us to approach migration in a more humane way. Hence we have developed the concept of the Ulysses Syndrome, studying how it affects mental health to live with fear, helplessness, social exclusion . . . unfortunately something common in many migrations.

Let us now comment briefly on the content of the book, which is divided into two main parts. The first one frames the content of the book at a historical and conceptual level. The second part delves into the issues raised and proposes a series of good practices.

This first part begins with the chapter, "The Children of Exile and the Ulysses Syndrome: The Memory of Pain", by Xabier Irujo which analyzes the hardships and sufferings of the Basque exile, especially in relation to the Spanish Civil War of 1936-1939 and the bombing of Gernika, one of the most dramatic events in Basque history.

Then in Chapter 2, "Basques that Come and Go, Basques from Oregon, Basques from Gabon: The Ulysses Syndrome in the Basque Migrations of Yesterday and Today," Joseba Atxotegi addresses the experiences of migration in an extreme situation in the history of Basque society. The text deals in a special way with the study of the very harsh personal circumstances experienced by the Basques who migrated as shepherds to the western United States, a true odyssey of loneliness and struggle against adversity.

Chapter 3, "Emigration as a Social Pathology: Impact, Causes, and Interpretations of the Basque Overseas Diaspora in the Nineteenth and Twentieth Centuries" by Oscar Alvarez-Gila, addresses fundamental Basque emigration to America, showing that it has had roots in the cultural and social ethos of the Basque people for hundreds of years and also analyzes the social and historical causes of this emigration.

Completing this first part of the book, Iñaki Markez's chapter "Migratory Policies and Institutional and Social Interventions Based on Human Rights" makes a complete analysis of the social and political factors related to the mental health of Basque migrants, pointing out the situations of helplessness experienced in many migrations.

In Part 2, entitled "Psychological and Psychosocial Studies on Basque Migrations: Recommendations of Good Practices in Mental Health in the Migration," the co-authors are more focused on the presentation their research, largely as professors and researchers.

In Chapter 5, "Psychological Support Program for Migratory Stress: A Pilot Study," Karmele Salaberría and Analia del Valle Sánchez address psychological intervention with immigrants with the Ulysses Syndrome. They show the efficacy of the techniques of intervention to help improve the mental health of immigrants.

Then in Chapter 6, "Acculturation Among Basques and Brazilians: Looking in the Mirror," Sonia de Luca, Nekane Basabe, and José Pizarro show the results of comparative research on identity and feelings of belonging between Basque and Brazilian migrations.

In Chapter 7, entitled "Immigrant Women Who Work as *Internas* and Mothers Who Are Here and There: A Critical Look from the Practice of Professional Intervention in Gipuzkoa," Katia Reimberg, Castello-Branco, and Heldy Soraya Ronquillo Peña show the difficulties in social integration, loneliness, and the experience of the Ulysses Syndrome in women who work in harsh conditions in the Basque Country.

In Chapter 8, "The Migratory Process and Psychological Adjustment among Recent Basque Immigrants in European Countries," Edurne Elgorriaga, Ainara Arnoso, and Izaskun Ibabe provide fundamental and often forgotten perspective: the Basque emigration continues, albeit to a much lesser extent, but in a context in which difficulties continue to exist in a world with ever-greater restrictions on migration.

In Chapter 9 "Migrations and Psychosocial Acculturation: The Case of the Basque Country," Nekane Basabe, Xabier Aierdi, and José Pizarro use their research on the psychosocial integration of immigrants to point out the importance of cultural factors in the integration of immigrants.

And finally in Chapter 10, "A Psychological and Psychosocial Analysis of the Radicalization of Young People of Immigrant Origin," Joseba Atxotegi analyzes the phenomenon of radicalization from the psychological perspective, pointing out that discrimination and barriers to integration are a very relevant breeding ground for radicalization.

# 1

# The Children of Exile and the Ulysses Syndrome

## The Memory of Pain

*Xabier Irujo*

The 160 shelters in Bilbao did not entail secure protection for the minors who were dying in alarming proportions because of the air-raids on open urban centers and without any military interest whatsoever, as in Gernika. This especially bloody bombardment convinced the Basque authorities to undertake a massive evacuation of minors to other points in Europe as the only effective measure to save their lives. Around 32,000 children were evacuated from Bizkaia between early May and August 1937, approximately 20 percent of all minors in the territory controlled by the Basque government. It was, without doubt, the biggest known operation of child evacuation in Europe to that time. In this context, on May 21, 1937, 3,860 children embarked in Bilbao on the *Habana* ship, with a capacity for 800 passengers, destined for the United Kingdom. They were accompanied by 200 teachers, priests, and assistants, and they arrived at the port of Southampton following a crossing of just under a day.

At the age of 80, María Luisa Patchett recalls how her home had been attacked by German planes:

> My mother had just had twins . . . she had them in the house and she used to listen for the planes coming over. She used to say to us: "Run . . . quick" . . . We used to hide and the planes [that] were coming over, they couldn't see us. . . . After they saw their house—where the babies were—catch fire following an air raid, Mother ran and we all ran with her terrified. She managed to save one of the twins . . . who is still alive but the other one died in the fire (quoted in Jahangir 2016).

In May 1937, several British news media published on their front pages the headline, "Terrorised as planes fly over tents," as the Basque children that were

FIGURE 1.1: The Habana, transporting 3,680 Basque refugee children to the United Kingdom in May 1937 on its arrival at the port of Southampton.

welcomed to the refugee camp in North Stoneham with an aerial flyover fled in all directions. They had been terrified by the air-raids they had experienced during a year of war in the Basque Country, and the local authorities had to put in practically a whole day's work in order to gather them up and calm them down.[1]

The pilots of an RAF base near the field had to be warned not to fly over the Eastleigh camp in order to avoid another child stampede. As the reporter for the *South Wales Argus* remarked, the children were so traumatized by the sight and even the sound of the planes that, when they flew overhead, they were frightened and "[w]henever one of these planes comes over we have to run about among them and shout 'Inglese' so that they will know the planes are not from the enemy" (quoted in Wade 2017). The refugees were at the time in canvas tents arranged in open fields and watched over by Boy Scouts and members of the Boys Brigade, but later the refugee children camps would be fenced in.

Besides the huge imprint that the war and the terror had left on them, these children were affected by what Joseba Atxotegi has termed the Ulysses Syndrome, an atypical set of depressive, nervous, dissociative, and somatic symptoms diagnosed in immigrants who have faced a multitude of extreme chronic stress factors stemming from the difficulties of the migratory process. These refugee children experienced multiple material losses and likewise the loss of their loved ones, and they lacked the support, status, and identity typical of minors in their own home. The massive evacuation of children in such a short space of time, and especially the traumatic migratory process, produced among these minors such intense levels of stress that in some cases it could even exceed their capacity to adapt, and it generated depressive symptoms among them (Atxotegi 2014, 18–23).

Among the elements that hinder the capacity to overcome the process of migratory affliction are separation from family and place of birth, the dangers of travel—often carried out in overcrowded ships—combined with the fear of being deported again to a war zone destroyed by bombing, lack of opportunities, and a complete lack of security and the feeling of being totally at the mercy of circumstance without the necessary parental support. To all this was added the perception—real or imagined—of suffering racial discrimination and social prejudice in the host country and the low or complete lack of competence in the language of that country, which is the principal element in the process of adaptation and assimilation to the new medium (ibid., 48–60).

As Atxotegi states,

> The symptoms of the syndrome include recurring fear and worry, tension, nervousness and irritability, disorientation, fatigue and insomnia, sadness, migraines, gastric and osteo-physical pains. These pains may affect the self-esteem of the person and generate a greater consumption of tobacco and alcohol as well as a decrease in their own productive capacity. Paraphrasing Homer's *Odyssey*, expatriates who find themselves in these circumstances find themselves seated on the banks of a river that is not theirs, without being able to stop weeping and spending hours yearning to return to their homes, ripping apart their spirits with tears, wails, and pains, and looking vainly toward the ocean that has brought them to this land.[2]

And, with the passing of years, when asked what their name was, they would respond that their name was no one "because no one is what everyone calls us."[3]

This was the situation for many of those children in North Stoneham. The poet of the Generation of 27, Luis Cernuda, worked there in what would be his first residence in exile. In his own words, "I did not know England, although it was a country that had interested me since childhood, most likely because of the attraction of opposites that is so vital in life, given that the tension between them is, at least in me, productive: my native south needed the north, to complete me" (Cernuda 1975, 919–20). There, the poet became a teacher to the young evacuees. One of them, José Sobrino Riaño, 15 years old and the son of a worker at the Altos Hornos de Bilbao foundry, fell ill with blood cancer just two or three days after his arrival and was sent to the John Radcliffe Hospital in Oxford. Lying there dying, he requested that Cernuda go to see him and recite a poem. On concluding, the child told him: "Now, please, don't go away, but I'm going to go back to the wall so you don't see me die" (quoted in Díaz Pérez 2011). And the child died.

Luis Cerneda recounts it thus: "You turned your head to the wall with the

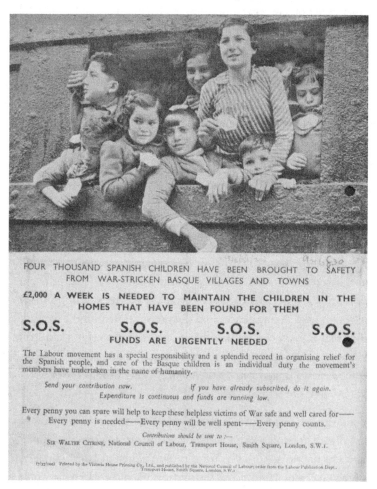

FIGURE 1.2: A flyer printed by the Victoria House Printing Co Ltd and published by the National Council of Labour, asking for funds to cover the needs of evacuated Basque children.

gesture of a child that feared demonstrating fragility in his desire. And the eternal long shadow covered you. You sleep deeply. And hear: I want to be with you: you're not alone" (Cernuda 1940, 207).

This happened on March 31, 1938. Cernuda visited his friend Rafael Martínez at Queen's Court and he told him the story with tears in his eyes.

> As soon as Luis saw him flanked by his sister and his mother (a last hope in the ocean) he told them what had happened with tears that he could not, however, repress, despite the intimate courage that it provoked in him to shed them. The three of them listened to him without saying a word, without interrupting him, astonished at Sobrino's story. Rafael's mother brought in a teapot and served four cups of tea. She also prepared a cheese sandwich, which Luis devoured in the blink of an eye. That is how hungry he was. Some minutes later, Cernuda told them that he had written a poem in honor of the child. Lola asked him to read it out. Luis took three sheets of paper out of his suitcase and read it out. In a short while he felt he needed some air or that something greater than him was overcoming him and stopping him from continuing. Nevertheless, he finished reading it out. As soon as he had finished, the four of them remained silent for a minute that seemed eternal. No one, not even Cernuda, knew how to react (Urroz 2012).

His friends attended the funeral in Rose Hill cemetery in Oxford on April 23 that same year.

The elegy to a dead Basque child in England expresses the desolation of any person, especially a minor, who could share that pain because they had experienced it themselves. In his poem, Cernuda speaks about the dead child through the earth that covers him, and he recalls his past days surrounded by the warmth of what had been, until that moment, his world, his home: "If I ever reach you beneath the earth, as young as your body, now covering a more far-reaching exile with death, the brief fleeting voice of friends, with a dark nostalgia, you perhaps may think that your life is a matter of forgetting" (Cernuda 1975, 180). Yet Cernuda concludes the poem by arguing convincingly that his life and, by extension, the experiences of his companions in exile, would not be abandoned and relegated to forgetting, because the poet himself is with him and will remember him: "Sleep soundly. And listen: I want to be with you; you're not alone" (Cernuda 1940, 207). The concern for the solitude of the dead and a dialogue with them is a theme in other works by Cernuda, but in this case the proximity of the writer and his interlocutor lends this poetic moment a significance that transcends the written word. And through his poetry we continue to remember that child in the North Stoneham camp called José Sobrino.

Many bitter memories have been registered in writing about the case of the bombing of Gernika and other tragic events in the war in the Basque Country, possibly in the thousands. In the specific case of Gernika, William Smallwood, nicknamed Egurtxiki by a group of Basque sheepherders in Idaho, collected the heartbreaking testimonies of 129 victims of the bombing (Smallwood 2012). Other testimonies come down to us via reporters who entered Gernika just hours after the last of the airplanes had abandoned the town. Such is the case of Maria Olabarria, who left us a shocking story:

> From where we were, we could see the bombs being dropped. The planes flew around overhead several times. It looked like they were looking for us. And it was true: they were looking for four women. They were there near a farmhouse. We ran toward the front door. It was locked. Then we huddled against the door frame, all seeking cover. I was in the middle. A plane flew over the farmhouse, shooting, with a machine-gun. It shot up the soil in front of us. Suddenly we heard an atrocious crunch: a bomb had dropped on the farmhouse. Trepidation forced me to throw myself to the ground amid stones and bricks. My older daughter, who was twenty-seven, died immediately, crushed. The other one, the youngest, who was going to get married, had enough time to grab my hand, squeeze it a little, and cry out "Oh!" She took a deep breath and, with her eyes fixed on mine, she died. I don't know how long I was there between my two dead daughters. Blood was pouring from the neck. After a while I was rescued.[4]

María Medinabeitia, who lost her mother in the Andra Mari air-raid shelter, also left her testimony:

> In Bilbao I saw the gravedigger of Gernika. I asked him if he had seen my mother. He said no. He added that in Gernika there were still many bodies that hadn't been identified, a lot—mostly body parts: heads, hands, legs, and so on—had been burned in fires that had broken out in the little Ibarra de San Juan square. The gravedigger calculated that more than two thousand individuals were dead in Gernika as a result of the bombing by Franco's planes (quoted in Gamboa and Larronde 2005, 174).

These are all pleas of pain, of memory, and of grief. Many oral and written testimonies of this historical event have been registered, but the pain of remembering is as strong as it is of forgetting, and most of the victims of the Gernika bombing, as in many other tragic or bloody human events, have always preferred to forget. I interviewed Joxe Iturria on several occasions during the summers of 2013 and 2014 in his home in Lesaka. Iturria was one of the few surviving witnesses present during three of the most dramatic bombings in the war in the Basque Country: the first bombing of Durango on September 25, 1936, the second on March 31, 1937, and the bombing of Gernika on April 26, 1937. Iturria was in the Loiola barracks when the insurrection broke out, and so he experienced the events that took place during the initial days of the war. He experienced very difficult events. Following the bombing of Durango in September 1936, he had to transport the bodies of dead victims to the town cemetery in his truck, and he lost contact forever with people he had known in wartime Durango.

He was in Gernika on the day of the bombing, and he knew from experience that the Heinkel He51 pilots were flying in groups of three planes, in a chain, busy with gunning down "anything that moved" because those had been the orders of their superiors. As he explained to me, Iturria lay down on the ground, facing upward, because the pilots were also machine-gunning the bodies of people that, instinctively, were cowering and covering their faces or lying down flat on the ground. He remained like that for three and a half hours until the bombing ended at 7:40 a.m. Then the worst came. He went into the center to help anyone who needed it. Everything was burning. He passed by the Pasileku, where dismembered fragments of human bodies were entangled up with the remains of animals from the fair, and that is how he arrived at the Andra Mari air-raid shelter. Standing on top of the shelter more than 15 hours later, he could still hear the shouts of people buried beneath tons of rubble that could never be rescued and would die there, burned or suffocated. Then Iturria stopped talking. He did not want to carry on talking after that point.

In fact, he never spoke about the bombing until he was 87 years old, when he told his children what he had experienced. I interviewed him when he was 98. He told me that his cousin, Periko Lasaga, had also been in Gernika on the day of the bombing. He was 10 years old and saw the planes bomb Gernika from a mountain to the east of the town, together with a group of *gudaris* (Basque soldiers). Like many other Basque children, he was sent off to school camps abroad until he returned to Lesaka in 1939. Lasaga worked for a construction company that Iturria ran for 45 years. When he told me this, I asked Iturria if he would go along with me to interview Lasaga. He told me, without hesitation, "you're going alone." After having worked together for 45 years, having lived practically next door to one another in Lesaka, and having enjoyed a close family relationship, they had never spoken about the bombing to one another. They could not do so, such was the pain. When we launched a book about Iturria's memories in Gernika, Lasaga could not attend. And this is not an isolated case; it is the norm.

And this trauma, which a person suffers individually and mostly in solitude, is likewise collective. The bombing of Gernika has come to be one of the most traumatic memories of what Carl Jung (1958) termed the collective unconscious (*kollektives Unbewusstes*) of the Basque people. As Maurice Halbwachs (1950, 35–75) contends, human groups possess a capacity to retain facts—whether traumatic or not—that transcend by a long way the cognitive capacity of the individuals that comprise the group. Yet in this case the bombing transcended, likewise by a long way, the collective memory of Basques to the point of forming part of the Western collective memory and becoming an icon of the transgression of human rights at a global level. The bombing demonstrated the urgent necessity for a series of legal measures relating to international humanitarian law and focused on aerial warfare, the first of them passed by the Non-Intervention Committee as early as June 1937. The attack on Gernika was carried out in complete defiance of international consuetudinary law and the conventions of aerial warfare established in the agreements of 1899 and 1907. The bombing, one more case in the persistent transgression of human rights and the norms of war, nevertheless confirmed the risk that such practices would become habitual practice. And that is what happened. The advent of World War II was sealed with the dropping of the most powerful bomb ever built up to that time on a civilian population.

The collective memory of a nation is represented by monuments that the group in question chooses to build, or consecrate, together with the continual production of representational forms around a remembrance or singular memory. In the digital era this phenomenon has generated a great flow of memory production in the form of particular narratives and images reproduced constantly and, therefore, readdressed over and over again, but also questioned and disputed through new images. The case of Gernika is paradigmatic in this regard, given that it constitutes one of the most disputed episodes in the twentieth century.

Barely hours after the bombing, Franco ordered a denial that Gernika had been bombed and, at the same time, that news should be spread by all the means at the disposal of the regime that the town had been destroyed by retreating "reds."[5] Headed by Luis Bolín, the press office of the regime repeated immediately the two orders of the *generalísimo*, and within a few days the official version of the regime covered the pages of the main print news media and radio programs controlled by the rebels. The message on Radio Salamanca included more than fifteen lies in just one paragraph:

> This is not the first time Aguirre, the mandarin of the Republic of Euzkadi, has lied. Aguirre declared today that a foreign air force in the service of national Spain bombed the city of Gernika and set fire to it in order to hurt the Basques in the most profound of their feelings. Aguirre is lying, he is lying; and he knows it. In the first place there is no foreign or German air force in national Spain. There is the Spanish air force, the noble and heroic Spanish air force, which has to fight continuously with the red aircraft, which are Russian and French and piloted by foreigners.

FIGURE 1.3: Telegram signed by General Carlo Bossi, Salamanca, April 27, 1937, in which he reproduces Franco's order to lie about the rebel aerial bombings and accuse the republican side of the destruction.

In second place, we did not raze Gernika. Franco's Spain did not set fire to it. The incendiary torch was the monopoly of those that razed Irun, of those that razed Eibar, and of those that tried to burn alive the defenders of the Alcázar in Toledo. If we did not know that Aguirre knows he is lying, which he is, like a common criminal, we would remind him that, among those who fought on the Bizkaian front, alongside the *gudaris*, there were Asturian miners, experts in destruction by flame and gasoline, and the barbarous dynamite of Marxist violence, whose collaboration Aguirre sought out like some petty king.[6]

And the lie likewise monopolized the media controlled by Nazi Germany, Fascist Italy, and Oliveira Salazar's Portugal. Just ten days later, the German ambassador in London, Joachim Ribbentrop, met with the British foreign secretary, Anthony Eden, and called his attention to the "incorrect and tendentious accusations" in the British press about "the alleged bombing of the Basque city by German planes."[7]

The efforts to erase this event from historical memory reached unheard of extremes, such as that of commemorating the destruction or razing of the site on the part of the red separatists on April 26, 1938, in Gernika itself, when work had just begun on clearing the debris from the town center. As the organizers of this act stated, "this Martyr Town wishing to celebrate in the most appropriate manner the anniversary of its liberation by the Glorious National Troops," the commission charged with doing so organized, as part of the "celebrations for the anniversary of the town's liberation," some "solemn funerals" in the Andra Mari church "for deceased natives, locals, and residents of the town as a consequence of its devastation by red separatists."[8] The acts would be crowned by a "solemn blessing and transfer of the images of the Sacred Heart of Jesus to the newly inaugurated premises of FET and JONS and the celebration of an outdoor campaign in the Plaza de la Unión with the blessing of flags and parades and an official banquet for the authorities."[9]

That Gernika had been bombed by "red separatists" constituted the official version of the Francoist dictatorship until 1975 and, subsequently, this position has never been refuted officially by the government authorities of the Spanish state or the Italian republic. It is true that, on April 27, 1997, on the occasion of the sixtieth anniversary of the bombing, the president of Germany, Roman Herzog, issued a message of reconciliation to survivors through the ambassador, recognizing Germany's responsibility in the massacre.[10] However, it is disturbing that the current government of Chancellor Angela Merkel, in a parliamentary response to a representative from Die Linke in the Bundestag, Andrej Hunko, avoided classifying the bombing as a "war crime" and "stressed classifying the bombing that destroyed the Basque city eighty years ago as an infraction of international public law."[11]

The construction, development, diffusion, and even commemoration of the lie, a position that likewise may come to form part of the collective imaginary of a human group, were intentional and increase the pain and suffering of the victims. Following the fall of Gijón, Iturria was captured and imprisoned in a concentration camp and, after being "purified" at a seminary in Gasteiz, sent to Zaragoza. As he recounts in his memoirs,

> One day I was allowed the luxury of going to the movies in the company of another soldier from here who, like me, had fought previously in the ranks of the Basque government. Before the movie they always screened a Nodo documentary, which showed propaganda and lies on behalf of the Falangist side. We sat there stunned in that theater as we heard how the town of Gernika had been blown up and razed brutally by the red army and the evil Basque separatists (Iturria 2013, 105).

This would always unsettle him, because "gu han gattuken ta bazekigu ongi ze pasatuzen" ("we were there and we know very well what happened") (ibid., 106). Yet the pain, which is the result of a human emotion and, therefore, not governed by the laws of pure logic and reason, but instead transcends them, affects likewise on many occasions the agents of these actions and even their descendants. The memory of the events that took place that day in Gernika also tormented some of those responsible for the massacre and sometimes pricked the consciences of their descendants. Such is the case of Dieprand von Richthofen, grandnephew of Wolfram von Richthofen, the architect of the bombing, and of Karl Benedict von Moreau, the nephew of Rudolf von Moreau, leader of one of the bombing squadrons that attacked Gernika. Even though neither of them knows a lot in detail about what happened in Gernika in April 1937, they are aware of the fact, and it has been a recurring theme in family discussions in both cases, to the extent that, during the commemorations on the eightieth anniversary of the bombing, both relatives went to Gernika and expressed that,

> As representatives of a family whose name is linked to the attack—against international law—by the Condor Legion against Gernika eighty years ago, I bow with humility and respect to the survivors. We share with their families their pain for the deaths and injuries caused. It is important that states, institutions, and representatives of civil society keep alive the memory of so much incommensurable pain that National Socialism brought to Gernika, and later to Europe and to the whole world. But, also, individuals and families have to face the memory of the past.[12]

And Richthofen signed off by saying:

> Both families have learned in Gernika and we have taken this transforming force of memory toward the future as a model for us. We have faced, from a critical attitude, up to the past of our relatives during the civil war and we have felt the weight of the past. Our memory has above all the objective to learn from what happened then and take responsibility in order to build the future.[13]

Scholarly memory also has the objective of learning from the past and building the future. On the night of the bombing, Fifi Roberts and her father, who had broken the siege of Bilbao and had brought, risking his own and his daughter's life, tons of food for the civilian population, were in Bilbao when they received news of the incident. She went immediately to Gernika with her camera and photographed the devastation of the town, although most of those photographs have remained unpublished until today. She kept them in an album until her death in Devon. In the late 1990s, Sally Insgram found them in a recycling plant in Winchester and rescued them from destruction on seeing the word "Guernica" on the front cover. Many years later she exhibited the photographs in an art gallery as part of the commemorative acts for the children's exile to the United Kingdom organized by the University of Southampton. And in 2016 she contacted Ana Tere Núñez, head of the Document Center for the Bombing of Gernika, through her friend Geoff Reynolds in Bilbao, whom she asked to pass on the album, which now resides in Gernika.[14]

Eighty years after the bombing, very important unpublished documents continue to appear for its study, and the memory of what happened that day continues to be handed down from generation to generation, while the image of what happened is becoming more complete and clearer via detailed study of the material evidence, testimonies, and documents at our disposal. Only the discovery and demonstration of the truth, alongside the unconditional acceptance of what happened that April 26, will be able to overcome the collective pain that these events in the past have generated, and thereby allow us to progress as humanity, and to develop, educate, and prosper individually as members of this humanity.

## Bibliography

Atxotegi, Joseba. *The Ulysses Syndrome: The Immigrant Syndrome with Chronic and Multiple Stress.* Ediciones El Mundo de la Mente, 2015.

"Alemania evita calificar el bombardeo de Gernika como 'crimen de Guerra'." *Público*, May 23, 2017.

Cernuda, Luis. *La Realidad y el deseo: poesías completas de Luis Cernuda.* Mexico: Editorial Séneca, 1940.

———. *Historial de un libro (la realidad y el deseo).* Madrid: Alianza, 1975.

———. *Invitación a la poesía.* Barcelona: Seix Barral, 1975.

Cloud, Yvonne. [Yvonne Kapp] and Richard Ellis. *The Basque Children in England: An Account of their Life at North Stoneham Camp.* London: Victor Gollancz Ltd, 1937.

Díaz Pérez, Eva. "Poeta herido, vagabundo." "Cultura" section, *El Mundo*, June 20, 2011.

"Donan imágenes inéditas del bombardeo de Gernika-Lumo. El centro de documentación ha recibido un álbum de una fotógrafa inglesa." *Deia*, June 3, 2017.

Gamboa, José María, and Jean-Claude Larronde, eds. *La guerra civil en Euzkadi: 136 testimonios inéditos recogidos por José Miguel de Barandiarán.* Milafranga: Bidasoa, 2005.

Halbwachs, Maurice. *La mémoire collective.* Paris: Presses Universitaires de France, 1950.

Irujo, Xabier. *Gernika 1937: The Market Day Massacre.* Reno: University of Nevada Press, 2015.

———. *Gernika: 26 de abril de 1937.* Barcelona: Crítica, 2017.

Iturralde, Juan [pseud. De Juan Jose Usabiaga Irazustabarrena]. *El catolicismo y la cruzada de Franco.* Vienne: EGI Indarra, 1960.

Iturria, Joxe. *Memorias de Guerra.* Gernika: Gernikako Bakearen Museoa Fundazioa / Gernika-Lumoko Udala, Gernika, 2013.

Jahangir, Rumeana. "Spanish Civil War: The Child Refugees Britain didn't Want," *BBC News,* July 17, 2016. At https://www.bbc.com/news/uk-england-35532286.

Jung, Carl Gustav. *Die Archetypen und das kollektive.* Zurich: Unbewusste, Rascher, Olten & Walter, 1958.

Maier, Klaus A. Guernica. *La intervención alemana en España y el "caso Guernica".* Madrid: Sedmay, 1976.

"Mensaje de las familias von Richthofen y von Moreau en el 80 aniversario del bombardeo de Gernika." *Gernika Gogoratuz,* April 26, 2017.

Olabarria, Zigor. *Gerra Zibila Otxandion.* Donostia: Eusko Ikaskuntza, 2011.

Reig Tapia, Alberto. Ideología e historia: sobre la represión franquista y la guerra civil. Madrid: Akal, 1986.

Smallwood, William. *The Day Gernika Was Bombed.* Gernika: Gernikako Bakearen Museoa Fundazioa/Gernika-Lumoko Udala, 2012.

Urroz, Eloy. *La familia interrumpida.* Mexico: Penguin Random House, 2012.

Wade, Martin. "The Child Refugees Who Escaped the Spanish Civil War and Found Safety in Newport." *South Wales Argus,* May 19, 2017. At https://www.southwalesargus.co.uk/news/15296559. the-child-refugees-who-escaped-the-spanish-civil-war-and-found-safety-in-newport/.

## Notes

1    "Terrorised as planes fly over tents," *News Chronicle,* Monday, May 24, 1937, 1; "Planes terrorise Basque Children," *South Wales Argus,* Monday, May 24, 1937, 1.

2    Interview with Joseba Atxotegi, Center for Basque Studies, University of Nevada, Reno, September 11, 2017.

3    Homer, *Odyssey,* cantos V.150 and IX.360.

4    Testimony of Maria Olabarria, aged 52, quoted in Paul Vaillant-Couturier, "La madre que vio morir a dos hijas," *La Voz,* May 26, 1937, 1–4 and "Más relatos impresionantes sobre la saña y la crueldad con que procedieron los rebeldes españoles en Guernica," *El Sol,* May 27, 1937, 2. In the original French: "Demain, Bilbao," *L'Humanité,* May 13, 1937, 1–3.

5    "Operazioni di Bilbao," Telegram from General Carlo Bossi. Salamanca, April 27, 1937, Archive of the Italian Foreign Ministry, Gabinetto del Ministro (1923–1943), Busta 7 (Uffizio Spagna Leg. 44, no. 1250).

6    Proa, 126, León, April 29, 1937. See likewise Radio Verdad, April 28, 1937, Archivo General Militar de Ávila, Caja 2103, Carpeta 10/ 1.

7    Note by Ray Atherton, adviser, in the Embassy of the United States in London, to the secretary of state of the United States, London, May 5, 1937, NARA, College Park, U.S. Ambassador Claude G. Bowers Files (Files 852.00/. . . , Boxes 3687 to 3701), Document 852.00/5602, 8.

8    "Festejos por el aniversario de la liberación de esta villa," in the Gernikako Bonbardaketako Dokumentazio Zentrua (GBDZ), Festejos por el aniversario de la liberación de esta villa.

9    Ibid.

10   Roman Herzog, "Message to the inhabitants of Gernika," Bonn, April 27, 1997.

11   "Alemania evita calificar el bombardeo de Gernika como 'crimen de Guerra'," *Público,* May 23, 2017.

12    "Mensaje de las familias von Richthofen y von Moreau en el 80 aniversario del bombardeo de Gernika," *Gernika Gogoratuz*, April 26, 2017, 3.

13    Ibid.

14    "Donan imágenes inéditas del bombardeo de Gernika-Lumo. El centro de documentación ha recibido un álbum de una fotógrafa inglesa," *Deia*, June 3, 2017.

# 2

# Basques that Come and Go, Basques from Oregon, Basques from Gabon

## The Ulysses Syndrome in the Basque Migrations of Yesterday and Today

*Joseba Atxotegi*

### The Basque Country: The Country of Migrations

It could be said that the Basque Country is the country of migrations. It is true that the Basque Country is small and for that reason these migrations have not given rise to large mass movements, but in proportion to their population, very few countries have experienced such intense migratory changes. In the nineteenth and twentieth centuries, almost half of the population born in the Basque Country emigrated, while at the same time another population, born outside of the Basque territory, settled there. Teaching in California, I have always heard Mexicans say that the U.S. border crosses them. Despite the distances separating us, as Basques we can say the same thing: migration (both emigration, leaving the country, and immigration, arriving in the country) traverses our history much more than we sometimes imagine.

Great knowledge of the social sciences is not needed to realize that such population movements have had a profound effect on the structure of Basque society. Unfortunately, this impressive social phenomenon has not been given the attention it deserves. Although this resistance is understandable given the complexity and potential perils of such an examination, no society can move forward without probing its realities, however complicated or contradictory they may be. I also believe, however, that there are many positive aspects related to this migratory mobility, enriching elements that are lost if not taken into account. Thus, for example, from the perspective of emigration, consider the millions of Basques scattered around the world—twelve million according to some estimates, including emigrants and direct descendants, out of a nation of two and a half million inhabitants presently. These émigrés and descendants could enable the Basque Country, with its small population, to play a much more significant role in the radically globalized world in which we live.

Many of these migrants in and out of the Basque Country lived through very difficult situations that may have caused them to suffered from the migrant syndrome, with chronic and multiple stressors—that is, the Ulysses Syndrome, a concept that I will describe in detail in the third section of this chapter. The Ulysses Syndrome is not a mental disorder, but a situation caused by stress, a very intense grief, and a mental health issue. The Ulysses Syndrome is what the French call a *souffrance*, not a disease.

## Emigration and Immigration in the Basque Country

I am going to refer to emigration and immigration in a general way to frame the issue and to state what we are talking about and the conditions under which this migration has occurred, with special reference to the extreme situations that lead to the appearance of the Ulysses Syndrome.

### Basque Emigration and Exile

José Navarro and Antonio Azcuénaga are a great example of the difficulties experienced in Basque emigration. They are two Bizkaians who were among the first Basques to emigrate to Idaho and who almost died crossing the desert between Nevada and Idaho. In the spring 1889, these two men were looking for better pastures for their sheep while crossing the Owihee Mountains from Nevada. They ended up exhausted, semi-conscious, suffering serious dehydration, and about to die, in Jordan Valley, on the border between Idaho and Oregon (Bieter and Bieter 2005, 1). Below I will analyze in detail, from the psychological point of view, this migration of Basque sheepherders, who endured extreme circumstances, to the western United States.

Another form of extreme migration is exile. Xabier Irujo (2012, 19) states that the Basque term *erbeste*, which means "to be in a territory or land other than one's own," first appears in the Basque Country between 1745 and 1749 in the First Carlist War, and again in 1802 after the French Revolution, in 1885 after the Second Carlist War, and in 1952 in full Basque exile after the war of 1936 (the Spanish Civil War). All this demonstrates the history of exile, many times in extreme circumstances, many Basques have experienced.

For Irujo (2012, 39), the Basque exile resulting from the civil war began as early as July 1936 when the rebellion triumphed in Navarre and Araba and tens of thousands of people fled to France and Bizkaia to escape the terrible repression. In the summer of 1936, after the uprising of General Emilio Mola, there were 1,757 executions in Navarre. Bilbao would double its population before its fall to Francisco Franco's troops in 1937, and, in the first stage of exile, many Basque children would go into exile outside the Basque Country, living in extreme circumstances, as discussed in an earlier chapter of this book.

The second stage, says Irujo (2012, 40), came after the fall of Bilbao. There was a third stage of exile, when the Basque government and thousands of refugees went to Barcelona. Finally, after the fall of Barcelona in 1939, the Basque government and the refugees went into exile outside the Peninsula, an exile that would last forty years, the length of the Franco dictatorship. We know many of the experiences of these people through their own testimonies, one of the most important being the book written by the president of the Basque government, Lehendakari (president) José Antonio Aguirre, which in English was translated as *Escape via Berlin: Eluding Franco and Hitler's Europe* (1944, 1991).

As an expression of the risks related to the exile, one could mention the "mysterious" disappearance of the prominent Basque exile, Jesús de Galíndez, in March 1956 in New York. It is also worth mentioning, as an expression of the odysseys undergone by these exiles, the trip of two small Basque fishing boats, the *Bigarrena* and the *Donibane II*, which escaped in 1939 from the French Basque Country to Venezuela, after a thirty-four-day voyage in difficult conditions (San Sebastián 2014, 184).

But throughout the history of the Basque Country there have been many more situations of very difficult emigration. I will mention only a few examples: the fishermen who settled in the polar climate of Newfoundland and arrived in small boats, in some cases not much larger than some small boats that arrive nowadays on the coasts of the Iberian Peninsula; heroic exploration trips like that of Elcano, who managed to complete the first round-the-world voyage; and the experiences of thousands of men and women who left the Basque Country as missionaries, living in extreme situations all over the planet (in my own family, I have had Jesuit uncles, one in China, persecuted during the Revolution, and another in Japan during World War II).

### Immigrants to the Basque Country Have Also Experienced Very Difficult Situations

As pointed out by José Ignacio Ruiz Olabuénaga and María Cristina Blanco (1994, 115), the Basque Country had been, until the nineteenth century, a society that sent out emigrants as administrators and sailors. In the second part of the eighteenth century, Basque emigration to the Americas tripled the Spanish average. Ten of the twenty-two Argentine presidents between 1853 and 1943 were descendants of Basques, as well as 40 percent of the parliamentary representatives in Chile. There were towns in which 25 percent of the population had emigrated to the Americas.

It is rare to find a Basque family that does not have relatives abroad, especially in the Americas, but also in Australia and the Philippines. To this must be added significant migration to large cities such as Madrid and Barcelona, and to Bordeaux and Paris in the case of the population of the French Basque Country. Madrid, especially, has many descendants of Basques, to the extent that the second soccer team in the city, Atlético de Madrid, one of the best soccer teams in Europe and one that long ago obtained better results than its mother team, Athletic Bilbao, was founded by the great Basque colony of Madrid.

Obviously, one factor greatly favoring migration is when another family member is already in the host country and is willing to sponsor other migrants. This is chain migration.

This emission of emigrants was completely compensated for in the second half of the nineteenth century when the Basque Country became a focus of constant immigration. Today, many of its inhabitants are immigrants, or the children and grandchildren of immigrants. Thus, Ruiz Olabuénaga and Blanco (1994) point out that among people over eighteen years of age, 57.3 percent in Araba, 47 percent in Gipuzkoa, and 61.9 percent in Bizkaia are immigrants or children of immigrants.

Ruiz Olabuénaga and Blanco (1994, 29) pinpoint the origins of this immigration in 1841 with the creation of the Altos Hornos Foundry, in 1843 with the creation of the Altos Hornos de Vizcaya Foundry, and in 1857 with the creation of the Banco de Bilbao. Of the 13,000 miners in the iron mines of Bizkaia at that time, only 20 percent were natives.

The extreme conditions in which many miners lived in the Gallarta and Ortuella mines led Dr. Enrique Areilza, director of the Bizkaia mining hospital, to write, "These men come here to work and live, not to die," as Yosu Montalbán points out in his book, *El Dr. Areilza, el médico de los mineros* (2018, 46). These miners were at great physical risks in their work, and accidents were very frequent, many of them fatal. These dangers and the accompanying racism directed against these miners appear in the novel *El intruso* by Blasco Ibáñez. The painful conditions in which this population lived also set the stage for the appearance of diseases, alcoholism, and so on.

This immigration continued with ups and downs, for example during the civil war, but it increased much more at the end of the 1950s as a result of the economic stabilization plan, when 600,000 immigrants, 32 percent of the population of the time, arrived within a few years. I myself have recorded the memory of a day in the late 1950s in the Magdalena neighborhood in Durango when I came across a man who had a large suitcase tied with ropes, accompanied by a child who would have been about my age. That boy and I stared at each other for a moment, which I will not forget, with expressions of curiosity and surprise. Each of us wondered what the other would be like, what he would think, and what he would feel. Years later, we ended up being friends.

But today in the Basque Country, in the context of globalization, new immigrants also suffer extreme conditions. Men, women, and even children migrate alone and live frightened, helpless, and far from their loved ones within the framework of a European migration policy that, since the late 1990s, has maintained borders practically closed to non-EU countries. And this is despite the huge demographic winter that looms all over Europe, including the Basque Country, with rates of 1.3 children per woman. As the Germans said when they allowed the arrival of refugees from the war in Syria: they are the children we did not have.

So we can see the story of Abdeslam, an immigrant from Cameroon who crossed the whole of Central and North Africa, arrived in El Aaiún, and crossed by boat to the Canary Islands from where, after being interned in a center for months, he was finally sent to the Peninsula and ended up in Bilbao. This immigrant's journey is perfectly comparable to that described by Homer in the *Odyssey*, since Ulysses went from Troy on the coast of Turkey to Ithaca on the coast of Greece. It is no exaggeration to say that the journey of Abdeslam is also an Odyssey.

It is very important to note that an important part of the wealth generated by the Basque Country and the well-being that we enjoy comes from the contribution of these immigrant men and women, who work in very difficult circumstances.

As for the psychological repercussions of these circumstances, in 2002, while researching the mental health of the new migrants in the extreme situation of the twenty-first century, I coined the terminology "Immigrant Syndrome with Chronic and Multiple Stressors," or "the Ulysses Syndrome," a psychological condition that I will explain next.

### Immigrants Living in Extreme Situations: The Immigrant Syndrome with Chronic and Multiple Stressors (The Ulysses Syndrome)

"But the days found him sitting on the rocks or sands, torturing himself with tears, groans and heartache, and looking out with streaming eyes across the watery wilderness. . . ." (*Odyssey*, Song V, 150,)

"You ask me my name. I shall tell you. My name is nobody and nobody is what everyone calls me." (*Odyssey*, Song IX, 360)

Human migrations have been frequent phenomena throughout history; however, each migration usually presents its own specific characteristics. Immigrants often come to host countries under their extreme conditions. For millions of individuals, emigration presents stress levels of such intensity that they exceed the human capacity of adaptation. These persons are, therefore, highly vulnerable to Immigrant Syndrome with Chronic and Multiple Stressors, known as the Ulysses Syndrome (in reference to the Greek hero who suffered countless adversities and dangers in lands far from his loved ones).

## Stressors

Immigrant Syndrome with Chronic and Multiple Stressors is characterized, on the one hand, by the fact that the individual suffers certain stressors or afflictions and, on the other, by the fact that she or he presents a series of symptoms from several areas of psychopathology. The most important stressors are:

1.  Loneliness and the enforced separation, especially in the case when an immigrant leaves behind young children.

2.  The sense of despair and failure felt when the immigrant, despite having invested enormously in the emigration (economically, emotionally, and so on), does not even manage to muster together the very minimum conditions to make a go of it.

3.  The need to fight for mere survival, that is, to feed himself/herself, to find a roof to sleep under.

4.  Fear and afflictions caused by the physical dangers of the journey undertaken (sailing on precarious boats, hiding away in trucks).

This combination of loneliness, the failure to achieve one's objectives, and the experience of extreme hardships and terror forms the psychological and psychosocial basis of Immigrant Syndrome with Chronic and Multiple Stressors (the Ulysses Syndrome).

Yet the harmful effects caused by the adversities and dangers that the immigrant must face are increased enormously by a whole series of unfavorable characteristics associated with stressful situations and the fact that the stressors involve the following dimensions:

1.   Multiple stressors (the greater the number of adversities and dangers, the greater the risk to the mental health).

2.   Chronic stressors (these situations of extreme hardship can affect immigrants for months on end, and even years); defenselessness (the feeling that whatever the individual does she/he will not be able to change her/his situation, namely, learned defenselessness) (Seligman 1975, 407).

3.   Overwhelming stressors (the enormous intensity of the stressors is quite unlike the stress associated with being stuck in a traffic jam or sitting an examination); the marked absence of any network of social support, an absence of social capital (Coleman 1984, 302).

4.   The symptoms themselves (sadness, weariness, insomnia, and so on) become an additional handicap that hinders attempts to survive.

To all this, we have to add the classic shocks the immigrant must undergo (coming to terms with a new language, culture, environment, that is, the acculturative stress) as well as the severity of the present extreme stressors.

What is more, the health system does not often provide adequately for these patients, either because their health problems are dismissed as being trivial (out of ignorance, a lack of sensitivity, prejudice, even racism), or because their condition is not adequately diagnosed and immigrants are treated as depressive or psychotic, thereby creating even more stressors. Nor are their somatic symptoms seen as being psychological problems, so they are subjected to a series of tests (such as colonoscopies, biopsies) and given inadequate, costly treatment. The health system becomes a new stressor.

## The Seven Griefs in Migration

From my perspective (Atxotegi 1999), there are seven griefs in migration:

1.   The grief for family and loved ones.

2.   The grief due to language: how a change of language is experienced by the immigrant.

3.  The grief of culture: customs, sense of time, religion, values.

4.  The grief of homeland: landscape, the light, the temperature, the colors, smells, humidity.

5.  The grief of social status: legality, working conditions, housing.

6.  The grief in relationship to the peer group: prejudices, xenophobia, racism.

7.  The grief due to risk regarding physical integrity: dangers in the migratory journey, dangerous jobs (accidents, professional illness) changes in diet.

These seven griefs can be experienced in a simple, complicated, or extreme way (Atxotegi 2002): simple grief occurs in good conditions and may be elaborated satisfactorily. Complicated grief occurs when serious difficulties exist for the elaboration of the grief, but it is possible to elaborate the grief. And extreme grief happens when the situation is so problematic, so difficult, that the grief cannot be elaborated. This is the case of the Ulysses Syndrome.

*Symptomatology*
The clinical expression of Immigrant Syndrome with Chronic and Multiple Stressors is a specific combination of symptoms:

1.  Symptoms in the area of depression include, fundamentally, sadness and crying, but do not include other basic symptoms such as apathy, low self-esteem, guilt, and thoughts of death, so that we are not dealing with a depressive disorder.

2.  It also includes symptoms in the area of anxiety-related disorders, such as tension, insomnia, recurrent and intrusive thoughts, and irritability.

3.  Somatic symptoms, above all migraines, fatigue, and osteoarticular complaints (we utilize the term *Im-migraine*).

4.  Symptoms of confusion (temporal-spatial disorientation, depersonalization, and derealization).

5.  To this symptomatology is often added an interpretation made from the perspective of the subject's own culture. Thus, it is typical to hear things

like "it is not possible that things can have turned out so badly for me," "I'm suffering such bad luck, I must be cursed," and "I'm the victim of witchcraft." It should be borne in mind that this symptomatology occurs in relation to the culture of the immigrant, since it is his/her culture that channels the expression of the symptoms and we find differences in the clinical conditions of migraines and tiredness, as pointed out by Marcos (1976), Bhugra and Gupta (2011), Crawford and Campbell (2012), and Berry (2011).

*Discussion on Differential Diagnosis: The Ulysses Syndrome Does Not Belong to the Area of Mental Disorder, but to the Broader Area of Mental Health*
I believe that environmental factors play a large role in situations of chronic stress (including other manifestations such as burn-out and mobbing) because stress is without a doubt one of the basic problems in mental health, although it is still neglected. Despite the fact that it is almost commonplace to make reference to bio-psychosocial approaches in the various official discussions of psychiatry, social aspects are still considered the drudgery of psychopathology. I believe, as noted in the introduction, that a direct and unequivocal relationship exists between the extreme stressors that these immigrants experience and the symptomatology of the Ulysses Syndrome.

The term *Ulysses Syndrome*, which I coined in 2002, is based on the definition of a syndrome as a series of symptoms. It is not necessary to refer to the World Health Organization's (WHO) classic definition of health as "a state of physical, mental and social wellbeing" (OMS, 1978, Alma Ata Declaration, 2) to understand that these immigrants in extreme situations and with a large number of symptoms are far removed from a state in which they enjoy a healthy life. However, psychological problems suffered by immigrants and their symptomatology, like women's disorders or minority problems, encounter prejudice and devaluation by certain sectors in psychiatry lacking sensitivity with respect to these social occurrences. At a general level, there is a clear discrimination against women that devalues manifestations such as fibromyalgia and chronic fatigue. As Foucault (1983, 2004) notes, psychiatric diagnosis is not objective or neutral but rather linked to power structures and ideology and forms part of "bio-politics."

One objection that could be made to this approach is that giving the name *syndrome* to this manifestation could be seen as a pathologizing of this segment of society. My response (as indicated above) is that the term *syndrome* is first and foremost descriptive (as a series of symptoms). The assertion that these immigrants suffer from a mental illness is not being made; these immigrants receive negative results on the Hamilton Questionnaire for both anxiety and depression, the two best known psychiatric evaluation questionanaires. The term indicates that they suffer a series of symptoms pertaining to the mental health sector, which is a wider area than that of psychopathology.

The question is whether it is more dangerous to confuse these mental health problems with depression, psychoses, adjustments, and disorders by not defining them. Does this not imply a greater risk of psychiatrization? And, on the other hand, is it not dangerous, as well as discriminatory, to consider that these individuals are well, that they have no mental health problems, despite having numerous symptoms? I believe that it is better to name these mental health problems.

On the contrary, by establishing the delimitation and denomination of the Ulysses Syndrome we are contributing to the avoidance of an incorrect diagnosis of these persons as depressive or psychotic. This is because there is no name for their suffering (thus converting these diagnostic errors into new stressors for the immigrants, to which one has to add the adverse effects of treatments, health care, expenses). On the other hand, nor do I agree with the idea that at a psychological level, there is nothing wrong with these people: supporting this idea would be to reject their numerous symptoms and to discriminate against the immigrants once more. That is to say, the attempt to name a reality that no one denies is positive (and our assertion, as with everything scientific, is subject to discussion and open to improvement). However, what does appear to be pathologizing and occurs with great frequency in clinical analysis are the adaptive disorders that immigrants experiencing Ulysses stressors are diagnosed as having: this latter approach considers the immigrants to be failing and to have deficits (only in this way can a disorder be considered), when the reality is quite different: they are experiencing inhuman stress factors to which there is no possible capacity of adaptation.

I believe that the Ulysses Syndrome is at one and the same time a syndrome and a prodrome; it forms a gateway between mental health and mental disorder. This syndrome is a subjective response when faced with a situation of inhuman stress, stress of such a character that it overwhelms the individual's adaptative capacities (living permanently alone, with no way out, with fear). However, if this situation is not resolved, there is a great risk that it finally becomes an illness. It is as if the temperature of a room were raised to 100 degrees. One would suffer dizziness and cramps, and discomfort would ensue from these symptoms, as they would correspond to an attempt at temporary physical adaptation to an increased temperature resulting in the failure of thermo-regulatory capacity and giving rise to a series of symptoms deriving from the attempt to compensate for and reduce the physiological effects of the temperature increase. If the temperature decreased, the symptoms would disappear. But if the situation persisted indefinitely, the risk of illness would continue to increase. The same occurs with the symptoms in the Ulysses Syndrome.

The Ulysses Syndrome is found in the area of preventative health care and the psychosocial sector more than in the area of the treatment. The objective of intervention would be avoiding the worsening condition of those who suffer from this manifestation so that they do not suffer a standard mental disorder (which means that work on the syndrome not only involves psychologists or psychiatrists, but also social workers). It is obvious that with the situations of stress that these immigrants face, a greater risk of alcoholism and psychosis is foreseeable. Treating a psychotic immigrant lacking in social support, with linguistic communication and cultural difficulties, is very difficult, which means that prevention is fundamental for those suffering in extreme situations.

I postulate that there is a direct, causal relationship between the enormous stress that these immigrants experience and their symptomatology, and that this goes much further than typical acculturative stress (related to language, culture, and nostalgia). Rather, we are confronted, unfortunately, with the worst possible nightmare: individuals in danger, alone, without the means to resolve their problems, feeling sick, without any way out of their situation and, furthermore, when they seek help, it is either not forthcoming or inadequate.

Loneliness, fear, despair; a lot of migrations remind us of Homer's verses: ". . . But the days found him sitting on the rocks or sands, torturing himself with tears, groans and heartache, and looking out with streaming eyes across the watery wilderness. . . ." (*Odyssey*, Song V, 150) and the part of the text in which Ulysses tells Polyphem: "You ask me my name. I shall tell you. My name is nobody and nobody is what everyone calls me" (*Odyssey*, Song IX, 360). It is clear that if a man has to become a nobody in order to survive, if he has to remain permanently invisible, he will have no identity and will never become socially integrated, nor will he enjoy mental health.

We live in bad times if mere mortals have to behave like heroes in order to survive. Ulysses was a demigod who nevertheless barely survived the terrible adversities and dangers he had to face, but the people who are arriving at our borders today are creatures of flesh and blood who, nevertheless, must suffer episodes that are as dramatic as, or even more so than those described in the Odyssey.

*What Does the Data Tell Us?*

The percentage of immigrants with Ulysses Syndrome in medical and psychological consultations is around 15 percent. Research in doctoral dissertations and articles shows these results (Athena Network, 2018). We can see that this syndrome occurs more frequently than psychoses, bipolar disorder, and adaptive disorders. I believe we are facing a reality that cannot be ignored in the health care system. Although men predominate, we can see that the proportion of female immigrants is similar.

## Analysis of the Ulysses Syndrome and the Seven Griefs in the Migration of Basque Sheepherders in the Western United States

In this section, I will describe in greater detail the psychological aspects of Basque migrations in the western United States, based on the data I have gathered in my contacts with the Basque community in Boise and from my study of the literature on these processes. Nevertheless, as Ricardo Ciérbide (1996, 44) indicates, it is not easy to interview the sheepherders. It is clear they have had a very challenging time, and they are somewhat reluctant to talk about their experiences, as is often the case with people that have lived through traumatic situations.

The migrations of Basque sheepherders to the United States began in the second half of the nineteenth century, and they, too, experienced extremely difficult circumstances, especially loneliness. The sheepherders spent months almost entirely on their own, living in great hardship, as described by the numerous testimonies that survive from that time. Their symptoms were referred to as being "sheeped" or "sage-brushed," which is highly consistent with the Ulysses Syndrome.

There were also cases of madness and suicide, as recorded by Ciérbide (1996, 87) based on information published in the *Elko Daily Free Press* and in the *Elko Independent*, which reported the case of a Basque sheepherder admitted to hospital because he was found wandering naked along a riverbank, claiming people were out to kill him. He could not speak a word of English. He eventually escaped from the hospital and was never heard of again. In November 1920, another sheepherder came down from the mountains saying he was ill. By the following morning he had committed suicide.

The excellent memoir *Sweet Promised Land* (1957, 2000) by Robert Laxalt, the son of a shepherd from Atharratze (Tardets) in the French Basque Country, describes magnificently, from the perspective of a shepherd's son, his father's life and that of the whole family. Laxalt explains how he saw his father for barely a few weeks each year, the dangers he was exposed to living up in the mountains in summer and down in the desert in winter, and the extremely hard life he led.

The first Basques to arrive in the American West were drawn by the 1848–1859 gold rush and were continuing a previous emigration, as they actually came by way of Argentina. In 1865, the advent of the railroad favored the transport of livestock, and sheepherding underwent a major expansion, to such an extent that by 1890 there was a shortage of space for herds in California, so some Basque sheepherders headed for Nevada and Idaho. In the 1920s, however, the United States adopted a much tighter immigration policy and many sheepherders arrived without the necessary papers, causing them a lot of stress. Thus, the 1924 Johnson–Reed Immigration Act restricted sheepherders from immigrating to the United States. Ciérbide (1996) states that the Basque community considered the 1934 Taylor Grazing Act which ended open grazing on public rangelands to be an anti-Basque measure.

The Basque influx recovered in the 1940s because of the shortage of sheepherders and increased further in the wake of the 1954 McCarran–Walter Act which introduced an immigration system of preferences based on skill sets. This influx came to an end in the 1970s when the appearance of synthetic fibers had a far-reaching impact on the wool trade. At the same time the economic recovery in Euskadi (the Basque Country), following the end of Franco's dictatorship and Spain's membership in the European Union, brought an end to a century of Basque migration to Idaho. Today's sheepherders are mostly Mexicans and Peruvians (Bieter and Bieter 2005, 164).

*Study of the Seven Griefs of Migration and the Ulysses Syndrome among Basque Sheepherders in the Western United States*
In this section, I will provide a preliminary introduction to the issue of the mental health of Basque sheepherders in the western United States. It is an extremely complex matter that has hardly been studied and clearly needs to be addressed in greater depth. I am, nonetheless, well aware of the limitations inherent to any pioneering work, and I naturally accept them.

I am going to adopt the perspective of the seven griefs, or stressors, of migration I considered above to analyze the Basque migrants, especially the sheepherders in the American West. As noted, these seven griefs of migration can be experienced under favorable, difficult, and even extreme conditions, with this last case triggering the appearance of the Ulysses Syndrome, as happened to many of the migrants in the American West.

With a view to understanding the aspects I am going to discuss in the next section, it is very important to put oneself in the shoes of these migrants suffering such hardship. As I have indicated in other studies (Atxotegi 2010, 2012), a great deal is said about migration, but it is also very important to focus on the process's protagonist, namely, the emigrant, who is not a statistic or a number, but rather a human being with a life and feelings. It is important to rehumanize the study of migrations, and in this case, the study of these sheepherders' experiences, living alone in a foreign land.

The following are the seven griefs to be analyzed:

### Grief over Family and Loved Ones

This is the aspect we most likely think of first when referring to migratory stress or grief: goodbyes and reunions. These experiences are very important for people because they affect our attachment, which is an instinct, according to the views of John Bowlby (1986). Attachment is one of the major paradigms of twenty-first-century psychology and psychiatry.

Yet there are different layers of stress regarding this grief, whereby it is not the same when a young, unmarried son or daughter leaves home to start a new life as when someone leaves behind young children, although this was admittedly not the case with the Basque sheepherders. This does apply, however, to recent migration in the Basque Country, with the arrival of many men and women forced to leave their little ones behind.

In the case of the Basque sheepherders, one of the main stressors was loneliness. They spent ten months a year alone in the mountains or deserts, accompanied solely by 2,000 or more bleating sheep. The worst part, they said, was having no one to talk to or meet. The biggest problems were not physical, although these were also present in the form of snakes, pumas, and dust storms, which were very dangerous. The stiffest challenges were mental.

Sabino Landa, who arrived in Idaho in 1920, wrote, "I missed my home and family so much. I had never been on my own like that before. I couldn't stop crying. I cried all day and all night." Another sheepherder explained: "I remember the day I received my first letter from my mother. I had to hide behind a tree because I couldn't stop crying like a baby" (Bieter and Bieter 2005, 38). Nevertheless, this extreme grief was not caused by separation from their parents, which is quite natural among adults, and part of the normal, straightforward grief of growing up, but instead by living in extreme solitude.

This was compounded by the fact a fair number of these migrants were minors, such as Marcelino Aldecoa, from the town of Ea, who migrated to America on his own at age sixteen. Dominique Laxalt himself, as we have already mentioned, is the protagonist of the memoir *Sweet Promised Land*, and emigrated when he was still a youth, leaving from the port of Le Havre. The father of Jerónima Echeverría, former professor in the History Department at California State University, Fresno, arrived from Bizkaia when he was fifteen years old. Martín Vizcay emigrated first to Uruguay and then to the American West when still a minor, as happens today with many migrants without papers in the Basque Country. This situation is already an extreme stressor, as the individual is still developing at this stage and requires a safe and protective environment in which to mature properly (Ciérbide 1996, 62).

The sheepherders came down from the mountains with such a need to talk that there is the anecdote of a man staying at a Basque boardinghouse who explained that when he came down for breakfast he just wanted to eat, "but goddam it, those sheepherders only wanted to talk, talking was their bread and butter. I knew why. I'd also been through the same." A sheepherder in Boise told me he needed to become human again after spending so many months with his animals.

The family details we have on this migration reveal that these men mostly married other migrant Basques. Nevertheless, this endogamy did not stop their children becoming thoroughly integrated in American society, with some soon achieving considerable success, such as Peter Cenarrusa, who became Secretary of State for Idaho, and Paul Laxalt, former senator for the state of Nevada. From the perspective of transcultural psychology, it is good when two phenomena are recorded at the same time, namely, maintaining strong ties with one's origins, as this diminishes the effects of migratory grief, and becoming closely attached to the new culture, as this leads to a social improvement essential for integrating within the host culture. Otherwise, any deficiency in social status soon rekindles migratory grief and has a profound impact on the migrant. This means a blend of the two strategies seems to be the most appropriate. The migrant Basque community in the American West has successfully pursued this blended strategy.

These isolated sheepherders found some consolation by carving on trees. It has been estimated that there are a million trees bearing these signs (not made solely by Basque sheepherders, of course, as there were also those from other areas in Spain, such as Santander and Leon, as Ciérbide (1996, 30) notes). These tree carvings or inscriptions on black and white aspens, for example, in the American West involved their partners, erotic drawings, and Basque farmhouses or *baserriak*. Juan Carlos Arizmendi from Luzaide (Valcarlos), who emigrated to Elko, explained that the sheepherders often carved their own names. From a psychological perspective, this can be understood as a way of remembering who they were, of not forgoing their identity while alone in an unfamiliar setting.

Dogs helped them to withstand their loneliness, as is the case today with the treatment of autistic children. Arizmendi explained that he lived with his dog and it gave him company; it was his family. The dog slept in the tent with him, and it woke him up every morning. He appreciated the dog's company to such an extent that he treated it as an equal; they ate the same food: stewed meat, pasta, and rice, and the dog deserved it, he explained (someone might see in this Basque sheepherder a forerunner of the animal rights movement today).

Ciérbide (1996, 65) describes cases of madness and suicide, indicating that loneliness consumes these men and renders them sad. When, years later, they cease being sheepherders, they find it difficult to converse. The trader, who brought their provisions every eight days, took his leave all too soon. It was the only opportunity the sheepherders had to talk, and they found it too brief.

The human mind, like nature itself, cannot tolerate a vacuum. And the risk is that the mind will end up filling this void in the interaction with others by conjuring up an imaginary world, the world of madness, hallucinations, and delirium, which occurs in certain cases involving vulnerable migrants. In most cases, nevertheless, an individual is capable of warding off this madness, albeit while experiencing great emotional stress, as in the case of the Ulysses Syndrome.

From a psychopathological perspective, one of the great dangers of loneliness, and in general of the Ulysses Syndrome, is that out of desperation individuals seek to escape from their plight through alcohol. It needs to be remembered, furthermore, that drinking is an accepted part of Basque culture, even though it poses numerous risks from a mental health perspective.

The extensive network of Basque boardinghouses, something of an institution in themselves, played an important part in bringing Basque migrants together, although the sheepherders, of course, only had a short time to enjoy them in the fall, until they managed to save enough money to leave the hard life of sheepherding and fully integrate within the social life of their host country.

This grief over family shows that the extreme stressors associated with the loneliness of living in isolation or emigrating at a tender age are more than sufficient to trigger the Ulysses Syndrome.

### Grief over Language

Learning the language spoken in the host country may be at least in part a source of pleasure and satisfaction, although it also requires effort. It is rarely easy for migrants, subject to an exhausting working day, to attend classes in the new language, and they often have few or no opportunities to practice because of the lack of contact with local people.

For the sheepherders, this grief became extreme and unbearable, as they had to spend the entire year on their own without being able to learn or practice English, and their isolation meant they could not actively learn the new language. This is similar to the present scenario in the Basque Country and throughout Europe affecting many migrants without papers, who live in hiding, often concealed in insalubrious storerooms and garages. During an appointment at my office, when I asked an undocumented African migrant about learning the language, he answered, "Look Doctor, you don't get to talk much when you're working illegally, okay?"

In the case of the Basque sheepherders' terrible isolation, there was the added problem experienced by those who arrived without papers from the 1920s and onward, making it more difficult to learn English for fear of being discovered if they interacted with local people, and thus making them even more vulnerable to extreme grief and the Ulysses Syndrome.

Regarding the stress linked to not knowing the language, there is the revealing anecdote (Bieter and Bieter 2005, 39) of the Basque sheepherder, alone in the mountains, who was approached by a group of Native Americans; the man was frightened and did not know what to do, so as a last resort he offered them a cup of coffee. After a while, one of his visitors looked him straight in the eye and said "you not good, you bad," and the sheepherder went pale and began to panic. But when he saw his visitors leave peacefully and go back the way they had come, the shepherd suddenly realized that what was very bad was not him, but his coffee!

In terms of the migrants' mother tongue, Basque, it should be noted that the extensive network of Basque boardinghouses throughout the American West enabled the migrant community to stay in touch and played an important part in keeping the Basque language alive, with all the emotionally healthy connotations this involves, although as John Bieter and Mark Bieter note, the Basque cultural aspects that have the greatest longevity are dances, festivals, and the cuisine.

From a psychological perspective, it is also important to mention the isolation caused by not being able to speak the language in the host country, increasing the risk of mental issues that may even lead to psychosis, as in the aforementioned case of the sheepherder found wandering naked and unable to speak a word of English. The inability to speak the language engenders mistrust and even paranoia that in some cases, such as the one described here, lead to madness.

The complexity of intragroup life in the migrant community, which was not nearly as idyllic as some would have us believe, was reflected in a document I consulted at the Basque Museum in Boise that told the story of a migrant from a village in Gipuzkoa who said that what she found difficult upon arrival in Boise was not having to speak English, but instead the effort required to speak

Bizkaian—the dialect of Basque spoken in the neighboring province of Bizkaia—because that was what most of the Basque migrants in Boise spoke.

## Grief over Culture

We understand the concept of culture here in its broadest sense, encompassing values, world view, dietary habits, dress, leisure, religion, among other factors.

Over time, these migrants and their descendants have ended up creating their own version of Basque culture. For example, when I was in Boise, I attended a Basque dance festival in Homedale, on the state line between Oregon and Idaho, and it was readily apparent that the Basque dances being performed and the accompanying rhythms were completely different, from those back in the Basque Country. The dancers themselves admit they see themselves as different when they visit the Basque Country. They have preserved the language but above all the dances and the music. Music is another major aspect of Basque culture widely acknowledged abroad because of its originality and possibly because Basque culture is largely oral.

It should be noted that these Basque migrants preserved traditions that had been lost in the towns and villages back home. A migrant from Ispaster even affirmed "we perform more traditional Basque dances in Boise than in my home town." (Bieter 2005, 160)

As Bieter and Bieter (2005, 133) note, compared to America's individualistic society, Basque subculture and Basque community spirit are valued in themselves. This was reinforced following America's identity crisis over Vietnam and the assassinations of the Kennedy brothers and Martin Luther King Jr. Many children of Basque migrants explained that their peers at school were truly envious to see how close the migrant Basque community was and how much they enjoyed their festivals, dances, gatherings, and food.

Food is an important part of a culture. In Boise, Basque migrants told me that food was what they most missed, although this is common to all migrants. In studies on acculturative stress in migration (Atxotegi 2010), in answer to the question about what they most missed of their culture, most migrants refer to food, rather than complex cultural constructs. Nonetheless, we will be referring in due course to food in relation to orality, a core component of the ideal Basque character.

Drinking, along with the negative connotations of alcoholism, is clearly one of the risks posed by the Ulysses Syndrome. Loneliness and isolation are an invitation to alcoholism. What is more, good food and hard drinking are key aspects of Basque popular culture. Bieter and Bieter (2005, 36) state that

Basques suffered during Prohibition, which was strictly imposed especially in Idaho (with a large German Protestant community). A Basque sheepherder wrote in 1915: "I have managed to save up a little money, but I'll be saving much more thanks to Prohibition, but we're still going to drink the place dry before it is enforced." The court records of the time are full of the names of Basques accused of alcohol possession.

Another aspect of Basque culture that helped migrants settle in the American West was the value invested in action and strength and the Basques' practical approach, which was very handy for successfully tackling the difficult working conditions they encountered in their host country.

In Basque culture, for example, sports involving strength and physical prowess are very popular and are associated with competitions linked to practical activities and traditional worklife: chopping tree trunks, hauling stones, and rowing, among others. The Basque words for truth and action both have the same root, *egi*, indicating that greater importance is given to what is done than to what is said. Regarding the value of strength, it should be noted that many of the typical jokes about Basques involve laughing about how brutish they are.

The influential priest J. M. Arizmendiarrieta, founder of the now powerful and globally important cooperatives in the Mondragón Corporation business group, compared the Creation to a commercial enterprise and maintained that God made man a partner in his own business, a shareholder in the undertaking of creation (Molina 2005, 413). In a sermon delivered to Basque migrants in Boise, another priest said that a Basque's life is like a game of jai alai or pelota: contest, guile, and strength. There is a popular Basque saying that clearly reflects this practical approach linked to action: "others will do things better, we just do things right."

Concerning this grief over culture, we should mention other aspects of Basque culture that favored the migrants' integration into the local community in Boise. For example, the Basques' religious devotion was as strong as that of the city's large colony of German Protestants, who had little time for great public expressions of affection.

Also in relation to religious devotion, it should be noted that the migratory phenomenon was so intense that it gave rise to a religious order called "Betharram" from the French Basque Country that focussed on attending to the migrants' spiritual needs. The Society of Priests of the Sacred Heart of Jesus of Betharram was founded in Bétharran by Saint Michel Garikoitz in 1832. As far as I know, only one other country of emigrants, Italy, also created a religious order, namely, the Escalabrinini, founded to provide spiritual succor for Italian emigrants. Nevertheless, as mentioned earlier, the Basque Country not only generated a large amount of emigration, like Italy, but also received over half its population as immigrants, which was not at all the case in Italy. Thus, I have posited the notion of the Basque Country as the land of migrations.

Even starting from the basis that there is an ideal Basque personality, social psychology also shows that within each human group, within each society there are more differences between the individuals that comprise it, than with the individuals of another society.

Given the close connection of the son with the mother (in the final part of the text, I will develop this aspect in relation to migration), it is necessary to point out the existence of traits of orality and mania in Basque popular culture. From this perspective, the passion for food would be a clear expression of orality and would constitute one of the central pleasures of the Basques. In Basque culture, the table is more valued than the bed. Restaurants are known as "temples" (it is often said that one can go to the Basque Country for anything, except to go on a diet). In the towns of the Basque Country, there are "gastronomic societies" that constitute one of the axes of social life. The enthusiasm for singing (as described by Strabo and Humboldt) is another oral characteristic of traditional Basque society: people sing in bars, around the table.

At the psychopathological level, orality is expressed in alcoholism and mania. From a psychoanalytic perspective, alcoholism is related to an attempt to avoid sadness and depression. Thus the Basque writer Pío Baroja, in his novel *Zalacaín el aventurero* (1909, 21), portrays the character Tellagorri as "a very determined man, a prototypical Basque, but when it comes to drinking wine or some other type of alcohol this situation becomes sad."

The relationship of mania and the limited influence of the father figure can favor the absence of limits, or the inhibition of sexuality, in genital expression.

From the perspective of mania, excesses of self-assessment, and euphoria, we can point out, for example, jokes about the grandiosity of the people of Bilbao, who refer to their city as the great Bilbao and their Port as a superport. In *Don Quixote,* only one character, the Bizkaian, understands the grandiosities of the hero from La Mancha, only the Bizkaian finds his delusions of grandeur normal and understandable.

Finally, regarding this grief over culture, it is also clear that living in isolation and working as a sheepherder were obstacles to cultural integration, which requires close contact with the local population and became another extreme stressor indicative of the Ulysses Syndrome.

## Grief over the Homeland

A "homeland" encompasses landscape, colors, aromas, light, temperature, and humidity as aspects that acquire considerable significance at an emotional level because when we are children we forge very strong links with the world immediately around us.

There are stories of Basque sheepherders who speak of their longing for the green of the Basque mountains. It was not always easy to adapt to the new country: "This is a sad country in which to spend your whole life," affirmed a Basque migrant at the beginning of the last century (Bieter and Bieter 2005, 35).

Loneliness was compounded by another major psychological predicament: being in an unknown foreign land; the feeling of being a stranger in an unfamiliar, untrodden setting with a tremendous fear of becoming lost, in the words of a sheepherder from Baigorri (Saint Etienne de Baigorry, 63).

Mention necessarily has to be made of the difficulties involved in adapting to extreme weather, with temperatures as low as -30 degrees Celsius up in the mountains in summer and down in the desert in winter. Esteban Allo, from Olite in Navarre, described how his breath froze and he could track its path (Ciérbide 1996, 50). Yet there were also positive aspects to the climate: they considered the damp cold in the Basque Country to be worse than the driest conditions in the American West.

## Grief over Social Status

Social status encompasses everything related to official papers, work, housing, and access to opportunities. Generally speaking, migration involves the quest for better social status.

The sheepherders' work was very hard. Nomadic, transhumant sheepherders traveled almost 1000 km each year with their flocks, through the desert in winter and the lambing season in spring, and then up into the mountains in summer, which only left fall for resting.

Many Basque migrants did eventually improve their lot after many trials and tribulations, although the figures show that only 1 percent became rich (Bieter and Bieter 2005, 163). Others, despite failing, did not return home. One said, "I don't want to be called a bad American" (Bieter and Bieter 2005, 41): they faced the danger of returning home after being fleeced, and never was the term more appropriate than for the migrant sheepherders.

The same thing applies to today's migrations in Europe. I have witnessed cases of Africans who say: "I can't go back empty-handed, they will think that if things have gone badly for me it's because I have the evil eye and they will shun me." Migrants have a great need to show that so much effort, so much suffering, has been worthwhile. Nonetheless, some had no choice but to return, as they could not stand so much stress and ended up making themselves ill. They had lost everything, or almost everything, they had invested in the journey, in their stay. The Basques in Boise eventually introduced a cash fund for repatriating those sheepherders who could not put up with so much hardship.

The situation of migrant Basque women was also very difficult. These women worked in the boardinghouses frequented by Basque men migrating to America. Their lives, too, were very hard, working interminably long working days. Lucy Garatea, for example, worked every day of the week, with only two hours off on Sundays. The women's tough lives led to premature ageing, according to Martín Vizcay (Ciérbide 1996, 72). Yet such hard work also had its rewards, and so the next generation of migrants recorded a number of successes, as in the case of Jerónima Echeverría, the daughter of a sheepherder who emigrated at the age of fifteen. She became a professor and senior editor of the *Journal of Basque Studies*. Nevertheless, Jerónima explains that Basque migrants around Fresno found it very difficult to get ahead in life (Ciérbide 1996, 62).

When the United States enacted its first legislation restricting immigration in 1921, many incoming Basques began to experience the downside of not having the necessary documents, the right papers, like many of the migrants from outside the European Union now living in the Basque Country, and this situation of intense stress is one of the triggers of the Ulysses Syndrome.

### Grief over Group Membership

People tend to identify with the group they belong to, and in migration that identification may be undermined when interacting with other groups. Migrants have to elaborate their grief over the reduction or loss of contact with the group they belong to, as well as cope with the stress of meeting and belonging to a new group. This grief refers to issues related to prejudices, xenophobia, racism, and so on.

Immigration rules such as the Johnson-Reed Act (1924) and the Taylor Grazing Act (1934) (Ciérbide 1996, 61) in the United States were very strict and were criticized for their lack of respect for human rights and for being discriminatory. Migrants were carefully screened on Ellis Island, in New York Harbor, to reject anyone with health problems, expelling the sick and disabled. María Yoldy explains the case of a young man from Rocaforte who was traveling with his father's group (Ciérbide 1996, 106). One of his fingers was shorter than normal, so he was sent home. Anyone found to have a mental disorder had an X put on their application form and also had to return home.

When the United States enacted its first legislation restricting immigration, many of the Basques who arrived had to suffer the difficult personal, vocational, and social experience of being undocumented. Nick Beristain was told by his boss: "I pay 225 dollars, but as you're here illegally I'm going to pay you 175, take it or leave it" (Ciérbide 1996, 45).

At other times, they were simply cheated after spending the whole year alone in the mountains: their employers told them the business was in difficulties and could not pay them. In these cases, the migrants' lack of social capital posed a huge setback, because they found it very difficult to defend their rights. Fortunately, in many cases the Basque associations of fellow countrymen at the boardinghouses helped them claim what was rightfully theirs.

Although Basque sheepherders were generally considered hard-working and honest, they also suffered from racism: the niceties leveled at the Basques included such insults as filthy, treacherous, and meddlesome, which is how they were described in the *Caldwell Tribune* in 1909, although it did admit that it was good that they had come because, like all migrants, they were paid less than local labor. Ciérbide (1996, 88) cites a 1906 text by R. Wilson in which the latter manifests his prejudices toward the Basques, saying that they are short men, almost all vagabonds, who only live to make money, and own neither water nor land. Basque sheepherders were known to be frugal, although for others they were mean and miserly. The truth is that, like most migrants, they did jobs that nobody else wanted to do; they did not cause their employers any problems, and they generated wealth, but they were still subject to racism.

As Ciérbide (1996, 88-9) states, they earned respect for putting up with things that others would not or could not do, always thinking of their loved ones. Senator Key Pittman testified before a court in 1913 that Basque sheepherders lacked intelligence and human decency and were like slaves because they accepted inhuman living conditions. Nevertheless, this affirmation was challenged, and on June 29, 1913, the *Elko Free Press* reported that Basques were homemakers and good husbands and fathers. Yet in August that same year, Senator Pittman responded saying Basques were short and of lesser intelligence.

In 1911, fortunately, the US Forest Service praised the Basques' work ethic and strength, as well as their ability to withstand the arduous life of wandering sheepherders.

As time passes, all migrants reassess their migratory project. The aforementioned memoir *Sweet Promised Land* (Laxalt 2000) provides a masterful account of this narrative, leaving it right to the end to tell us whether the old shepherd

Laxalt will return to Atharratze or remain in Nevada after fifty years without seeing the village of his birth, which he left when he was no more than a child.

It is interesting to address the subject of identity from the perspective of successive generations of migrants, as Bieter and Bieter (2005, 5) do, quoting Hansen: "what the son wishes to forget the grandson wishes to remember." We have already noted that these migrants retained a strong awareness of their Basque identity, preserving dances, festivals, and traditions that have disappeared in their hometowns; it is an identity with positive connotations, rather than being in opposition to something, which is the best way of forging an identity. On the specific subject of the complexity of identity, there is an old Jewish joke that tells the story of a rabbi who is shipwrecked and has to spend many long years on a desert island. When he is finally found, he shows his rescuers what he has built on the island, taking them to see the two synagogues he has constructed. His rescuers, somewhat mystified, ask him why he needed two synagogues when he was living alone on a desert island. The rabbi answers: "it's very simple. I built one synagogue for my prayers, and the other to avoid at all costs: I can't stand the sight of it!" This is very much in keeping with the Basque saying "you can live without friends, but never without enemies."

In terms of the complexity of experiencing one's own identity, Martín Vizcay, from Orondritz (Olóndriz), describes the rivalries that emerge between Basques from one or the other side of the Spanish-French border while they play the card game *mus* or bet on pelota matches at the Basque center in San Francisco. In terms of social psychology, it is preferable to construct rich, complex identities.

**Grief over Physical Risks**

This refers to the risks run by someone emigrating and having to face numerous environmental and often hostile changes: contact with new diseases, dangerous jobs, and so on. Personal safety is a basic psychological need, like attachment, as noted in the now seminal studies on psychology by Abraham Maslow.

Even the journey itself to America involved hardship and had its own dangers. The ship taking Juan Achabal, from Ispaster, sank. He was miraculously rescued by another ship. He arrived in America with just the clothes he was wearing, as he had lost all his belongings. Yet his story had a happy ending, as years later John Achabal ended up being one of the wealthiest men in the United States. The *Idaho Statesman* reported that on returning home in 1925 he had a brand-new sports car shipped over from Detroit, and all the kids in his village ran along beside him trying to touch the fabulous vehicle. There can be few images as iconic of the psychological aspects of migration as that of Juan/John's triumphant ride around the streets of Ispaster. So much endeavor, so many set-backs in far-off America had all been worthwhile! (Bieter and Bieter 2005, 43).

As an illustration of the difficult conditions in which these journeys were made, migrants tell of eating the stones in prunes to get all the nourishment they could out of the dried fruit because they were so hungry. They also told how they were given bananas to eat on the ship, and as they had never seen them before they ate them whole, skin and all.

The sheepherders faced numerous risks on these migrations. There was the risk of not being cared for in the event of emergency, since they lived in isolation. In *Paroles de bergers du Pays Basque au Far West*, Gaby Etchebarne (2005, 66) narrates the case of a sheepherder struck down by crippling sciatica while on his own high up in the mountains, where he was looking after 2,000 sheep.

There was the risk of being attacked by pumas, rattlesnakes (one sheepherder talked about hopping through the pastures like a dancer for fear of being bitten), bears, and coyotes, especially in spring when the sheep are lambing (Esteban Allo, from Olite, explained how on one occasion bears and coyotes killed 450 lambs.) (Ciérbide 1996, 48). Tarantulas were another danger according to a sheepherder from the Erro Valley (Ciébide 1996, 46).

There were high winds, mountain blizzards, and also whiteouts, in which massive windstorms and snowstorms made it impossible to see anything for days on end. The sheepherders were forced to abandon their flocks to survive.

There was the fact of living almost constantly without shelter, up in the mountains in summer and down in the desert in winter, in places with such unsettling names as Death Valley or Funeral Mountains.

There was the threat of danger from violence in the American West, as featured in so many Hollywood Westerns, to the extent they have become a whole genre in their own right. Initially, the sheepherders were nomads and vagrants, and they came into conflict with ranchers and cowboys. On April 13, 1903, the *Nevada State Herald* reported a pitched battle between Basques and cowboys, with numerous fatalities. The cowboys dragged the sheepherders along with their horses and then finished them off. The dead men's companions then murdered the cowboys during the night when they were sleeping. Ciérbide describes how the Basques suffered major persecution in western Nevada at the beginning of the twentieth century (Ciérbide 1996, 88).

Yet many of these sheepherders were tough and were used to long treks and the dangers of smuggling across the Spanish-French border in the Pyrenees. During the nineteenth-century Carlist Wars, uniforms were brought across by smugglers. Not even the village priests in the Basque mountains considered smuggling or *gaulana* (meaning "night work" in Basque) to be a bad thing; it was a way of life, although admittedly a highly risky one, but it prepared the men both physically and mentally for the adversities of the American West.

Adrien Gachiteguy (2005) tells of sheepherders who died after falling asleep before reaching safe shelter due to exhaustion. He describes the case of a young sheepherder who awoke one morning to discover a completely snow-covered landscape in which there was not a single sheep to be seen. In desperation, he went in search of another sheepherder, who reassured him and helped him to find the sheep: they were buried under the snow. In 1947, the US army had to intervene to rescue sheepherders because of the unusually heavy snowfall that year.

Gaby Etchebarne (2005, 23) notes that 20 percent of the sheepherders died through illness or suicide. She tells the story of a sheepherder who came down from the mountain to have a wound treated and explained: "I didn't do this to myself on purpose. Others do, though: they just can't take it anymore!"

## Psychological Characteristics of Basque Culture in Relation to Emigration

With respect to migration, there are two contrasting poles in Basque culture; these two poles are very marked, as in a dialectical or thesis–antithesis relationship. There is a centripetal pole and a centrifugal pole: a kind of cardiac systole (a contraction) and diastole (the expulsion). Interestingly, the heart, the organ that represents emotions, affectivity, in Basque is called *bihotz*, which translates to "two noises" and shows what the ancient Basque language, spoken by the immigrant Basque shepherds, already knew; from thousands of years ago, the heart had two noises.

There is a centripetal pole with an almost atavistic link to the territory: the world related to the hamlet, the farmhouse (*baserri* in Basque), and the mountain pastures. This link is so strong that in the Basque rural areas people are not known by their surname but by their hamlet or farmhouse name. Thus, my mother, for example, who is from the Iturbe hamlet of Garay, in Bizkaia, is surprised that in the investigations on the origin of the Basque emigrants, the hamlet from which the emigrant comes is not taken into account anymore. "From many of my neighbors of the other villages we had no idea of how they were called, for us the name of the hamlet was what identified us as a person."

This tendency indicates an intense link to the land, which is also seen in the popular poem "Altzateko Jaun" (The Lord of Altzate) by Xabier Lete, in which the isolation and lack of contact with outer civilization is poetically exalted and taking refuge in the mists of the Larrun, a mythical mountain of the

Franco-Spanish border, is idealized. "Altzateko Jaun" is based on a legend of the mountains of Navarre about one of the oldest lords in the Basque Country unwaveringly clinging to his land. The poem reads:

| | |
|---|---|
| Alzateko Jaun, gure izetearen testigu zuzena | The Lord of Altzate, a witness of our conduct, |
| makurtu gabeko zuhaitz lerdena . . . | a tall tree that does not lean . . . |
| | |
| bainan guztiok jakin dezagun bidea | But for everyone to know what the road is, |
| nondik dijoan | |
| Alzateko jaun, hor zaude zu. | there you are, Lord of Alzate. |
| Bidasoaren ezker-eskuin udaberrian | In spring the banks of Bidasoa bloom, |
| lore gorriak | |
| ixilikako ur izkutua: | hidden and silent water |
| lurrak badaki kontu hoien berri | The earth already knows those stories |
| eta hor dago ixil-ixilik. | and there it is in silence, in silence. |

Another great popular poem, "Xalbadoren heriotzean," is a posthumous eulogy to a famous poet shepherd of the Pyrenees, Fernando Aire Etxart, known as Xalbador, who died in 1976—a man who preferred his mountains to any contact with the outside world. This echoes a very peculiar characteristic of Basque history: that of being a country that has never invaded another country. On the contrary, Basque culture idealizes retreat into its mountains and its myths.

| | |
|---|---|
| Nun hago, zer larretan | Where are you, in what meadow shepherd |
| Urepeleko artzaina, | of Urepel climbing the mountainsides |
| Mendi hegaletan gora | you escaped |

But at the other pole there is also a powerful impulse to go as far as possible from the country. As mentioned above, during the last century much of the Basque-born population emigrated to all parts of the world. There are several times more Basques or descendants of Basques living abroad than in the country itself! Michel, a son of Xalbador, the poet shepherd, who took refuge in its mountains, was a sheepherder in America. It is impossible to further contrast their two lives. The father lived attached to the pastures next to the *baserri* while the son went to the other end of the planet!

From a psychological perspective, the powerful image of the Basque woman and especially of the Basque mother, of the *amatxu*, generates an enormous oedipal conflict that feeds these two poles: a desire to return to the maternal womb, to the mists of the mountains full of witches and mythological beings, dancing as in Lete's song, and another desire to escape, the farther better to overcome the incestuous impulses.

It could be argued that the more men emigrate, the more important the role of women who remain. The important role of women in Basque culture could be linked, among other factors, to the high percentage of men who emigrate. Even in the seventeenth century, 75 percent of the population of Bizkaia was female. In Basque culture the most important gods are feminine: Mari, a woman, is the most important god, while her husband, Sugaar, has a very secondary role.

This migration of men is linked to a society where families often included ten children or more, with a differential-type inheritance, according to the Todd model (1990), in which only one child would inherit the house and this led many of the other children to emigrate to the Americas, Australia, among other destinations.

For the anthropologist Andrés Ortiz Osés (1980), this Basque matriarchy has much older roots and is related to a collectivist conception of society. The persecution of the *akelarres*, witches' covens—made up mostly by women and persecuted by men—demonstrates the struggle between the matriarchal and the patriarchal model.

The son is intensely linked to the mother in traditional Basque culture. Thus in the movie *Ocho apellidos vascos* (Eight Basque surnames) this situation is very well picked up when Patxi, a Basque sailor, returns from Newfoundland after months of sailing to visit Getaria, his hometown. He has barely kept in touch with his daughter. He does not even know when her birthday is. That is up to the mother. Children are above all brought up by their mothers in traditional Basque culture, while the fathers are friendly but more distant.

So that, in my opinion, in relation to migration there are two contrasting poles in Basque culture. The two poles are very marked, as in a relationship of dialectical type, thesis-antithesis. This centripetal pole and centrifugal pole show, as I have indicated, an intense orality, a very primitive connection with the Basque land, a connection so radical that it could be found on the edge of the fusion. And this conflict with fusional impulses could be a great psychological motor to emigrate. But obviously these considerations, these hypotheses, will have to be demonstrated in further research.

## Bibliography

Atxotegi, Joseba. 1999. "Los duelos de la migración: una perspectiva psicopatológica y psicosocial." In *Medicina y cultura*, edited by Enrique Perdiguero and Josep M. Comelles. Barcelona: Editorial Bellaterra.

——. 2010. *Emigrar en el siglo XXI: estrés y duelo migratorio en el mundo de hoy. El Síndrome del inmigrante con estrés crónico y múltiple-Síndrome de Ulises*. 2nd edition. Llançá: Ediciones el mundo de la mente.

——. 2012. *Los trastornos mentales, un enigmático legado evolutivo. Por qué la evolución ha seleccionado la psicodiversidad y no ha eliminado los trastornos mentales?* Llancá: Ediciones "El mundo de la mente".

Atxotegi, Joseba, and María Morales. 2010. "Características de los inmigrantes con Síndrome de estrés cróncio y múltiple del inmigrante o Síndrome de Ulises." *Norte de salud mental* 8, no. 37: 23–30. Athena Nework. At http://www.laredatenea.com/.

Agirre, Jose Antonio. 1944; 1991. *Escape via Berlin: Eluding Franco and Hitler's Europe.* Reno: University of Nevada University Press.

Barandiarán, José Miguel. 1972. *El mundo en la mente popular vasca.* Donostia: Auñamendi.

Baroja, Pio. 1976. *Zalacaín el aventurero.* Madrid: Astral.

Basabe, Nekane, ed. 2004. *Identidad, Migración y Cultura.* Bilbao: Inguruak. *Revista vasca de Sociología*, no. 38.

Berry John. 2011. *Cross-Cultural Psychology.* Cambridge: Cambridge University Press.

Bieter, John, and Mark Bieter. 2005. *Un legado que perdura. La historia de los vascos en Idaho.* Vitoria-Gasteiz: Eusko Jaurlaritza.

Bhugra, Dinesh, and Susham Gupta, eds. 2011. *Migration in Mental Health.* Cambridge: Cambridge University Press.

Bowlby, John. 1980. *La pérdida afectiva.* Barcelona: Paidós.

Ciérbide, Ricardo. 1996. *Vasconavarros en el Oeste americano. Memorias de un viaje y otras historias.* Tafalla: Edit Ainzúa.

Coleman, James. 1984. *Foundations of Social Theory.* Cambridge, MA: Belknap Press of Harvard University.

Crawford, Michael, and Benjamin Campbell. 2012. *Causes and Consequences of Human Migrations.* Cambridge: Cambridge University Press.

Douglass, William. 1973. *Muerte en Murélaga.* Barcelona: Barral.

Etxebarne, Gaby. 2005. *Paroles de bergers. Du pays basque au Far West.* Donostia: Editorial Elkar.

Foucault, Michael. 1984. *El nacimiento de la clínica.* México: Siglo XXI.

———. 2004. *Biopolítica.* México: Siglo XXI.

Gachiteguy, Adrien. 2005. *Les basques dans l'ouest americain.* Bayonne: Edit Iru errege.

Gorroño, Iñaki. 1979. *Experiencia cooperativa en el País Vasco.* Durango: Leopoldo Zugaza.

Homer. 2015. *Odyssey.* London: Peguin Books.

Ibáñez, Blasco. 1999. *El intruso.* Madrid: Editorial San Antonio.

Irujo, Xabier. *Expelled from the Motherland.* 2012. Reno: Center for Basque Studies, University of Nevada, Reno.

Laxalt, Robert. 2000. *Dulce tierra prometida.* Donostia: Editorial Ttartalo.

Marcos, L. R. 1976. "Bilinguals in Psychotherapy: Language as an Emotional Barrier." *American Journal of Psychotherapy 30*: 552–60.

Molina, Fernando. 2005. *Jose María Arizmendiarreta.* Mondragón: Ediciones de la Caja Laboral Popular.

Montalbán, Yosu. 2018. *El Dr. Areilza, el médico de los mineros.* Bilbao: Muelle de Uribitarte Editores.

Ortiz Osés, Andrés. 1980. *Matriarcalismo vasco.* Bilbao: Servicio de Publicaciones de la Universidad de Deusto.

Reeve, Johnmarshall. 2002. *Motivación y emoción.* Madrid: McGraw-Hill.

Ruiz Olabuénaga, José Ignacio, and María Cristina Blanco. 1994. *La inmigración vasca. Análisis tri-generacional de 150 años de inmigración.* Bilbao: Universidad de Deusto.

San Sebastián, Koldo. *El exilio vasco en América*. 2014. Vitoria-Gasteiz: Eusko Jaurlaritza.

Seligman, Martin. 1975. *Helplessness: On Depression, Development, and Death*. San Francisco. W. H. Freeman.

Todd, Emmanuel. 1990. *La invención de Europa*. Barcelona: Busquets.

# 3

# Emigration as a Social Pathology

## Impact, Causes, and Interpretations of the Basque Overseas Diaspora in the Nineteenth and Twentieth Centuries

*Oscar Álvarez-Gila*

### When Basques were migrants . . .[1]

Migratory movements (to, from, and within the Basque Country) must be understood as one of the fundamental elements that gave birth to modern present-day Basque society, whose influence spread beyond pure demographics to impact its economic growth, social evolution, political development, and even cultural features (Álvarez Gila 2013). On the one hand, due to the process of industrialization that started in the 1860s in the area surrounding Bilbao as a consequence of working the iron ore mines of Somorrostro, the central part of Bizkaia received huge numbers of immigrants who changed the region dramatically along with an accelerated process of industrialization and modernization (Montero García 1995). The total population living on the so-called Left Bank (the highly industrialized space between Bilbao and the coast along the river Nervion/Ibaizabal) grew from 62,417 inhabitants in 1877 to 304,364 in 1930. Even though many newcomers to the area arrived from other parts of the Basque Country, most of the immigrants actually came from non-Basque regions of Spain. It is calculated that, by 1975, about 84 percent of the inhabitants of the Left Bank had been born or had family roots outside the Basque Country (González Portilla and García Abad 2006).

On the other hand, and seemingly paradoxically, by the 1840s Basques had also started emigrating in massive numbers abroad, mainly to the Americas, and specifically to destinations such as Argentina, Uruguay, Cuba, and the United States. However, migration overseas was not a new practice for nineteenth-century Basques. In fact, it had had deep, long-standing roots in the cultural and socioeconomic ethos of Basque people for centuries, since the first European conquerors and settlers arrived in the Americas, and continually thereafter. In the late Middle Ages, for instance, there are mentions of the presence of Basque sailors and merchants throughout Europe, from Seville to Bruges (Álvarez Gila and Angulo Morales 2014); and throughout the early modern era, plenty of Basques were settled in most of the most vibrant cities in Spain (Angulo Morales 2016). But the "discovery" of America changed these patterns dramatically. The Americas soon became the main destination for a majority of Basques who abandoned their country to settle down anywhere else. As a result, the presence of Basque immigrants in the New World can be dated back to the very early moments of colonization of the continent (Aramburu Zudaire 2005). As subjects of both Spain and France, Basques from both sides of the Pyrenees Mountains had the right to move and settle within the boundaries of the Spanish and French colonial empires—and in effect, that is what they did. References to the activity, presence, success, and failure of Basque immigrants can be found in any region of the Americas controlled by either of the two crowns that the Basque Country belonged to (Vázquez de Prada and Amores Carredano 1991). The historical heritage of almost any village, town, or city in the Basque Country itself still preserves a lot of reminders left by wealthy returnees (known as *indianuak* or *amerikanuak*) with the aim of showing their countrymen stories of success and empowerment, from the early sixteenth to the twentieth centuries, and beyond (González Cembellín, 1993; Paliza Monduate, 1998, 2001).

The abrupt culmination of French and especially Spanish colonialism in the Americas by the first quarter of the nineteenth century stopped the free movement of Basques to these territories for a while, but it was not able to bring it to an end. In fact, soon after the new independent Latin American nations started their own path to nation-building, the demand for manpower to colonize and make economically profitable the immense regions taken recently and violently from the hands of Native Americans turned immigration into a necessity in the eyes of political leaders. One of the most influential authors was Argentinian Juan Bautista Alberdi. In his renowned book *Bases y puntos de partida para la organización política de la República Argentina* (1852) he proposed immigration as a way of assuring the future economic and social success of Latin American countries, summed up in the motto "to govern is to populate":

> To govern is to populate in the sense that to populate means to educate, to better, to civilize, to became richer and bigger spontaneously and quickly, as has happened in the United States. . . . But in order

to civilize by means of population, it is mandatory to make it with civilized peoples; if we want to educate our America in freedom and industry, it is necessary to populate it with people from the part of Europe that is more advanced in freedom and industry, as happens in the United States (Alberdi, 1852).

No one can deny this vision emerged from quite a racist perspective, because it was based on a hierarchy of human races and peoples. Nonetheless, this proposal became rapidly accepted by most Latin American politicians, which opened up a legislative race to attract European immigrants. The successful example of the United States, whose economic and demographic landscape was changing rapidly thanks to increasing flows of settlers from Europe, contributed to making the ideas of Alberdi and his followers popular among the political leaders of most Latin American countries. Therefore, in a short span of time, most of these countries had passed their own legislation to promote European settlement. The response to such dreams and efforts was nonetheless disparate: some countries enjoyed quite a successful outcome from the process (for example, Argentina, Uruguay, Brazil, and, to a certain extent, Chile and the still Spanish island of Cuba); many others, on the contrary, did not (Mörner 1985; Míguez 2003). As José C. Moya emphasizes:

> The surplus population created by Europe's demographic expansion and economic modernization did not simply head for countries with flourishing economies. It moved toward specific environments. 96 percent of the 56 million Europeans who left their continent in the century or so after Napoleonic Wars settled in four regions: North America . . . where 67 percent of the total settled; the River Plate (formed by eastern Argentina, Uruguay, and southern Brazil), which attracted more than 20 percent of the total; Australasia, with 7 percent; and in smaller numbers, South Africa. These regions comprise the bulk of the non-European Temperate Zone and have warm-to-cool climates with an annual precipitation of 50 to 150 centimeters, thinly spread aboriginal population, some of the world's best pasture and wheat-producing lands, immense herds of cattle and flocks of sheep, consistent surplus production of grains and, with the exception of South Africa, largely Caucasian populations (Moya 2003, 13).

Such a large volume of people on the move soon became one of the major topics of social and political discussion, both in the European countries of departure and the American countries of arrival. Nonetheless, its impact in both regions was undisputable, leaving its imprint in the way the present-day world was constructed and still is today.

### Basque Participation in Modern European Emigration Overseas

Basques were among the first European peoples to join these new emigration flows in massive numbers. One of the first questions that emerges when speaking of a demographically based social phenomenon such as migration is linked to the problem of quantification, summed up in the following question: How many Basques migrated to the Americas? In a country that, taken as a whole, has today a population of just over three million people,[2] it is still difficult to present accurate data about the flows that brought Basque people from their hometowns to relocate in other places, regions, or even countries. On this matter one could say that no major advances have been made since José Manuel Azcona Pastor asserted in 1992 that, "it is impossible to ascertain exactly how many Basques migrated overseas" (1992, 52).

It is true that some research has attempted to present a depiction as close as possible to what the real figures of Basque emigration could have been. For this purpose, historians must overcome several hurdles, and usually with no or little success, because the task is really hard to achieve. Among these obstacles, three stand out with regard to the use of the statistics and other available quantitative quasi-statistical sources.

First, the main problem is that Basques do not exist, at least from a statistical point of view. Since the implementation of an internationally comparable system of state-based official statistics, usually managed and recorded by national and/or supranational bureaus, the tendency has been to use political nationalities as the basic unit for quantification. Basques are, therefore, included among either Spanish or French migrants. It is true that in some cases, thanks to qualitative information, we can guess approximately at the relative importance of Basque representation in these official figures. Something like this happens, for instance, in historians' research on the early period of European immigration to Uruguay. As Magnus Mörner (1996, 22) says, "between 1835 and 1852, a total of 32,934 immigrants" arrived in Montevideo, "of which 17,765 were French and 8,281 Spanish"; yet whatever the case, he states, "we know that both groups were actually composed almost entirely of Basques" (see also Marenales Rossi 1991, 127–53).

Second, even when the statistical records somehow differentiate Basque emigration—or, at least, give clues that can be used to obtain a more precise view of Basque emigration within the wider Spanish or French numbers—the data is still far from collecting all the migratory movements from and to the Basque region. Such local and regional statistics or quasi-statistics were more common in the Northern Basque Country, under French rule. Henry de Charnisay, for example, sums up in a list of all the quantifications of French-Basque emigration to the Americas collected by the departmental authorities of the Basses-Pyrénées, to which the Basque Country belongs:

| Author | Researched | Number of Departures |
|---|---|---|
| Barrère | 1831–1841 | 8,547 Basques (of which, 6,912 were men and 1,635 women) |
| Azevedo | 1832–1841 | 7,357 from the French Basque Country and Béarn (5,900 men and 1,457 women) |
| Picamilh | 1832–1858 | 35,000 emigrants from the Basses-Pyrénées (of which, 30,000 obtained passports) |
| Echeverry | 1832–1881 | 61,847 emigrants from the Basses-Pyrénées "overseas" |
| Etcheverry | 1832–1897 | 79,262 emigrants from the Basses-Pyrénées "to South America" |
| Butel | 1847–1872 | 64,000 emigrants from the Basses-Pyrénées "to South America" |
| Chandeze | 1857–1891 | 61,248 emigrants from Basses-Pyrénées "to South America" |
| Levasseur | 1880–1889 | 15,474 emigrants from Basses-Pyrénées "to South America" |

Source: Charnisay (1996, 114–15).

Less information is available, surprisingly enough, from the Spanish side of the Basque Country. The late implementation of statistical collection by the Spanish state on international emigration, which only started in the early 1880s, and the lack of an adequate disaggregation of data on a regional basis make it more difficult to determine what the movement from the Basque Country was like. Data is therefore fragmentary. Ángel García-Sanz Marcotegui (1989), for instance, accepts an annual average of about one thousand emigrants departing from Navarre between 1879 and 1883. Fernando Muru Ronda (1996, 207), meanwhile, states that for the period 1911–1928, the annual average number of departures from the Spanish Basque Country was also about one thousand people, with a pronounced drop from the first half of the 1910s on (about three thousand departures every year), and also because of the negative impact of World War I, which hindered transatlantic traffic.[3]

Third, there are other movements that are by nature impossible to analyze using only official statistical data. One of them is illegal emigration, that is, the departure of emigrants to the Americas without giving any preceptive report to the authorities, on account of their not having obtained a passport or permit to emigrate or belonging to groups for whom emigration was forbidden: for example, young men waiting to be called up for military service. As we have seen before, few sources even attempt to give an approximative approach to the possible scope of illegal emigration; most of them simply ignore it. The second of these other movements is the question of return migration, which is not usually included as an observable item in most available statistics. We do not know how many of those Basques who, after crossing the Atlantic to try their luck, actually settled there forever or how many chose to come back home for whatever reason.

Among the few scholarly estimates made about the extent of Basque emigration, the most valuable and widely accepted today is still the amount proposed for the period between 1840 and 1950 and the whole Basque Country (both the Spanish and French regions together) by William A. Douglass and Jon Bilbao, who speak of a possible range of 200,000–250,000 Basque emigrants (Douglass and Bilbao 1975, 136–37).

However, instead of focusing on the actual absolute figures, it is more important to put them into their demographic context in the Basque Country. For example, Basque emigration seems to be exceptional within the practices of both Spain and France. Using data published during the nineteenth century by French state officials, Mörner (1996, 25) stresses that, "in [the period] 1875–77 no less than 24 percent of the total overseas emigration departing from France came from the department of the Basses-Pyrénées, which only comprised a tiny 0.5 percent of the total French population by then." One could say something similar, even though the percentage difference is not as remarkable as in the case of the Northern Basque Country, about Spanish-Basque provinces, which are among the Spanish regions with higher participation levels historically in overseas migration, alongside other northern regions such as Galicia, Asturias, Cantabria, and Catalonia. Whatever the case, all contemporary witnesses coincide in stating that, qualitatively speaking, emigration was a truly major phenomenon in the Basque Country and its impact was visible in many aspects of everyday life. It is because of this that, by the first decade of the twentieth century, when Basque emigration abroad was at its highest historical peak, Pierre Lhande (1910, xvii) could say that, "in order to be a real Basque, three conditions are needed: to have a Basque-sounding last name that denotes one's origins, to speak 'the language of Aitor', and . . . to have an uncle in the Americas."

Similar approaches can be taken as regards the main destinations of Basque migratory currents. It is widely accepted that Argentina and Uruguay were the main points of arrival for Basque immigrants throughout the nineteenth century: according to Douglass and Bilbao (1975, 137), four out of every five immigrants could have selected either of these countries. Moreover, as William

A. Douglass and Gloria Totoricagüena (1999, 263) state, "even if we take into account the wisest estimates, it is evident that Argentina was" and still is, "the country that has received the largest number of Basques in the last two centuries." Up to the 1880s, similar numbers of Basques from both sides of the Franco-Spanish border emigrated, but thereafter Basques from the southern provinces started to be more numerous. Some indirect information estimates that Basques made up about 10–15 percent of the total population of Argentina by 1910.[4] Unlike Argentina and Uruguay, Cuba still remained under Spanish colonial rule throughout the nineteenth century. As such, the Spanish governments always tried to direct the main overseas emigratory flows of Spanish subjects to this island. These attempts were partially successful, and therefore Cuba became the third largest point of destination for Basques. This situation even lasted after the Spanish-American War of 1898, the end of the colonial rule, and the independence of Cuba in 1902; indeed, Cuba continued to be a point of attraction for Basques until the eve of the Great Depression of 1929, when overseas migration abruptly stopped. In Latin America there were other minor destinations like Chile, Brazil, and Mexico. Finally, from the 1850s on, the United States emerged as the only main focus of Basque immigration outside the Latin American cultural space; and the Basque emigratory process to the United States would last longer than its counterparts, finally coming to an end in the 1960s (Álvarez Gila 2004, 325–30).

## On the Causes: The Fever of Migration

In 1882 Julien Vinson—a renowned French scholar on the Basques, their language, and their culture—summed up as follows the most widely accepted reasons for why so many Basques were abandoning their homeland to migrate overseas:

> Assertions made by emigrants when asking for their passports establish that the causes for their departure are low salaries, increasing difficulties in living in their homeland because of the rarefaction of livelihoods, invitations by emigrants that preceded them and who send home remittances, the example of those that have returned after amassing huge fortunes in a short period of time, the measures put in place by travel agencies to facilitate the payment of passages, and, finally, the ardent propaganda of emigration agents (Vinson 1882, 28).

To a certain extent, one of the historiographical debates that has been going on for decades about Basque emigration deals with the problem of this very same topic of the causes of migration. As Vinson pointed out, some causes—probably the most important—were economic, either from a reactive or proactive point of view. One year earlier, for example, the provincial government of Bizkaia had ordered an inquiry to be made in every town in the province to elucidate whether emigrants were "escaping from poverty" in their homes or "looking for better opportunities" in the Americas.[5] Answers were inconclusive: to a certain extent, every migrant had a set of reasons that usually included several elements, and only in a few cases did one of these two different factors prove more important than the other. Lucas Mallada, reflecting on late nineteenth-century Spanish migration, admits that these two ways of understanding economic migration—one proactive, that is, the pull of booming economies; and the other reactive, in other words the push of crisis and poverty—are intermingled: "everywhere there is wealth in the world, myriads of people will arrive in order to enjoy it, thus creating a pole of attraction; on the contrary, where resources are scarce or get exhausted, people are expelled" (Mallada 1890, 6). By the mid-twentieth century, the historiography on international migration accepted the pull-push theory, in which the conditions at both the point of departure and the place of arrival are considered to be equally relevant when it comes to explaining any migratory movement (Dorigo and Tobler 1983). Therefore several economic reasons have been given to explain the Basque exodus: from a crisis in the traditional agricultural sector to the lack of industry, especially in the Northern Basque Country, as well as the availability of cheap land for agriculture in the Americas and the differences in prices and salaries between the places of departure and the countries of arrival (Sánchez Alonso 1995).

Social factors have also been proposed. For example, the fear of military service, introduced in most European countries during the nineteenth century, is commonly said to be one of the reasons behind Basque migration. It is true that the desire to avoid this obligation, which was understood by many people to be a waste of time, could be behind a lot of personal decisions to flee overseas, but it remains unconvincing as the only explanation for the migration boom (Sarmiento and Álvarez Gila 2018). The prevalent model of family and inheritance systems in the Basque Country was also supposed to play a role: since the very first moments of massive migration, it had been commonplace among social thinkers and researchers to establish some kind of connection between inheritance rules and liability to emigrate. As Totoricagüena concludes, the core argument of those who defend this connection was based upon the idea that:

. . . [t]he fueros guaranteed the practice of selecting one of the former owner's offspring to be the new owner, and other siblings could be disinherited, although in practice they were usually provided with dowries. This meant that in every family there were most likely three or four siblings that were candidates for emigration. Even today in certain villages the traditional rules of male primogeniture are followed, in other areas a female is selected, while in parts of Nafarroa the heir or heiress is chosen according to individual merit without reference to gender or birth order. Until recently, the remaining siblings would have to depend upon the new owner for employment, accommodation, care, etc. and although family members, there usually was not enough work to finance the entire extended family. Unmarried siblings had the right to stay with the family farmstead as long as they stayed single, some married other heads of household, others turned to religious professions or the military. For thousands, a more viable alternative to alleviate hardship was emigration (Totoricagüena 2000, 106).

The inheritance hypothesis of Basque migration, although suggestive, has nevertheless been subject to criticism due to several flaws. Authors like Charnisay, Douglass and Bilbao, Martha Marenales Rossi, and Azcona Pastor, among others, present quite solid evidence about this link, but on the other hand, there is still some unexplainable complexity behind it. In fact, the most commonly made mistake about this topic is the same idea, as expressed by Totoricagüena, that there is only one inheritance system in the Basque Country, which is not true at all (Fernández de Pinedo 1995, 18). The differences between inheritance systems do indeed modulate rhythms and protagonists of migration, but do not explain the mere existence of migration as such.

Nevertheless, even though none of these factors alone is sufficient to explain the prevalence of emigration within Basque society during this period, all of them have to be taken into account within a complex system of different, interrelated factors that, once we put all of them together, are responsible for the huge dimensions the phenomenon took on in the Basque Country. In fact, contemporary witnesses were well aware of the dimensions of what many of them did not hesitate to define as an "exodus" (Álvarez Gila 2004, 340). Moreover Moya (1999), departing from an in-depth study on overseas migration from several regions in the Iberian Peninsula, including among others the northern Navarre, underscores the fact that, for those contemporary observers who witnessed the growing process of migration that had been taking place since the mid-nineteenth century, migration was seen as a kind of "plague" or "fever": it was conceived of as spreading like an infectious disease, being transmitted from one town, valley, or county to the contiguous ones by the means of contagion. Rocío García Abad (2003, 348) explains that the "utilization of terms such as 'fever', 'plague', and 'epidemic' refers to a fast dissemination of both information and behavior on migration."

The use of medical terminology to describe the most prominent—and, from the point of view of most opinion-makers, also the most threatening—socioeconomic phenomenon at that moment was commonplace, not only among Basque thinkers, journalists, politicians, and Catholic clerics, but also in other European regions all over the continent (Farías 2010, 50). It was therefore related to other similar "social fevers" such as the "gold fever" that attracted thousands of adventurers to places like California in the 1850s and Alaska in the 1890s, or the "investing fevers" that have usually been behind the major financial crisis of capitalism since the nineteenth century. In all of these cases, the metaphoric allusion to a kind of disease is linked to three main semantic contents: its irrationality, a high degree of contagiousness among the social fabric, and its perdurability even when the causal factors or triggers have disappeared.

But more than a mere symptom, emigration was above all a true degenerative disease that undermined the bases of any healthy society, including that of the Basque Country. Between 1883 and 1883 José Colá y Goiti achieved what was at the time an unthinkable goal: his book on Basque migration, a compilation of a series of articles that had appeared in several Basque newspapers over a number of years, was published in Spanish, Basque, and French by the public bodies of the local administration in both the Southern and Northern Basque Country. His work, *La emigración vasco-navarra*, as it was titled in its first Spanish edition, marked the line that other journalists would follow in the years to come; like Colá y Goiti, "many other writers did not hesitate to attack directly the reasons that were driving so many emigrants toward the Americas. They considered emigration to be a calamity," because it would provoke "an irremissible depopulation of Basque fields and the total abandonment of agriculture and industry . . . if the government of the nation and the local authorities did not decide firmly to stop the causes that were stimulating the departures of young people toward the American continent" (quoted in Muru Ronda 1996, 195–96).

As with any contagious disease, there had to be some kind of vector to transmit it. Writers, journalists, politicians, and other "thinkers" on the "migratory problem" soon found a source for the blame: travel agents, colonization companies, and American governments that, more than informing people, were actually deceiving poor aspiring Basque emigrants by offering them an unrealistic and false vision of their possibilities in the Americas. For example, as Spanish congressman Piernas Hurtado wrote, it was considered that "those that in virtue of ignorance or innocence, either because of an adventurous spirit or the fever of emigration, are candidates to emigrate [should be] considered as irrational, inconsistent, human beings and, therefore, prone to be prey in the hands of unscrupulous agents" (quoted in Gil Lázaro and Fernández Vicente 2015, 22). This was a fever of migration, moreover, behind one of the seven capital sins: greed. Emigrants were assumed to have gone in pursuit of the immoral desire of quick enrichment, attracted by "a gold fever," as the Navarrese newspaper La Tradición Navarra put it in the mid-1880s (Azcona Pastor 2004).

The Spanish (and Basque) press soon coined a very graphic denomination for these people and their activitiy: ganchos (literally, "hooks," meaning "hoodwinkers"). In the Northern Basque Country, an even more poetic but sinister name was also conceived: uso martxantak ("dove traders"):[6] an allegoric image in which the innocence of the scammed immigrants contrasted with the purest picture of evil, slave trading. The solution seemed to be easy: the Basque authorities would have to ban the activity of all such hoodwinkers (Azcona Pastor 2010), in order to avoid the further spread of "the bastard promises of speculators that, in a criminal manner, make their victims hallucinate with pompous offers and build their own fortunes, taking advantage of the efforts and lives of thousands of poor wretches, credulous peasants that are drawn into the abyss of inevitable misfortunes" (El Eco Vascongado, Bilbao, September 18, 1860, quoted in Apaolaza Ávila 2009, 10).

There are great doubts about the actual scope of influence these hoodwinkers had on the decision-making of future immigrants (Camus-Etchecopar 2008, 26–27). Of course, almost all the agencies that could make a profit from emigration would try to do as much as they could to attract more people. Thus, different propaganda systems were employed by representatives of shipping companies specializing in transatlantic trade, which basically wanted prospective emigrants to choose their vessels (Branaa 1995); or by local agents of American colonization businesses that wanted to fulfill the minimum required number of recruitments demanded by their headquarters (Santiso González 1993); or even official representatives of American independent states appointed to inform people about the possibilities for newcomers that sought to start a new life overseas. Argentina and Uruguay, for example, established a network of consulates in every European region whose population was prone to emigrate, such as the Basque Country (Santiso González 1998). But more than creating the desire to emigrate, most of this organized propaganda was just profiting from a preexistent situation. In fact, the channels most migrants used, not only for getting information about possible destinations and job opportunities, but also (and more importantly) for getting material and personal aid during their set-tlement in the new country, depended more on personal links: information directly coming from the Americas, sent through person-to-person channels—especially pri-vate correspondence—and, furthermore, calls from relatives of friends already living overseas to join them, in what it is widely known as the chain-migration system.

In any event, the impact of decades of published opinion against emigra-tion in the Basque Country managed to leave its impact. It could not stop the flows, as attacks were directed at the wrong targets, but at least it was able to generate a common state of opinion in which emigration was, more than any-thing else, possibly the purest incarnation of evil.

## Interpretations of Emigration: From Hope to Destiny to *Herri Mina*

As a result, one of the arguments offered by politicians, journalists, and Catholic clergymen in the Basque Country in their fight to stop the phenomenon was based on what they believed to be the dangers of migration. And all means, both traditional and cutting edge, were to be used for this purpose. In the Basque Country, the tools used to spread propaganda against emigration and influence public opinion had to take into account the particular sociolinguistic situation with a mismatch between the official languages of the states (Spanish and French) and the tongue most commonly used by a large part of the population (Basque)—in the case of Basque speakers, a segment of the population especially prone to migrating. Thus, the channels to bring the message to their targets ranged from those that historians most typically tend to use in their analyses, like written lan-guage (books, newspapers, and pamphlets), to other means based primarily on oral transmission, usually in Basque. The customary tradition of *bertsolaritza* (im-provised oral versification) and its profound importance in the social practices of leisure and information dissemination within the Basque-speaking part of soci-ety contributed to making it one of the most privileged channels (Mehats 2005, 93–121). A good example of the premeditated use of *bertsolaritza* is the 1853 *bertso* contest in Urruña (Urrugne), in the Northern Basque Country. An open competi-tion was called for any *bertso* writer or improviser to compose a poem "explaining the regrets of a Basque that had departed to Montevideo" (Goicoetxea Marcaida 1998). In the decades that followed, local and regional authorities in the Basque lands followed the same path and—as in the case of the provincial government of Gipuzkoa in 1883—financed "the publication of verses in the Basque language" to convince Basques not to migrate, which "would be freely given to blind men that work in this industry, and they would then spread them to the remotest of the houses" (quoted in Zavala 1984, 12–13).

The main argument of this propaganda (the identification of migration as very dangerous and unsafe behavior) relied even more on the same medical metaphors to explain migration. Moreover, the risks of emigration could actually be understood in two ways: as a social disease (noted above) and also as a threat to the physical and mental health of the emigrants themselves. The propaganda tended to resort to the latter in order to be more effective, assuming that the recipients of the messages would, preferably, respond as desired if they were asked about their private safety rather than about general concerns of society as a whole.

Joseba Atxotegi (2009, 40) describes a mental disorder, the so-called Ulysses Syndrome, which is linked to the specific situations and challenges any emigrant has to face personally during every migratory process: what he refers to as "the seven mournings of emigration." He also defines mourning as "the process of personality restructuration that takes place when there is a detachment from—or a loss of—something that has great significance for the subject" (Atxotegi 2009, 37). In the case of emigration, it is a "partial mourning," because the lost object does not disappear; rather, it is unreachable, therefore the mourning could be recurrent. According to Atxotegi, the seven mournings of the emigrant would be for family, relatives, and loved ones; the mother tongue; the culture and the *land* (landscape, colors, luminosity) of the homeland; social status at the place of origin; contact with the group of belonging; and the risks to the physical integrity of emigrant (the dangers of traveling, accidents, prosecution, defenselessness).

Descriptions of the life of emigrants abroad, specifically of the innumerable hardships they were supposed to be enduring and the adversities they were supposed to be suffering, actually formed the bulk of most of those texts, either written or orally transmitted, distributed to modulate Basque public opinion on emigration. And, what is more interesting for us, the topics these texts tended to refer to were, in most cases, the same ones identified as the mournings of emigrants.

One large group of descriptions is linked to the sentiment of loss on account of having to abandon both the social and physical landscape of the homeland. Here, the contrast between the original hopes of emigrants and what they find in the Americas used to be the main line of argument. There are indeed plenty of sources, especially of *bertsos*, underlining this sentiment of attachment to the remote homeland and family. This is usually termed *herrimina* (literally, "pain for the homeland" or "homesickness") in Basque (Pérez 2016, 390). One of the best-known songs by the Basque *bertsolari* Jose Maria Iparragirre, written when he was traveling to Uruguay as an emigrant in 1858, reflects some of these elements (Mendibil 1999, 282):

Gazte-gaztetatikan,            Since I was young
herritik kanpora,              I have spent my time
estranjeri aldean             out of my country
pasa det denbora.             in foreign lands.
Errialde guztietan            Everywhere there are
toki onak badira,             pleasant places
baina bihotzak dio            but your heart always says:
"zoaz Euskalerrira."          "go to the Basque Country."

Lur maitea uztea              To leave your beloved land
da negargarria.               is painful.
Hemen gelditzen dira          Here you leave
ama ta herria.                your mother and your town.
Urez noa ikustera,            I cross the ocean
bai, mundu berria.            to see the New World.
Oraintxe bai naizela          Now I deserve
errukigarria.                 to feel sorry.

Agur, nere bihotzeko          Farewell, my beloved mom
amatxo maitea!                of my heart!
Laister etorriko naiz,        I will come back soon,
kontsola zaitea.              cheer yourself up.
Jaungoikoak nahi badu         If it is God's will
ni urez joatea,               that I must cross the ocean
ama, zertarako da             mother, why should you
negar egitea?                 cry?

A second group of descriptions is focused on the perils that await Basque emigrants from the very first moment of their departure. According to an article that appeared in *El Eco Vascongado* (Bilbao 1860), the main problem was that emigrants "do not seem to know the sufferings they will be exposed to, because they have absolutely no knowledge of the news sent by those that live in remote climes, and that have learned from their painful experience the terrible mistake they made, whose consequences must nonetheless endure" (quoted in Azcona Pastor 2010, 1065). Far from the love of relatives, the protection of the authorities, and the guidance of priests, emigrants were like errant vessels that wandered aimlessly with no help to confront the knocks of misfortune. Under these conditions, obtaining a job could be hell rather than the first step toward heaven: in 1889 the *El Gorbea* newspaper of Vitoria-Gasteiz published a letter sent by "an emigrant" to his wife, describing the horrors of what the journalist dared to describe as a renewed form of slavery: "I cannot rest any day or night. I sleep above a board, and when I go to sleep my heart becomes darker than the night itself. Food is unpalatable. It is still two hours before dawn when we have to start working; and we only have one hour to rest during the whole day. Here we live worse than dogs" (quoted in Apaolaza Avila 2009, 11).

Diseases were also part of the darker side of the migratory experience, as emigrants were admonished firmly. In an 1877 article, *La Voz de Vizcaya*, a Basque newspaper in Bilbao, felt sorry for "our youth that, instead of finding jobs in this country, prefer to go to unknown lands in search of imaginary fortunes and guaranteed diseases" (ibid., 10). Which kind of diseases? In tropical regions like Cuba and Brazil, lack of adaptation to new climatic conditions was the main threat to the migrants' health. To emigrate to these places, as explained in an 1864 an article in the *Euscalduna* newspaper in Bilbao, meant to spend a hardworking life "beneath the heat of a tropical sun, suffering the diseases that anyone not adapted to that climate and that land suffers, because nature was made there in a different way, and many die because of this" (Azcona Pastor 2010, 1069). "We sent laborers, strong men, plenty of life;" denounced another newspaper a few years later; "they return us misery . . . men turn into all skin and bones, dead bodies . . . As are all the hopes that brought them to these countries also dead" (*La Voz de Guipúzcoa*, 1912, quoted in Apaolaza Ávila 2009, 12).

Harsh labor conditions were also behind the more typical spread of mental rather than physical diseases. Among them, one particularly well known among Basque immigrants in the United States was produced by the impact of the circumstances in which sheepherding—the main economic activity of Basques in the American Far West—was carried out. When the Basque Museum of Boise, Idaho, opened in 2013, the name given to its permanent exhibit about the Basque experience in that state was clear and concise: "*Artzainak*: A Life of Solitude and Hard Work."[7] It became commonplace in the American West to tell stories about Basque sheepherders who had gone crazy while spending so many months alone in the open range, with only sheep for companionship. In fact, another story told about these same Basque sheepherders recounted that, because of the lack of contact with any other human beings, except for a few other Basques like them, after decades of living in the United States, they were still unable to speak English. Deprivation of social contact and lack of adaptation gave rise among other factors to a very negative image of the Basque community as a whole. For instance, Iker Saitua quotes a quite interesting description taken from an article published by the *Washington Post* in April 1907:

City wanderers in the mountain meadows of the California Sierras occasionally meet silent, dark visaged men who follow herds of sheep alone with their dogs. As the stranger rounds some sudden corner in the dusty highway the sheep, blocking the road divide and hurry by his buckboard. Then back in the dust of their hoofs the stranger sees the shepherd. The ragged man with the staff and the mongrel collie at his heels may raise his stick in mute salutation as he passes; he may slouch by without a word, though there be no other human being within thirty miles of the spot. A minute and he is lost in the wilderness around the turn of the road. This man is a Basque shepherd, one of the strange exiles from the Pyrenees who find a new home in the California mountains. He is content to live alone with his flocks and his dogs four months out of the year up in the cool meadows of the mountains, setting no man save the casual traveler. In the wintertime when the sheep are on the valley ranges he loses himself somewhere in the shoddy valley towns along the Sacramento, not to reappear until the summer wind shrivels up the valley grass and sends the sheep back to the mountains (quoted in Saitua 2018, 106).

Among the more tragic outcomes of this situation was the case of Domingo Malasechevarria. In 1952 he was executed in the State Prison of Carson City, Nevada, after being sentenced to death for having committed murder. The roots of the crime, as local journalists assessed, were to be found in his past job as a sheepherder: "During those years he also herded sheep in Douglas Co., NV. But things were not going well. His brothers had returned home, and had settled down more or less, while he was fighting loneliness in the Nevada desert. Domingo's disposition was turning sour. He had become antisocial and a loner" (San Sebastián 2015, 193). After having suffered a previous two-year jail sentence, "he underwent psychiatric evaluation at the Nevada Mental Hospital in Sparks" (*Reno Evening Gazette*, October 10, 1947): "[t]otally broke and with a reputation for violence, none of the stockmen wanted to hire him. Soon he had become a vagrant that wandered in Humboldt Co., living off charity and scrounging some handouts from a compatriot. In Sep. 1951 he was interned in the section of public welfare in the Humboldt Co. General" (San Sebastián 2015, 193). Finally, he committed the murder that brought him to death row.

## Epilogue

In his 1910 book on Basque emigration, Lhande devotes a whole chapter to the "psychology of the emigrant" (Lhande 1910, 144). In contrast with the previous images we have just seen, Lhande depicts quite an optimistic view of the personal and social outcomes of migration. According to him,

The Basque people have a curious mixture of hot enthusiasm and positive psyche. Their ardent imagination makes them forecast the way; their impulsive will makes them try it; their practical sense brings them with the same path toward changing landscapes. I think that this is a gift that Basque emigrants have the privilege of not being like Italian or Russian Jewish emigrants, that lack cohesion, personality (Lhande 1910, 146–47).

But at the same time, he does not dare to admit that among Basque emigrants there also exist a "spirit of return," a "melacholy," a "poetic hope."

To what extent was this optimistic view closer, or indeed more distant, from the reality most Basques experienced in their migration? The answer is, in fact, neither the former or the latter, but a mixture in several degrees of the two of them. Overseas emigration was a chapter in the history of modern Basque Country whose impact was as major as it is unknown. Like other migrant people before and after them, Basque emigrants were confronted with the demands of adapting to a totally new environment: new landscapes, new jobs, new languages, new climates, and, even more importantly, the undesired outcomes of separation from their own cultural environment. But like other migrant people before and after, Basques soon managed to recreate a replica of their home society in the countries in which they settled: a network of associations, mutual-aid societies, spaces for leisure and sport, moments and places for socialization, and, even more seriously, enterprises such as newspapers and schools flourished for more than a century to serve the Basque colonies of the Americas.

Even before the syndrome had been given a name, emigrants knew at least some of the ways to face up to their symptoms.

## Bibliography

Atxotegi, Joseba. *El síndrome de Ulises. Síndrome del inmigrante con estrés crónico y múltiple. Emigrar en el siglo XXI*. Figueras: Ediciones El Mundo de la Mente, 2009.

Alberdi, Juan Baustista. *Bases y puntos de partida para la organización política de la República Argentina*. Valparaíso. Imp. de El Mercurio, 1852.

Alsina, Juan A. *La inmigración europea en la República Argentina*. Buenos Aires: Félix Lajoauane Ed, 1898.

Álvarez Gila, Óscar. "Las nuevas Euskal Herrias americanas: Los vascos y las emigraciones ultramarinas (1825–1950)." In *Historia de Euskal Herria. Historia General de los Vascos*. Volume 4. *La crisis de la civilización de los vascos del Antiguo Régimen y estrategias de revolución liberal e industrial: 1789–1876*, edited by Joseba Agirreazkuenaga Zigorraga. Donostia-San Sebastián: Lur Argitaletxea, 2004.

———."Changes on the Perception of Ethnic Identity after the End of Mass Migration: The Basques in the United States." *Amnis. Revue de Civilisation Contemporaine Europes/Amériques* (online journal) (2013), 12. At http://amnis.revues.org/1977.

Álvarez Gila, Óscar, and Alberto Angulo Morales. "Between Trade, Religion and Ethnicity. The Catholic Church's Ethnic Institutions in the Spanish Empire, 16th-19th Centuries." *BOGA: Basque Studies Consortium Journal* 1, no. 2 (2014): 1–14.

Angulo Morales, Alberto. "Los hidalgos norteños en el centro de un Imperio. Madrid (1638–1850)." In *Recuperando el Norte: Empresas, capitales y proyectos atlánticos en la economía imperial hispánica*, edited by Alberto Angulo Morales and Álvaro Aragón Ruano. Bilbao: Universidad del País Vasco/ Euskal Herriko Unibertsitatea, 2016.

Apaolaza Ávila, Urko. "Ameriketara joandako emigranteen irudia Euskal Herriko prentsan (1876– 1936)." *Kondaira* 9 (2009): 1–22.

Aramburu Zudaire, José Miguel. "América y los vascos en la Edad Moderna. Una perspectiva histo- riográfica." *Vasconia* 34 (2005): 249–74.

Azcona Pastor, José Manuel. *Los paraísos posibles. Historia de la emigración vasca a Argentina y Uruguay en el siglo XIX*. Bilbao: Universidad de Deusto, 1992.

———*Possible Paradises: Basque Emigration to Latin America*. Reno: University of Nevada Press.

———,2010. "Las campañas de prensa antiemigración: José Colá y Goiti y el caso vasco-navarro." In *Congreso Internacional 1810–2010: 200 años de Iberoamérica*. Santiago de Compostela: Universidade de Santiago de Compostela, 2004.

Branaa, Eric. "Découverte des archives de Charles Iriart, principal artisan de l'émigration basque moderne aux États Unis." *Ikuska* 9 (1995): 23–41.

Camus-Etchecopar, Argitxu. "A Historical Comparative Study of Basque Institutions in the United States." Ph.D. Dissertation, University of Nevada, Reno, 2008.

Charnisay, Henry de. *L'émigration basco-béarnaise en Amérique*. Biarritz: J&D Éditions, 1996.

Dorigo, Guido, and Waldo Tobler. "Push-Pull Migration Laws." *Annals of the Association of American Geographers* 73, no. 1 (1983): 1–17.

Douglass, William A., and Jon Bilbao. *Amerikanuak. Basques in the New World*. Reno: University of Nevada Press, 1975.

Douglass, William A., and Gloria Totoricagüena. "Identidades complementarias. La sociabilidad y la identidad vasca en la Argentina entre el pasaado y el presente." In *La inmigración española en la Argentina*, edited by Alejandro E. Fernández and José C. Moya. Buenos Aires: Biblos, 1999.

Farías, Ruy G. "La inmigración gallega en el Sur del Gran Buenos Aires, 1869–1960." Ph.D. Dissertation, Universidade de Santiago de Compostela, 2010.

Fernández de Pinedo, Emiliano. "Los movimientos migratorios vascos, en especial hacia América." In *Españoles hacia América: la emigración en masa, 1880-1930*, edited by Nicolás Sánchez-Albornoz. Madrid: Alianza, 1995.

Garcia, Joxerra, and Patri Urkizu. *Bertsolaritzaren Historia*. Volume 1. Donostia: Etor, 1991.

García Abad, Rocío. "Un estado de la cuestión de las teorías de las migraciones." *Historia Contemporánea* 26: 329–51, 2003.

García-Sanz Marcotegui, Ángel. "An Estimate of Navarrese Migration in the Second Half of Nineteenth Century (1879–1883)." In *Essays in Basque Social Anthropology and History*, edited by William A. Douglass. Reno: University of Nevada Press, 1989.

Gil Lázaro, Alicia, and María José Fernández Vicente. *Los discursos sobre la emigración española en per- spectiva comparada. Principios del siglo XX—Principios del siglo XXI*. Alcalá de Henares: Instituto de Estudios Latinoamericanos (IELAT), Universidad de Alcalá de Henares., 2015

Goicoetxea Marcaida, Ángel. "Un aspecto de la Antropología social en las Fiestas Eúskaras: la emigración a Uruguay y los Montebideoko Kantuak." In *Antoine d'Abbadie. Congrès International (Hendaye, 1997)*. San Sebastián and Bilbao: Eusko Ikaskuntza; Euskaltzaindia, 1998.

González Cembellín, Juan Manuel. *América en el País Vasco: Inventario de elementos patrimoniales de origen americano en la Comunidad Autónoma Vasca*. Vitoria-Gasteiz. Eusko Jaurlaritza, 1993.

González Portilla, Manuel, and Rocío García Abad. "Migraciones interiores y migraciones en familia durante el ciclo industrial moderno en el área metropolitana de la Ría de Bilbao." *Scripta nova. Revista electrónica de Geografía y Ciencias Sociales* (online journal)10, no. 218, 2006. At http://www.ub.edu/geocrit/sn/sn-218-67.htm.

Lhande, Pierre. *L'émigration basque*. Paris: Nouvelle Librairie Nationale, 1910.

Mallada, Lucas. *Los males de la Patria y la futura revolución española. Consideraciones generales acerca de sus causas y efectos*. Madrid: Tipografía de Manuel Ginés Hernández, 1890.

Marenales Rossi, Martha. *La aventura vasca. Destino: Montevideo*. Montevideo: Editorial Gamacor Producciones, 1991.

Mehats, Claude. *Organisation et aspects de l'émigration des basques de France en Amérique: 1832–1976*. Vitoria-Gasteiz: Eusko Jaurlaritza, 2005.

Mendibil, Gontzal, ed. *Iparragirre. Erro-urratsak. Raíz y Viento*. Igorre, Bizkaia: Keinu., 1999

Míguez, Eduardo José. "Foreign Mass Migration to Latin America in the Nineteenth and Twentieth Centuries—An Overview." In *Mass Migration in Modern Latin America*, edited by Samuel L. Baily and Eduardo José Míguez. Wilmington, DE: Scholarly Resources Books, 2003.

Montero García, Manuel. *La California del hierro: las minas y la modernización económica y social de Vizcaya*. Bilbao: Beitia, 1995.

Mörner, Magnus. *Adventurers and Proletarians: The Story of Migrants in Latin America*. Pittsburgh: The University of Pittsburgh Press, 1985.

———."Inserción del fenómeno vasco en la emigración europea a América." In *Emigración y redes sociales de los vascos en América*, edited by Ronald Escobedo Mansilla, Ana de Zaballa Beascoechea, and Óscar Álvarez Gila. Vitoria-Gasteiz: Universidad del País Vasco/Euskal Herriko Unibertsitatea, 1996.

Moya, José C. "La 'fiebre' de la emigración: el proceso de difusión en el éxodo transatlántico español, 1850–1930." In *La inmigración española en la Argentina*, edited by Alejandro E. Fernández and José C. Moya. Buenos Aires: Biblos, 1999.

———. "Spanish Emigration to Cuba and Argentina." In *Mass Migration in Modern Latin America*, edited by Samuel L. Baily and Eduardo José Míguez. Wilmington, DE: Scholarly Resources Books, 2003.

Muru Ronda, Fernando. "Prensa local y emigración vasca contemporánea (siglos XIX y XX)." In *Emigración y redes sociales de los vascos en América*, edited by Ronald Escobedo Mansilla, Ana de Zaballa Beascoechea, and Óscar Álvarez Gila. Vitoria-Gasteiz: Universidad del País Vasco/Euskal Herriko Unibertsitatea, 1996.

Paliza Monduate, Maite. "Los indianos y las bellas artes: el caso del Valle de Carranza, Vizcaya. Escultura y pintura, siglos XIX y XX." In *Arte e identidades culturales: Actas del XII Congreso Nacional del Comité Español de Historia del Arte. Homenaje a D. Carlos Cid Priego*. Oviedo. Universidad de Oviedo, 1998.

———. "Los indianos y la construcción del ensanche de Bilbao." *Kobie. Antropología Cultural* 10 (2001): 205–24.

Pérez, Pío. "El canto del pastor no espanta las ovejas: memoria y nostalgia en los versos improvisados." *Revista de Dialectología y Tradiciones Populares* 71, no. 2 (2016): 389–414.

Saitua, Iker. "'Distilling Spirits.' Imigrantes vascos, cultura de la bebida y prohibición en el estado de Nevada, 1910-1920." *Historia Social* 90, no. 1 (2018): 45–66.

San Sebastián, Koldo. *Basques in the United States: A Biographical Encyclopedia of First-Generation Immigrants.* Volume 1. *Araba, Bizkaia, and Gipuzkoa.* Reno: Center for Basque Studies, University of Nevada, Reno, 2015.

Sánchez Alonso, Blanca. *Las causas de la emigración española, 1880–1930.* Madrid: Alianza, 1995.

Santiso González, María Concepción. "La contratación de jornaleros en la emigración hacia América. 'Ganchos' y ofertas de trabajo en Guipúzcoa, 1840–1860." *Ernaroa* 9–10 (1993): 115–53.

———.*Cien años de torrente emigratorio hacia América: diáspora vasca y enganchadores (1830–1960).* Bilbao: Fundación BBV, 1998.

Sarmiento, Érica, and Óscar Álvarez Gila. "Serviço militar e emigração. Reflexões, possibilidades e problemátias a partir do caso español." In *Pontes entre a Europa e América Latina (XIX–XXI): Histórias de migrações e mobilidades,* edited by Lená Medeiros de Menezes and Chiara Pagnotta. Rio de Janeiro: Labimi/UERJ, 2018.

Totoricagüena, Gloria. "Comparing the Basque Diaspora: Ethnonationalism, Translationalism and Identity Maintenance in Argentina, Australia, Belgium, Peru, the United States of America, and Uruguay." Ph.D. Dissertation, London School of Economics, 2000. At http://etheses.lse.ac.uk/1592/1/U145019.pdf.

Vázquez de Prada, Valentín, and Juan Bosco Amores Carredano. "La emigración de navarros y vascongados al Nuevo Mundo y su repercusión en las comunidades de origen." In *La emigración española a Ultramar, 1492–1914,* edited by Antonio Eiras Roel. Madrid: Tabapress, 1991.

Vinson, Julien. *Les basques et le Pays Basque. Moeurs, langage et historie.* Paris: Librairie Léopold Cer, 1882.

Zavala, Antonio. Ameriketako bertsoak. Tolosa: Auspoa, 1984.

## Notes

1   This chapter has been written within the scope of the Consolidated Research Group of the Basque System: "The Basque Country, Europe and America: Inter-Atlantic Links and Relationships" (IT938-16).

2   By 2013, according to the data from the Spanish and French national censuses of 2011, in all seven historical territories of Euskal Herria there was a total of 3,127,326 inhabitants. See http://www.gaindegia.eus/es/node/5751 (last consulted December 1, 2018).

3   These numbers are, nonetheless, problematic. Muru Ronda states that data were collected and tabulated by himself using Spanish official statistical data from the *Dirección General de Emigración* (General Office of Emigration). He does not explain, though, if he is covering a four-province Spanish Basque Country (including Navarre) or not, which makes it more difficult to compare his calculation with the estimates of other researchers.

4   Juan A. Alsina (1898, 45) states that by the end of the nineteenth century, 9 out of every 100 people living on the banks of Buenos Aires were Basque.

5   Foral Archive of Bizkaia, "Archivo de Gernika." *Estadísticas varias,* leg. 1. "Estadística de interrogatorio sobre emigración de los pueblos de Vizcaya. Abando/Zollo" (1881).

6   "Uxo marxant batzuek arribatu dute, / berrogoi bat dozena behar omen dute, /herriz herri dabiltza propien berexten" ("Several dove traders have arrived, / it is said they will need about four dozen, / they go to every town, selecting unwary people"). Garcia and Urkizu (1991, 356–57).

7   See https://basquemuseum.eus/see/current-exhibits/the-basque-sheepherder/.

# 4

# Migratory Policies and Institutional and Social Intervention Based on Human Rights

*Iñaki Markez*

Nongovernmental Organizations (NGOs) provide rescue and assistance that European governments avoid or simply do not offer. We have a great deal of information from NGOs on their activities and on the results of their assistance to and recovery of many thousands of people. Furthermore, and as different NGOs and humanitarian agencies have pointed out, detained persons are seriously deprived of their rights on migration journeys and in the facilities set up by European governments.

## How Have We Arrived at This Point?

At the start of the new millennium, in the 2000s, Silvio Berlusconi's Italian government began to restrict entry to migrants, the majority of whom were from sub-Saharan African countries, by means of agreements with Muammar Gaddafi, the leader that governed Libya for over forty years with support from European leaders. Between 2000 and 2004, agreements regarding migration were reached according to which Libya was provided with logistical support in exchange for containing migratory flows by strengthening its border control. The agreements also provided financing to build migrant detention camps in Libya.

Europe had looked the other way since the influx from Syria began in 2011, which would become the "Syrian crisis" in 2013, even though many other displaced persons came from Eritrea, Sudan, Ethiopia, Yemen, and neighboring countries. Article 78 of the EU Treaty regarding emergency situations was not activated until May 2015, after the major displacements to the Turkish and Libyan coast, and from there, across the Mediterranean, to Greece and Italy. Over 160,000 people reached each of those two countries that year and the following one.

The European Union (EU) dismantled Operation Mare Nostrum, the rescue and anti-people-smuggling mission along the Italian and Libyan coasts, under-taken by Italy, acting alone and with a small budget (€9 million per month), which ran from October 2013 to November 2014. Its results were 588 operations, 100,250 people rescued, and 728 people smugglers arrested, all of which was a major and important result. The Italian government asked the EU to take over and for the 28 member countries to help to bear the cost. The EU response was not favorable. The United Kingdom, France, and Spain refused, arguing that the rescue operations generated a "pull effect," and even going so far as to say that, "we must avoid the duty to rescue, otherwise more will come." The reality is that there is no "pull effect." However, there is a "flight effect" from war and hunger.

The EU replaced Mare Nostrum with two police and military operations: the military Operation Sophia, with police intervention by the navy and/or armed forces to destroy the "death boats" anchored in or crossing the Mediterranean; and Operation Triton, which began in November 2015 and was funded by the EU (€2.9 million/month) as a border control mission conducted by Frontex (the European border control agency), with rescue operations being left on the side-lines. The major shipwrecks in the Mediterranean started at that time.

This all occurred in a complex geopolitical situation, with instability in Turkey following the victory of President Recep Tayyip Erdoğan's AKP (Adalet ve Kalkınma Partisi, Justice and Development Party), the so-called state "self-coup," leading to the curtailing of freedoms, wide-scale arrests, an election result highly criticized by EU observers, many reports of torture, and so on. The agreement between the EU and Turkey established that the Turkish government would take back refugees that had reached Greece. The EU would likewise accept one refugee through the legal channel for each deportee. Furthermore, the EU undertook to provide €6 billion to revive the negotiations for Turkey to join the community club and to exempt Turkish citizens from needing visas. A year after the signing of the agreements, there was a surge in criticism from human rights (HR) organiza-tions and European governments that were suspicious of the Ankara government.

This was compounded by geostrategic movements in the area, the strength-ening of Iran as a regional power after the signing of the nuclear agreement, and traditional alliances: Russia and Iran with the Syrian regime, and Jordan and Saudi Arabia with the United States. This was all occurring in an area of upheaval and great confusion in international policy.

There have been mass deaths on an unprecedented scale in recent history. According to a report by the International Organization for Migration (IOM), a UN-related organization, the Mediterranean, with over 5,600 deaths in 2016, heads the blacklist that includes around 1,100 people dying in the countries of

North Africa. Between 2014 and the end of 2018, 17,200 people died or disappeared. Meanwhile, the systematic breach of human rights is justified by the EU, the media, and part of civil society.

Around 89,000 refugees and migrants—19,000 of whom were children—had reached Europe (particularly Greece, Spain, Italy, and Bulgaria) between January and September 2018, from countries such as Syria, Iraq, Nigeria, Guinea, Bangladesh, and Morocco. Guaranteeing their protection at all stages of the path is a priority. Therefore, UNICEF is working in Europe and in the countries of origin and transit, such as Turkey, Lebanon, Libya, Mali, and Niger. In 2018, for example, 14,000 children and teenagers were educated in Greece, Italy, Serbia, and Bulgaria. Yet the different European governments have only met 18 percent of the envisaged undertakings.

Greece and Macedonia make up the main route into Europe for the refugees, for two reasons: because the geography and their porous borders make it easier for people smugglers and because it is the quickest way to get into Hungary and, from there, to try to reach Germany and the Scandinavian countries, their Eldorado. A refugee from Syria (or from Afghanistan, Sudan, Ethiopia, Eritrea, Iraq, and so on) would typically cross Turkey, make their way to Greece, then to Macedonia, Serbia, and reach Hungary. At present, the Hungarian parliament is dominated by xenophobic, fascist, and paramilitary members of parliament, and the country has built a border fence to keep refugees out. And the Council of Europe has tolerated all of this.

Money has been given to Libya, then to Turkey, and now to Morocco, Niger, and Mali to contain these thousands and thousands of migrants. EU migration policy, rather than addressing and improving living conditions in the refugees' countries of origin, has become a security issue through the externalization of the border.

### The Human Cost: What Is Happening in Europe?

The violations of human rights committed on the European borders against migrants and refugees have become an everyday occurrence. Since 2000, over 25,000 people have died trying to reach Europe. Over 10,000 minors have disappeared from a collective in which nine out of every ten minors make the journey alone. Gender violence is part of everyday life, not only because women are usually the ones carrying and looking after the children on the migratory journey, but also because they are raped, attacked, and suffer sexual abuse, or because they must turn to prostitution for their and their family's survival. The differences and inequalities between men and women are perpetuated every day, and this inequality implies violence. And one should not forget other consequences for women's physical health: unwanted pregnancies, the risk of STDs,

HIV, hepatitis, and so on, as well as greater vulnerability to associated harm. We remember with sadness that, now two years ago, the women of Aleppo committed suicide to avoid being raped; many attacks against civilians were highlighted by the UN Security Council, as people had nowhere to live.

Migrants and refugees are illegally being expelled from Bulgaria, Greece, and Spain, without access to asylum, abused by coast and border guards, or kept in prolonged detention as a deterrent to those fleeing from countries in conflict such as Syria, Eritrea, Afghanistan, and Somalia. Closer to home we have seen pictures from Ceuta and Melilla, from Fuerteventura and Lanzarote, of migrants being shot, drowned, beaten, crushed, detained, and handed over to the Libyan or Moroccan police.

Blame can be directly laid at the door of the EU member states, with the worst being Italy for the violations of the human rights of the migrants and refugees who are denied entry and access to asylum and and are detained in Libya or are returned from there to their countries of origin from which they are escaping. They are responsible for the abuse and torture at the Libyan detention centers, for the hidden deaths in the Sahara Desert, and for the daily deaths and disappearances on the Mediterranean route (Safont 2018). For the last two decades, European governments have been pushing for agreements between Italy and Libya to prevent the arrival of migrants and refugees to Europe by means of arbitrary detentions and deportations in that country.

Many people drown at sea or suffocate to death in the trucks in which they are being smuggled. There is a lot of violence at the borders, and they are denied the right to seek asylum. Their flight ends up with their dying at the European borders. Or they are trapped in Libya, Morocco, Ukraine, and Turkey, where they are destitute and lack economic and social rights.

In light of that, it must not be forgotten that the EU, which allocated €1.9 billion between 2007 and 2013 to its foreign borders, invests 9 times more in that regard than in its spending on refugees, except for Spain, where spending on its border was 32 times more than the amount invested in aid and resources for refugees (see table 1), sums of money that mainly come from the EU. The situation has subsequently remained unchanged.

**Table 1. Funding for Refugees and External Borders in Some States, 2007–2013**

|  | Funding for Refugees | Funding for External Borders |
|---|---|---|
| Bulgaria | €4,295,548.61 | €38,131,685.92 |
| Greece | €21,938,521.14 | €207,816,754.58 |
| Spain | €9,342,834.50 | €289,394,768.35 |
| Italy | €36,087,198.41 | €250,178,432.52 |
| Malta | €6,621,089.03 | €70,441,716.30 |

A total of €628 million were reserved for the European Fund for Refugees for 2008–2013.

Turning its southern border into a fortress is a EU priority as far as migration policy is concerned, as the EU is focused on closed borders rather than on human rights obligations or on improving asylum procedures and on covering the needs of refugees.

According to the IOM, by 2017, Spain was expected to be ahead of Greece as the destination of undocumented immigrants resorting to sea crossings to seek refuge in Europe. While the Eastern Mediterranean route, mainly used by refugees to reach Greece from Turkey, has seen a drop in the influx due to pressure from the Turkish government, the Western Mediterranean route, which leads to Spain, has increased, even though the main flow continues to be that to Italy from the central part of the Mediterranean. However, it seems that the number of fatalities on all the routes is clearly higher.

Yet there is also a pathology of emigration. There is a tendency to use hospital resources as an initial care option in response to the lack of adequate family and social support that they had in their country of origin. It seems there is no greater pathology but rather greater difficulties to address for the intervention with those sub-groups. Yet does a pathology of emigration really exist? This fundamentally young collective is the generation at the crossroads of the "place from where paths leave in different directions" and the "difficult situation where they do not know how to behave" faced by the many immigrants who have managed to integrate in the host society, but with ambivalent feelings and experiences, as they are between two cultures, two countries, two languages, and two loyalties. There is a basic identity crisis that puts them into a confusing situation, increasing their insecurity, causing anxiety and ambivalence, and leading to dissociative and regressive responses.

## Asylum Law is Being Breached in Europe

In many European countries, refugees are detained in camps, kept apart with fences and barbed wires, and beaten, expelled, deported, or left to die in the thousands along their desperate journey, which recalls the tragic images of Germany or invaded territories in the 1930s and 1940s. But it is the twenty-first-century, and tragic situations have become the reality of most EU countries.

Denmark, Switzerland, and Germany, in the *länders* of Bavaria and Baden-Württemberg, have passed laws allowing refugees to be stripped of their money and goods, as well as mass expulsions; Sweden, Finland, and Austria have limited asylum requests; Hungary, Bulgaria, the Czech Republic, and Slovakia reject Muslim refugees; Greece, the great welcomer, has allowed the European border control agency, Frontex, to patrol its coasts and expel refugees to Turkey, after signing a migratory agreement worth €3 billion.

Authoritarian behavior, demanding that officers use firearms if necessary to prevent illegal border crossings, forcing them to turn back at sea, and even leaving them to drown if they were breaking the law, have become the modus operandi, along with several countries erecting hundreds of kilometers of fences along their borders (barbed wire, cement, razor wire, and metal borders) to stem the flow of refugees, even though they have only managed to shift that flow somewhere else. The borders of Hungary, Serbia and Croatia, Slovenia and Croatia, and Austria and Slovenia have closed. The migrant transit to the United Kingdom is impeded in Calais. This is Europe's new wall. Together with the customs' controls that undermine free movement in the EU, it is the end of the Schengen space in which people may freely travel without controls across internal borders, but, as the result of the voluntary flow, some countries have reintroduced temporary controls on their borders with other states.

The EU measures are criminalizing the migratory phenomenon. Alleging the fight against transnational people trafficking and smuggling criminal networks, they have generated categories in the illegal immigration and migratory flows. The policies of European countries have become the unexpected fuel of the mafia business by closing safe borders and fostering the informal routes for immigrants and asylum seekers, with threats to their safety, rapes, disappearances, and frequent violence.

The deep-rooted stereotypes in society are reflected in the conduct of police officers, judges, and, even, at times, in that of legal aid lawyers, according to an Open Society report that stresses the racial bias in the justice systems of twelve member states of the European Union, including Spain. In Spain, researchers have found the existence of a clear institutional bias. They give the example of the disproportionate representation of non-nationals in crime rates and prison population statistics.

## A Refugee Crisis?

Dictatorships, wars, poverty, environmental degradation, persecution, repression, and hunger, among other factors, are the causes of those refugee and migrant movements and, to a great extent, are the result of the interventions of different EU states.

This refugee crisis is rather different from the EU one. Yet there are other issues on the table (the Ukrainian and Greek crises, the Euro, Brexit) in the EU that have been put on the backburner, given the size of the human drama. Refugees are those suffering the crisis, not the ones that cause it.

The community institution established after World War II began to be questioned over time. Border control has been reinforced instead of pursuing an integral policy to address the arrivals or causes of the political and migratory problem. Funds allocated are for security on Europe's "external border" to build walls, fences, for more police, returns, detention camps. These are situations that recall earlier tragedies and holocausts, such as in the 1940s or in the Balkans. Furthermore, Italy and Greece, majority recipient countries that have received little aid for health care, nutrition, hygiene, schooling, or attention to life for those populations, have been shunned.

We are facing a humanitarian challenge in Europe. The uncivil war in Syria, in which 4,600,000 Syrians have been forced out of their country, is one factor behind this huge refugee movement.

Europe has not reached its reception capacity and is very far from it. Eighty-five percent of Syrian refugees are taken in by four neighboring countries: Lebanon, Jordan, Iraq, and Turkey (Table 2). A refugee- and migrant-exporter country, such as Ethiopia, takes in a greater number of people than the whole of Europe.

**Table 2. Recipient population in different territories**

|  | Population | Taken in |
| --- | --- | --- |
| Jordan | 6.6 million | 2.7 million |
| Turkey | 78 million | 2.5 million |
| Pakistan | 190 million | 1.6 million |
| Lebanon | 5.9 million | 1.5 million |

**European Union** >500 million 160,000 proposed and 5,651 received (3.5 percent)

There is not a common policy that guarantees the right to political asylum, but there is such a policy for police-military operations and to control "economies in crisis" such as that of Greece.

Turning immigrants into the scapegoat of the crisis for the popular classes (and media) that do not identify with the states means they lose the guarantee of economic and social rights.

The migratory flows do not threaten sovereignty because they do not introduce delinquency or unfair competition on the job market, and they do not erode the identity of the states or their peoples. It is a fallacy.

The repressive policies regarding migratory flows criminalize people and punish them with criminal sanctions that may mean their being deprived of liberty without a court ruling, such as in the CIEs (Centros de Internamiento de Extranjeros, migrant holding centers), facilities halfway between prisons and reception centers.

Three conclusions can be reached from the evolution of some asylum and migration data: the EU is not the area with the greatest number of refugees, despite the increase in the two last years; nearly one out of every five asylum seekers from Syria have come to Europe; and those seeking asylum do so from the routes that economic migrants use.

## The Response of the European Union

The response is disappointing. The Commission has tried to coordinate policies and discourse from the European Agenda of Migrations, but the member states have shown a lack of empathy and solidarity within the Council. During the Council of Ministers meeting on June 20, 2015, the Italian prime minister and the Lithuanian prime minister clashed, and things became very heated. The outcome was the prevalence of the voluntariness of the fair distribution of refugee quotas, a desolate landscape. The states established the number of places that they would offer for relocation and resettlement. The majority of states offered fewer places than those originally proposed by the Commission.

Refugees looking for work are given German classes in Germany. It was announced that Germany would accept 800,000 asylum applications in 2015 for those coming from Greece or Italy and for the Kosovar, Albanian, Serbian, and Ukrainian refugees who sought it. The number would subsequently prove to be far, far smaller. Only 18,415 resettlement places were covered by member states out of the 20,000 proposed by the Commission. It was noteworthy that the 22,504 places were only reached thanks to the offers of Norway, Switzerland, Liechtenstein, and Iceland. The stinginess and the blocking by countries such as Spain, Hungary, and the United Kingdom were highly instrumental. Their arguments were based on the risk of a "pull effect" from the potential asylum seekers and the impossibility to absorb the people who arrived and were a breeding ground for racism and xenophobia that soon made themselves heard. In reality, it was a "push effect." The lack of political will and empathy by the European Council has been clear. It is more feasible for the EU, with a population over 500 million, than for Lebanon, Turkey, or Jordan to assume the impact of arrivals that represent less than 1 percent of its population. The facts have shown how wrong the people are who advocate militarizing the border and being stingy with the number of places offered.

The only priority for Brussels is now to contain the flows of displaced persons in Turkey, Greece, and the Balkans, and to keep them as far away as possible from the European hubs. They do not see the explosive situation at their gates.

In 2015, thousands and thousands of men, women, and children tried to reach their European dream while fleeing the horror of war. The Syrian conflict

began in 2011 and its impacts in the form of citizen awareness raising and mobi-
lization were felt in 2015. The political class did not react until images circulated
of the body of a boy named Aylan, who had drowned off the Turkish coast, and
then of Omsram, sitting in an ambulance waiting for his wounds to be treated.
And that is the reality of hundreds and thousands of other children who were
lucky enough to have survived that holocaust. Or even when a lorry showed
us the horror of people smuggling in Central Europe, or dozens of images of
people drowning in the Mediterranean or dying of cold in the Balkans made
the affluent consciousness react. Meanwhile, institutions and leaders could not
agree on what to do. Society seemed numbed about the drama in Syria, Libya,
Afghanistan, Somalia, Eritrea, and Iraq.

The European Union does not respect citizen and human rights, and it has
passed on its "responsibility" to periphery countries such as Turkey, Libya, and
Morocco, where human rights are absent. It has been the breakdown of the
founding principles and legal commitments of the EU. The "crisis" has affected
essential aspects of EU identity: the idea of a space in which to defend and protect human rights, solidarity between member states, and the very compliance
of the obligations acquired by the states. Suspension of the application of the
legislation regulating the free travel space to stem the arrival of asylum seeks and
immigrants as well as failure to comply with the commitments to provide in-
frastructure as well as human and material resources increase the "hot returns,"
which are in breach of international law. The Spanish government set the prec-
edent with the approval of the rejections at the Ceuta and Melilla borders in
the Citizen Security Act.

### Agreement of the European Union to Address the Migrant Crisis

In June 2018, the European leaders agreed that all EU countries must help, as
a voluntary and shared endeavor, the migrants rescued in the Mediterranean,
in order to alleviate the burden of Italy and Greece. However, they did not establish the details of by whom and how that would be done. The agreement
indicates that "secure migration centers" would be established and discrimi-
nates between those looking for "genuine" asylum and those who are "illegal
migrants, economic ones, who will be returned to their countries." Neither have
details been given of what a "secure center" means, and some people fear that
those would be a type of prison for the migrants who reach Europe.

Several countries in central Europe, including Hungary and Austria, have
rejected the EU project to relocate the 160,000 refugees in the overcrowded

camps in Greece and Italy. Furthermore, Italy is the main destination of the
people rescued in the overloaded boats that leave from Libya.

Alarming figures are given about the migrants who arrive. There has been
no increase in the number of people who try to enter Europe through its coasts,
which include those fleeing from the war in Syria and other conflicts in Africa.
They have fallen according to data from the IOM. During the third quarter of
2017, 146,287 arrivals to Europe were recorded, 137,771 by sea. Less than half
of the total recorded for the same period in 2016. However, even though the
number has fallen, the tolerance of governments and citizens for the problem
seems to have disappeared.

Driven by intolerance and xenophobic and racist discourse, anti-migration
movements and politicians have emerged throughout the length and breadth of
Europe. These include Hungarian prime minister Victor Orban, and Austrian
chancellor Sebastian Kurz, who will be president of the EU Council and who
said that the migration issue will be "his main priority." And one should not
forget that the regulation of immigration must be an "integrated and coordinated" approach. Matteo Salvini, the Italian Minister of the Interior and leader
of the xenophobic Lega Nord (Northern League), has said that he is "satisfied"
and "proud" about the result.

The existence of real differences is not necessary for immigration to be
rejected and discriminating policies to exist, even with popular support. They
just have to exist in the collective imaginary, an imaginary construction just
has to be established and then fostered and magnified. This has all too often
been the case, leading to racist and xenophobic currents of opinion. What was
idiosyncrasy, exoticism, due to the different product, becomes *hate-syncrasy*
toward others. It is beyond discussion that as immigration figures increase
without a correlation in the rise of social resources for those high collectives,
not only are migration numbers and the risk of citizen unrest going to grow,
but also racial violence, discrimination, and xenophobic behavior. Fear of
unemployment and of citizen insecurity, along with the unease about govern-
mental policies and the non-growth of social resources, are the reasons put
forward for the increase in racism and xenophobia.

The conclusions adopted after the meeting of the European Council in
Brussels left much to be desired, as they recommend "exploring" the setting up of
"regional disembarkation platforms" in third countries and contemplating further financial support for migrant-receiving countries in southern Europe, including Spain, or transit ones in North Africa, particularly Morocco. Furthermore, the
text warns the NGOs operating in the Mediterranean that "they must respect the

legislation and not obstruct the activities of Libyan Coastguards." They are thus backing Italy's position, which has prevented several ships from disembarking the migrants rescued at sea, forcing them to return to Libya or merely paying little heed to something as fundamental as the right to life.

More recently, on August 22, 2018, 116 migrants and refugees came over the Ceuta border fence and reached Spanish territory. The following day, the Spanish Minister of the Interior confirmed that those persons had been returned to Morocco by means of applying the agreement between the Kingdom of Spain and the Kingdom of Morocco on the movement of people and the transit and the re-admission of foreigners who have entered illegally, signed in Madrid on February 13, 1992. That month, numerous signatories, representatives of very different sectors of civil society in the Spanish state, signed a manifesto regarding the returning of migrants and refugees to Morocco, harshly criticizing that modus operandi.

They criticized the lack of a legal basis according to immigration legislation for the authorizing of the return of any person who comes under the Spanish immigration authorities. They pointed out the numerous and repeated allegations by international and social organizations regarding the torturing and degrading treatment of migrants in Morocco. The current government showed with these measures that its migratory policy involved hot returns, thus embracing the arguments of the previous government and contradicting its criticism of border rejections. They denounced the downward spiral that deferred hot returns represent, not only because they do not respect the required legal safeguards, but also because they are a further step in the externalization of border controls that are so costly in terms of human rights—along with the political and economic considerations for Morocco that the government does not reveal—and migratory polices that compromise the moral dignity of this society and the humanist values on which it should be based. Meanwhile the Court of Justice believes that Spain is in breach of European community law by justifying public order measures regarding foreigners in accordance with what is indicated by the Convention Implementing the Schengen Agreement (CISA).

## Essential Measures to Redirect Migratory Policy

*1) For the refugees:*

A summit should be proposed to the European partners to conduct a review of the Schengen Agreements, abolish the Dublin Regulation, and dismantle Frontex. It is dangerous to accept what is imposed by Germany, which amended its asylum legislation without consulting other countries.

There should be a reassessment of the definition criteria by updating the notion of safe countries and adapting the link between the first country of arrival in European territory and the asylum process.

Legal channels should be implemented to seek asylum and, in particular, to guarantee the possibility of seeking asylum in embassies and consulates of the transit, neighboring, and origin countries.

There should be an increase the European offices processing asylum applications and assurance of the presence of UNHCR, particularly in the neighboring countries.

Humanitarian visas should be activated in a timely and flexible manner.

The requirements for transit visas should be relaxed in order to allow those from countries in conflict to cross. They are not economic migrants.

There should be an increase in resettlement programs in keeping with the number of refugees, with a fair and inclusive distribution among the states. Accept the mandatory quotas.

*2) For the economic migrants:*
Entries should be relaxed, and not only for the qualified migrants, since the working classes are those who need to emigrate to be able to send money back to their countries.

There should be an introduction, along with the residence permits already in force in all Euro zone countries, of worker "mobility" documents, in accordance with the countries of origin and according to the needs of the host countries.

A common European co-development policy linked to the migratory flows should be encouraged.

A common strategy with the border countries should be prepared to fight the mafias and, under the UN mandate, to act on land and at sea to help the failed states.

## What Can Europe Do?

Pope Francis has called for "migrants and refugees to be welcomed, protected, promoted and integrated" in a program that was not deemed worthy of any attention by the Spanish Episcopal Conference. He argues that the safe and legal entry of migrants should be established by issuing humanitarian visas in an extensive and straightforward way, fostering family reunification, including of grandparents, and increasing the humanitarian corridors for the most vulnerable refugees, without arbitrary and collective expulsions, particularly if people are returned to countries that do not guarantee fundamental rights.

A greater effort is needed from politicians and decision makers to understand this problem and for there to be the political will for the public administrations to commit to solve the current difficulties, including universal access to public health like any other person. There is a pressing need for us to change our viewpoint, so that neither the status of refugee or migrant is considered a risk factor.

An urgent response is needed to the dramatic events that we have witnessed during the last two years. There has been a clear division in each European Council regarding the recent actions of the member states. There is the core of founding countries, with the support of Denmark and Ireland, which have shown solidarity and follow the tradition of being recipient countries for asylum seekers and refugees. There is also a periphery that is not committed to the community solidarity. Germany has put forward, to an overcautious France, the need to embark on reforming the European asylum system with specific proposals, overcoming the controversies regarding the imposition of restrictions in the entry criteria, opening decent refugee centers, and establishing common basic standards for the 28 member states regarding the conditions to receive refugees.

A far-reaching reform of the European asylum and migration policy is essential and needs to include the setting up of legal channels to submit asylum applications at consulates and a fair distribution of the number of refugees, along with the implementation of adequate European management mechanisms to address migrations (work, family).

Changes to the Common Foreign and Security Policy are essential and need to include border control and acting at the source of the causes that lead to the mass exit of people. Diplomatic channels should be exhausted and direct action (arms embargos, the setting up of humanitarian corridors in the conflict zones) used to provide humanitarian aid on the people reaching the borders.

Progress has to be made in the reflecting on political integration and the institutional improvement of the decision-making process. They have so far opted to invest in more fences, barbed wire, walls, police, and other security resources, and they have sidelined the humanitarian values that have traditionally differentiated us from other global players.

The government, the state, is still failing to meet the requirements sought by the social collectives addressing this huge tragedy and has not yet disclosed the resources implemented in the returns: the number of legal aid lawyers and interpreters involved; the number of police officers who have acted as investigating officers and clerks in the different procedures; the activities carried out to identify the persons; the activities aimed at identifying the existence of situations of special vulnerability (minors, international protection seekers, and victims of human trafficking); the nationality lists of the returned people; and guarantees provided by Morocco, Libya, and other countries that they will not be subject to abuse.

## The Citizen Response

The response to the refugee crisis has meant renouncing what remained of the European project. There are critical responses and also aspirations for another political model for Europe in the citizen movements that have emerged. There has been anger and indignation at the impact of highly emotional and symbolic stimuli, such as the photography of the body of the child Aylan Kurdi on the Turkish coast.

First, we have to break down a certain lying institutional discourse by the authorities and a large part of the media, which has generated racist and xenophobic behavior. Then, individuals, social movements, community, professional, and institutional collectives may put forward initiatives aimed at changes in the specific care and the reception policies for thousands of people with all their rights. Even though there is resistance, migrant reception networks have also emerged in response in European cities.

The institutional response has been very positive, with initiatives such as those of the Madrid, Barcelona, A Coruña, Pamplona-Iruñea, Zaragoza, Valencia, and several more city councils, along with those of hundreds of small towns, with the involvement of their mayors, autonomous communities, and so on, pressured by citizen movements that were activated to receive the refugees and launched proposals to create a European cities-refugee network. Initiatives are possible that go beyond the action of the states and can be implemented in a coordinated manner at the European level, with public resources and from civil society.

There should be policy and welfare initiatives driven from the grassroots, by collectives and social initiatives. Health professionals have an important role to play regarding violence and must deal with family and basic needs.

The first impetus is humanitarian: it is necessary to alleviate asylum and refugee needs. Psychosocial support and support during the transit are needed. Easing access to food and housing, empathic reception, empowerment, and strengthening family ties are among the measures required. And the dignity of people must always be respected, regardless of their origin and situation.

It is currently the state that decides who is a refugee and who is not. Citizen reception infrastructures will have to be constructed to receive those who arrive, and the institutional-legal framework and the logic of action also need to be transformed. That European cities-refugee network would be an example of a cosmopolitan, cross-border policy, serving the rights of people, which goes beyond national limits and requires different types of responses.

There is no doubt that refugees will continue to come to Europe in waves, they will walk as many thousands of kilometers as necessary, and they will sail as many hundreds of miles as needed, because they are looking for a decent life away from the repression, illness, hunger, and death in their countries of origin. It is up to us to guarantee all the rights of everyone.

## What Can Be Done in the Field of Mental Health?

There must be greater general socio-health care, which until recently only covered those with residence permits and all minors, regardless of their administrative status. The public health system currently provides universal care to the whole immigrant population that seeks it. However, fear of detention, expulsion, and being returned to their country of origin is a curb on the normal exercising of the right to health. Some NGOs have offset the shortcomings while that option did not exist, and even continue to do so.

Mental health professionals have been discussing the need for specific teams to care for those sectors of the population. The significant number of mental disorders in an already large affected population, numerically speaking, and that continues to grow, with their many specificities, could be better addressed by means of the aforementioned specific teams. They already exist in other European networks and schemes for those and other groups (exiles; people who have been tortured, raped, abused; former prisoners; and so on) and have produced very interesting therapeutic results. It is also true that, in pursuit of a successful integration, those sufferers could and must be cared for by the standard mental health care networks.

Some requirements to be taken into account include understanding of the reality, with impetus needing to be given to studies focused on immigrant health that consider sociocultural, clinical, and epidemiological aspects.

There is a pressing need to recognize the social role of professionals and training mental health professionals skilled in the cultural factors of the human groups to be cared for is also necessary. Empathy with the foreigner has to be fostered, and that requires training in interculturality in order to drive greater levels of awareness about cultural diversity and preparation with cognitive resources, necessary to perceive and analyze social inequalities, with transformation proposals and to be critically positioned in the social intervention.

It is necessary to encourage psychosocial support, given its protective effect against possible life stressors. Greater family and social support means lower symptomatological incidence. Awareness-raising actions and dissemination of the health reality of the immigrants will therefore have to be encouraged, along with health promotion interventions through the usual social and health stakeholders.

We must move, in short, toward the mix of "us" and "them," something that is then pending but inevitable, with open intervention, integration, and reception policies, by constructing equality mechanisms in this social framework dominated by diversity. The migrant population does not bring confrontation and unwanted competition. They do want better living conditions than the ones they had in their country of origin, and they do come with a baggage of experiences, memories, lifestyles, landscapes, aesthetics, and so on that are different but that are also compatible and enriching. If our viewpoint is different, mutual enrichment will be possible.

We make a global recommendation to stress the need for the authorities involved, both the public and private powers-that-be, and society overall to consider the phenomenon as a process of normalization and therefore a social program to address the difficult and painful migration process.

There should be a border control policy based on respecting human rights, with far-reaching changes to immigration legislation to guarantee legal channels for migration, approval of the regulation of asylum legislation to guarantee access to the asylum procedure in consulates, and an assurance that border externalization agreements are ended with third parties that do not guarantee human rights or protect people in transit.

## Bibliography

Amnesty International. The Human Cost of Fortress Europe. Human Rights Violations Against Migrants and Refugees at Europe's Borders (January 5), 2014.

Joint NGO statement ahead of the European Council. The NGOSs stronly condemn new EU policies to contain migration. Madrid, (2016): 27-6.

Ferrero Turrión, Ruth. Seguridad y derechos humanos, la crisis de refugiados como crisis de valores de la UE. Madrid: IEEE, Instituto Español de Estudios Estratégicos, 2016.

Lucas, Javier de. El Mediterráneo: el naufragio de Europa. Valencia: Tirant Humanidades, 2015.

Markez, Iñaki. Menores Inmigrantes: acceso a las drogas de la generación uno y medio. San Sebastián: Mugak 47 (2009): 29-32.

Markez, Iñaki, Paloma Favieres, Gabriela López Neyra, and Nabil Sayed-Ahmad. El bienestar psicosocial de las personas migrantes y refugiadas. Cuadernos Técnicos 19. Madrid: AEN, 2017.

Naïr, Sami. La Europa mestiza. Inmigración, ciudadanía y codesarrollo. Barcelona: Círculo de Lectores/ Galaxia Gutenberg, 2010.

———. Refugiados. Frente a la catástrofe humanitaria, una solución real. Madrid: Editorial Memoria Crítica, 2016.

Safont, Laura. "Lo que ocurre en el Mediterráneo central no es capricho de Salvini." Público, July 9, 2018.

# PART II

# Psychological and Psychosocial Studies on Basque Migrations

## Recommendations for Good Practices in Mental Health in Migration

# 5

# Psychological Support Program for Migratory Stress

## A Pilot Study

*Karmele Salaberría and Analia del Valle Sánchez*

Immigrants' main resource for coping with the immigration process is their physical and mental health. Immigrants are, in general, strong people because they have given themselves the chance to seek new horizons and to project themselves toward a different future, but the migration process can weaken them. This process involves elaborating grief and the loss of what they left behind in the country of origin, dealing with multiple psychosocial stress situations, adapting to a new culture, and rebuilding a new identity.

Migratory stress is characterized by its multiplicity because it affects many life areas; it is chronic because it can be prolonged for years; it is intense and disruptive due to the loss of control associated with different situations; moreover, the immigrant often lacks social support to cope with it. All this constitutes a permanent long-term overload that requires effort and the immigrants' willingness to adapt (Atxotegi 2009). In addition, being members of social minorities, immigrants also suffer from the emotional consequences of prejudice, stigma, and discrimination (Hatzenbuehler 2009; Meyer 2003). Some of the sources of stress that an immigrant may experience are displayed in Table 1.

### Table 1. Sources of migratory stress

- Hardships encountered to reach the host country.
- Fears that increase during the trip.
- Looking for a job.
- Processing documentation: residence and work permit.
- Possibility of detention and expulsion if they are in an irregular situation.
- Search for housing and registration.
- Processing of healthcare coverage.
- Achieving economic income to meet basic needs.

- Payment of debts incurred from emigrating and sending money to their country of origin.
- Coping with prejudice about immigrants.
- Achieving family reunification.
- Overcoming illnesses, vital moments of their loved ones in the country of origin, without being able to travel or from the exhaustion of trying to make the journey.
- Construction of affective and social links that can help them feel contained in the host country.
- Legal procedures to receive the visit of a relative or friend from their country of origin.
- Uncertainty about a possible event, like an illness or an accident, which can turn the immigrant into an invalid and place him/her in a situation of dependence.

Studies conducted to compare the health status of the immigrant and native population reveal that, in general, an immigrant's health is poorer (Bischoff and Wanner 2007; SAHMSA 2015). Immigrants have higher levels of anxiety, depression, and somatization than the indigenous population (Bhugra 2004), according to findings in studies conducted in Germany (Wittig, Lindert, Merbach, and Brähelr 2008), Belgium (Leveque, Lodewiycks, and Vranken 2007), and Spain (Elgorriaga 2011; Salinero, Jiménez-García, De Burgos, Chico, and Gómez-Campelo 2015; Salaberria and Sánchez, 2017). David Ingleby (2005) and other authors argue that inappropriately treated mental health problems can adversely affect immigrants' adaptation and subsequent integration (Bourque, van der Ven, Fusar-Poli, and Malla 2012; Morgan and Hutchinson 2010; Pumariega, Rothe, and Pumariega 2005).

In view of the problems of immigrant health, management of psychological assistance encounters some difficulties such as the use of the healthcare system by immigrants, adherence to psychological treatment, and the lack of psychological support programs geared to immigrants' specific needs and that have been assessed (Hoffmann, Asnaani, Vonk, Sawyer, and Fang 2012; Rubén, López-Zenón, Domenech, Escobar, Whitehead, Sullivan, and Bernal 2016).

With regard to the immigrant population's access to health services, immigrants face some obstacles, such as fear of being identified when they are in an irregular situation, the lack of access, misgivings about whether the professionals can understand them and respond adequately, the influence of cultural and religious ideology on healthcare, the unstable socio-work situation (working in internal domestic service, periodic changes of address, pressing economic needs), and ignorance of the language(Díaz Olalla 2009; Sayed-Ahmad Beiruti 2010). Thus, despite the high levels of stress and the disadvantaged socioeconomic situation suffered by the immigrant population, due to the abovementioned factors, they do not seek health services or, when they do so, it is through the emergency service or through police intervention (Llop, Vargas, Garcia, Aller, and Vazquez 2014; Sarria, Hijas, Carmona, and Gimeno, 2016).

Another healthcare challenge when working with the immigrant population is adherence to psychological treatment. Several authors have noted the high rate of therapeutic dropouts among immigrants and persons belonging to minority groups (Aponte, Rivers, and Wohl 1995; Sanz, Elustondo, Valderde, Montilla, and Miralles 2007). The reasons put forward are diverse: geographical displacement, changes of residence and employment, being unaccustomed to using mental health services, and lack of networks of informal support. It is therefore of interest to know which factors are related to treatment dropout.

Taking into consideration the medical difficulties and psychological needs of the immigrant population, two levels of intervention could be established: a first level of psychological support for migratory stress, as primary prevention, to facilitate the expression of the feelings of grief, help to cope with psychosocial stress, and support cultural adaptation (Government of Canada 2008; Gimeno-Bayón 2007; Muiño 2009; de Pedro 2010); and a second, specialized level when mental disorders are present, applying empirically validated therapies that have been shown to be useful for ethnic minorities (Watters 2002; Pérez-Sales 2009; Muiño 2009).

There are hardly any specific psychological support protocols for migratory stress that have been assessed from the therapeutic standpoint. In a meta-analytic review of 65 studies with quasi-experimental designs, Timothy B. Smith, Melanie Domenech, and Guillermo Bernal (2010) conclude, on the one hand, that the most effective treatments were those that were culturally adapted and that addressed the therapeutic goals identified by the participants and, on the other, they stress the need to investigate and develop therapeutic strategies for the immigrant population.

Hence, the aim of this work is to develop and evaluate a psychological therapy for migratory stress, to analyze its results across evaluations, at the group and individual level, and to present its scope and limitations.

## Method
### Design
The study was conducted with a design of A-B-A cases plus follow-ups at three, six, and twelve months.

*Participants*

The inclusion criteria for this study were as follows: (a) being over 18 years old; (b) wishing to participate voluntarily in the program after having been informed; (c) not being a refugee; (d) not undergoing a process of mourning the death of a family member in the last three months; and (e) being able to fill out the questionnaires and having a minimum knowledge of the Spanish language. From the psychopathological viewpoint, not presenting a psychotic disorder, an addictive disorder, a severe affective disorder, an eating disorder, or chronic illness serious were also taken into account.

A total of 156 immigrants contacted the psychological support program, of whom 24 did not keep the appointment. Of the 132 participants who came to the first interview, 54 did not meet the inclusion criteria (35.18 percent had a mental disorder, 12.96 percent came to request information, 7.41 percent were victims of workplace harassment or abuse and were referred to specific services, 7.41 percent had experienced the recent death of a family member, 5.5 percent wished to return to the country of origin, 5.5 percent were refugees, 11.96 percent did not know the language, and 5.55 percent were pregnant, which prevented their regular attendance to the sessions).

Of the 78 immigrants who began the pretreatment assessment, 13 did not finish it. Therefore, the final sample consisted of 65 first-generation immigrants residing in Gipuzkoa (northern Spain), whose main reason for migration was economic, and who requested help in the psychological support program.

*Assessment Instruments*

**Sociodemographic and Migratory Variables**

We designed an initial interview to collect sociodemographic data (age, sex, marital status, housing, education, employment, and economic situation), and migratory data such as place of origin, date of departure from their country and legal situation, as well as health status (previous psychiatric history, diseases, and health card possession).

**Migratory Stress Variables**

The Ulysses Scale (Atxotegi 2009, 2017) was used, in the context of an interview, to assess the level of migratory stress. The scale is divided into seven sections, collecting data on the immigrant's level of stress in different areas: family (range 0–60), acculturative stress (range 0–27), failure (range 0–48), survival and fear (range 0–24), epidemiological factors (range 0-6), vulnerability (range 0–18), and other variables (range 0–9). Each item is scored from 0 to 3. The maximum score that can be obtained on the scale is 192 points. A score between 30 and 60 points is considered moderate stress, and more than 60 is considered extreme stress. The internal consistency alpha coefficient is .74 in this study.

**Psychopathological Variables, Self-esteem, and Target Behavior**

The Symptom Checklist -90-R scale was applied (SCL-90-R; Derogatis 1975; González de Rivera, De las Cuevas, Rodríguez-Abuín, and Rodríguez-Pulido 2002) to assess the presence of general psychopathological symptoms. The scale consists of ninety items, with five response options rated on a Likert-type scale, ranging from 0 (*Not at all*) to 4 (*very much*). It assesses nine dimensions of symptoms (somatization, obsession-compulsion, interpersonal sensitivity, depression, anxiety, hostility, phobic anxiety, paranoid ideation, and psychoticism). In addition three global indices are provided that reflect the subject's distress: the global severity index (GSI), positive symptoms total (PST), and positive symptom distress index (PSDI). The internal consistency of the questionnaire ranges between .81 and .90 and temporal stability between .78 and .90. This questionnaire has been used in several works on immigrants' mental health carried out in different countries (Haasen, Demiralay, and Reimer 2008; Valiente, Sandín, Chorot, Santed, and González de Rivera 1996).

The self-esteem scale (Rosenberg 1965) was used to evaluate the individual's sense of satisfaction about him- or herself. This instrument consists of ten general items scoring from 1 to 4 on a Likert-type scale. The total score ranges from 10 to 40, with higher scores indicating higher self-esteem. Its test-retest reliability is .85, and the internal consistency alpha coefficient is .92. The cutpoint for the adult population is 29 (Ward 1977), which was used with the immigrant population in Norway (Oppedal, Røysamb, and Lacklud 2004).

To assess the level of difficulty of the participants' target behaviors (the ones they wished to address), we used a self-report in which participants made a list of five behaviors that they wanted to improve and that would constitute a significant benefit to their everyday life. These five behaviors were rated according to their degree of difficulty from 1 (*least difficult*) to 10 (*most difficult*) with a total range from 5 to 50.

**Treatment**

A psychological support program focused on problem-solving and addressing anxious-depressive-somatic symptoms, and the confusion arising from migratory stress was elaborated. Its purpose was to enhance the immigrants' development of skills to deal with stress and the difficulties that emerge in their daily lives. The components of the program appear in Table 2 in the order in which they were addressed. They were also presented to the participants in the form of a workbook that served as a reminder of the sessions and to carry out homework. The theoretical basis for the construction of the program were cognitive-behavioral programs for coping with complicated grief (Falicov 2002), chronic stress (Polo-Lopez, Salaberria, and Echeburúa 2015), adaptive disorder (Strain, Klipstein, and Newcorn 2010), and psychological strength empowerment (Remor, Amorós, and Carrobles 2010).

**Table 2. Components of the psychological therapy**

- Psycho-education about the psychological implications of the migration process and the most important symptoms.
- Management of anxious symptoms: breathing and relaxation techniques.
- Sleep and feeding habits.
- Temporal-spatial reorganization: daily, weekly, and monthly organization.
- Administration of money and debt incurred in their country of origin or in the host country.
- Improvement of mood: positive activities.
- Working with thoughts: positive self-instructions, search for solutions, reappraisal exercises, development of thinking flexibility.
- Increasing self-esteem and identification of strengths.
- Progress in social relations: search for social support networks, associations, religious communities, etc.
- Relapse prevention: summary of the process, recommendations in the face of conflictive situations, implementation of the learned strategies, etc.

The program acted as a primary attention facility to listen to, understand, contain, help, and provide emotional support based on the following premises: adaptation is achieved through learning, respect for differences, the importance of stress as the cause of symptoms, and the recovery of participants' healthy resources as a way of maintaining self-control and avoiding confusion.

*Procedure*

To obtain the sample, we advertised the program through a fact sheet and a bookmark with the address and telephone number that immigrants could call to request attention. Information was disseminated in telephone call centers and in various institutions that help immigrants: SOS-Racism, Caritas, the Red Cross, and various city council social services. When an immigrant contacted the program, we made an appointment for the first interview. In the interview, we determined whether the admission criteria were met, explained the program and the objectives, handed out an information sheet that described the intervention program and a letter of consent. If the immigrant agreed, we carried out the assessment, which could last between two and three sessions. The program was applied at intervals of one weekly session or a session every one and a half weeks, depending on the immigrant's ability to attend the appointments. It consisted of eight sessions of an hour and a half. After completing the program, we evaluated the participant and carried out the 3-, 6-, and 12-month follow-ups. Evaluation, treatment, and follow-up were carried out in the Faculty of Psychology at the University of the Basque Country by a clinical psychologist expert in cognitive-behavioral therapy.

*Data analysis*

Data were analyzed with the SSPS-23 statistical program for Windows. Descriptive analysis (means and standard deviations) was calculated for the quantitative variables, and analysis of frequencies and percentages were used for the qualitative ones. We applied the Kolmogorov-Smirnov test to verify the assumptions of normality and, as they were not met in some variables, we used non-parametric analysis. To evaluate the effect of the program, we used the Friedman test, and to compare the results between pre- and posttreatment and between posttreatment and the follow-ups, we used Wilcoxon, and *r* for the effect size. To compare the participants who completed the program with those who did not, we used Mann-Whitney's *U*, and *r* for the effect size of the quantitative variables, and Chi-square and Kramer's *v* for the qualitative variables.

To determine the evolution of each participant, we calculated Jacobson and Truax's (1991) reliable change index (RCI). The index is calculated for each subject by subtracting the posttest or follow-up scores from the pretest scores and dividing this result by the standard error of the difference between the scores of two applications of the test (Sdiff).

$$\text{RCI} = \text{pre-post/Sdiff}; \quad \text{Sdiff} = \sqrt{2}\,(SE)^2; \quad SE = SD\,\text{pre}\,\sqrt{(1\text{-r pre-post})}$$

An RCI higher than 1.96 is unlikely ($p < .05$) to occur unless there is a really significant change and therefore, it is reasonable to assume that this person has recovered. The cut-off points are established in four categories: recovered (>1.96), improved (1 1.96), unchanged (0.1–1), and worse (<0) (Ogles, Lumen, and Bonesteel 2001).

## Results

Table 3 presents the sociodemographic and migratory characteristics of the sample of 65 immigrants:

**Table 3. Sociodemographic and socio-work characteristics**

| Sociodemographic variables | N=65 | % | Migration characteristics | N=65 | % |
|---|---|---|---|---|---|
| Provenance | | | Time outside your country | | |
| Central America/Caribbean | 23 | 35.4 | 0–1 year | 18 | 27.7 |
| Northern Latin America | 22 | 34 | 1–3 years | 19 | 29.2 |
| Southern Cone | 13 | 20 | 3–5 years | 11 | 16.9 |
| Africa | 7 | 10.7 | 6–10 years | 17 | 26.1 |
| Sex | | | Debt incurred | | |
| Male | 9 | 13.8 | Without debt | 40 | 61.5 |
| Female | 56 | 86.2 | With debt | 25 | 38.5 |
| Age | | | Housing | | |
| 18–30 years | 22 | 33.8 | Shared flat | 32 | 49.2 |
| 31–40 years | 29 | 44.6 | Assistance flat | 9 | 13.8 |
| 41–60 years | 14 | 21.6 | Family unit | 14 | 21.5 |
| Marital status | | | Internal | 10 | 15.4 |
| Single | 22 | 33.8 | Living in shared room | | |
| Married/living with partner | 29 | 44.6 | 2 people | 20 | 30.8 |
| Separated | 12 | 18.5 | 3 people | 4 | 6.2 |
| Widowed | 2 | 3.1 | 4 people | 3 | 4.6 |
| Partner | | | Parents and children | 5 | 7.7 |
| Without a partner | 25 | 38.5 | Residence permit | | |
| With partner | 40 | 61.5 | Yes | 37 | 56.9 |
| In the host country | 23 | 57.5 | No | 28 | 43.1 |
| In the country of origin | 17 | 42.5 | Work permit | | |
| Children | | | Yes | 34 | 52.3 |
| Yes | 43 | 66.2 | No | 31 | 47.7 |
| No | 22 | 33.8 | Registration | | |
| Academic training | | | Yes | 57 | 87.7 |
| Primary studies | 19 | 29.2 | No | 11 | 12.3 |
| Secondary studies | 24 | 36.9 | Health insurance card | | |
| Professional training | 9 | 13.8 | Yes | 54 | 83.1 |
| University studies | 13 | 20.0 | No | 11 | 16.9 |

The participants were mainly from Latin America, mostly female (86.2 percent), with an average age of 33.31 years (*SD* = 9.09), that is, young adult population. Moreover, 44.6 percent were married or living with a partner, and 66.2 percent had children; 36.9 percent had secondary education studies. Only 26.1 petrcent had lived for more than six years outside of their country, and 47.7 percent did not have a work permit. Concerning job status, 35.4 percent were unemployed at the time of coming to the program, and, of those who were employed, 18.5 percent worked in cleaning and catering service, and the majority (46.2 percent) worked in domestic service and caring for older dependents.

Of the 65 participants who began the psychological support program, 34 completed it (52.3 percent) and 31 participants (47.7 percent) did not finish it. The reasons for not finishing the program are as follows: 19 participants (29.2 percent) failed to attend because they found work and could not reconcile their working hours with the program appointments; 8 participants (12.2 percent) left the sessions without giving any explanation; and 4 (6.2 percent) did not complete them because they reported they felt better. Between the posttreatment evaluation and the 3-month follow-up, 9 participants left, of whom 5 communicated that they were moving to other countries. Of the 25 participants who carried out the 3-month follow-up, three did not perform the 12-month follow-up, which was finally completed by 21 participants.

We performed a comparative analysis between participants who completed the program and those who did not complete all of the variables evaluated at pretreatment (Table 4). Participants who completed the program had more children living with them in the host country (35.29 percent), a greater proportion had been victims of aggression (18 percent), but they presented less stress and cultural distance than those who did not complete the program. They also had more self-esteem and less symptomatic intensity that those who did not conclude the program. The differences were small.

**Table 4. Comparison of participants who completes
and those who did not complete therapy**

| Variables | Completed | Did not complete | Chi-square | Kramer's v | Mann-Whitney U | r |
|---|---|---|---|---|---|---|
| | N= 34 | N=31 | | | | |
| | 52.3% | 47.7% | | | | |
| Children in host country | N | N | 8.31** | 0.44 | | |
| Yes | 12 | 4 | | | | |
| No | 8 | 19 | | | | |
| | | | | | | |
| Victim in host country | N | N | 6.02* | 0.30 | | |
| Yes | 6 | 0 | | | | |
| No | 28 | 31 | | | | |
| | M    SD | M    SD | | | | |
| Ulysses Scale | | | | | | |
| Total | 59.35  13.50 | 68.58  14.49 | | | 334.50** | 0.31 |
| | | | | | z=-2.53 | |
| Cultural stress | 5.85   2.39 | 7.97   2.69 | | | 314.50** | 0.35 |
| | | | | | z=-2.82 | |
| Self-esteem | 28.21  4.44 | 25.72  3.44 | | | 325.50** | 0.29 |
| | | | | | z=-2.32 | |
| SCL-90-R: PSDI | 2.37   0.57 | 2.63   0.54 | | | 364.00** | 0.24 |
| | | | | | z=-1.96 | |

PSDI: positive symptoms distress index

*p < .05. **p < .01. ***p < .001.

From the point of view of the effect of the therapy, Table 5 presents the scores in the different assessment instruments across the evaluations. In the pre-treatment evaluation, the immigrants presented low levels of self-esteem, below the cut-off point of the scale (29), high levels of psychopathology, corresponding to the 90th percentile of the general population norms of the SCL-90-R, and a high level of difficulty of target behaviors.

As can be seen, after treatment, there was a decrease in psychological distress, in the perception of difficulty to achieve the target behavior, and an increase in self-esteem. The participants' improvement between pretreatment and posttreatment assessment was large, as evidenced by the effect size of all the measures. Between posttreatment assessment and the 6-month follow-up, the improvement was still increasing in the subscales of interpersonal sensitivity, depression, paranoid ideation, and psychoticism, as well as the global severity index and the level of difficulty the target behavior. Between the 6- to 12-month follow-up evaluations, improvement was maintained at a general level.

### Table 5. Effect of the program and evolution over time

| | Pre | | Post | | 3 m | | 6 m | | 12 m | | Chi² | Pre-Post | | Post-6m | | 6-12m | |
|---|---|---|---|---|---|---|---|---|---|---|---|---|---|---|---|---|---|
| | N=65 | | N=34 | | N=25 | | N=22 | | N=21 | | | | | | | | |
| | M | SD | M | SD | M | SD | M | SD | M | SD | | Z | r | Z | r | Z | r |
| **SCL-90-R** | | | | | | | | | | | | | | | | | |
| Somatization | 1.66 | 0.86 | 0.60 | 0.46 | 0.53 | 0.42 | 0.49 | 0.42 | 0.37 | 0.36 | 28.41*** | -4.78*** | 0.58 | -1.36 | | -2.3* | 0.3 |
| Obsession-compulsion | 1.79 | 0.77 | 0.80 | 0.57 | 0.60 | 0.45 | 0.47 | 0.37 | 0.48 | 0.39 | 27.87*** | -4.40*** | 0.53 | -2.37* | 0.32 | -0.76 | |
| Interpersonal Sensitivity | 1.94 | 0.74 | 0.81 | 0.53 | 0.65 | 0.51 | 0.55 | 0.45 | 0.47 | 0.40 | 42.49*** | -4.92*** | 0.59 | -2.35* | 0.31 | -2.60** | 0.3 |
| Depression | 2.46 | 0.66 | 0.88 | 0.51 | 0.78 | 0.59 | 0.57 | 0.40 | 0.53 | 0.39 | 45.87*** | -5.08*** | 0.62 | -3.18** | 0.42 | -1.88 | |
| Anxiety | 1.76 | 0.87 | 0.52 | 0.43 | 0.46 | 0.41 | 0.37 | 0.37 | 0.33 | 0.36 | 44.13*** | -5.09*** | 0.61 | -1.38 | | -1.78 | |
| Hostility | 1.30 | 0.99 | 0.43 | 0.55 | 0.40 | 0.56 | 0.28 | 0.39 | 0.33 | 0.41 | 17.80*** | -4.14*** | 0.50 | -1.19 | | -0.34 | |
| Phobic Anxiety | 0.93 | 0.86 | 0.29 | 0.45 | 0.20 | 0.31 | 0.19 | 0.31 | 0.15 | 0.22 | 28.93*** | -4.24*** | 0.51 | -0.91 | | -2.21* | 0.3 |
| Paranoid Ideation | 1.77 | 0.82 | 0.76 | 0.54 | 0.57 | 0.49 | 0.45 | 0.39 | 0.41 | 0.44 | 36.61*** | -4.66*** | 0.56 | -2.39* | 0.32 | -1.70 | |
| Psychoticism | 1.23 | 0.62 | 0.40 | 0.34 | 0.22 | 0.24 | 0.14 | 0.18 | 0.15 | 0.21 | 46.70*** | -4.72*** | 0.57 | -3.17* | 0.42 | -1.38 | |
| GSI | 1.72 | 0.58 | 0.64 | 0.39 | 0.51 | 0.38 | 0.41 | 0.32 | 0.38 | 0.30 | 44.96*** | -5.02*** | 0.61 | -3.08** | 0.41 | -2.58** | 0.3 |
| PST | 61.02 | 12.99 | 37.20 | 19.30 | 32.20 | 21.49 | 27.41 | 19.08 | 26.33 | 20.07 | 44.28*** | -5.01*** | 0.61 | -2.93** | 0.39 | -2.49* | 0.3 |
| PSDI | 2.49 | 0.57 | 1.48 | 0.39 | 1.30 | 0.49 | 1.26 | 0.35 | 1.27 | 0.27 | 33.21*** | -4.74*** | 0.57 | -2.20* | 0.29 | -1.51 | |
| **Self-esteem** | 27.06 | 4.17 | 32.97 | 3.43 | 34.04 | 3.89 | 34.86 | 4.41 | 34.86 | 4.20 | 23.67*** | -4.73*** | 0.57 | -1.11 | | -1.43 | |
| **Target behaviors** | 40.41 | 6.33 | 16.71 | 6.91 | 14.52 | 8.03 | 12.64 | 6.30 | 12.52 | 5.97 | 44.81*** | -5.08*** | 0.61 | -2.91** | 0.39 | -1.22 | |

GSI: global severity index; PST: positive symptoms total; PSDI: positive symptoms distress index

*p < .05. **p < .01. ***p < .001.

GSI: global severity index; PST: positive symptoms total; PSDI: positive symptoms distress index
*p < .05. **p < .01. ***p < .001.

From a qualitative point of view, the types of target behavior the patients addressed during the psychological support program were grouped into categories: the type of target behavior, the percentage of patients who proposed those goals, and the level of difficulty with which they perceived them.

**Table 6. Types of target behaviors and perception of the level of difficulty**

| No. | Category | Examples | Percentage of participants who mention it | Level of difficulty (0–10) |
|---|---|---|---|---|
| 1 | Depressive symptoms | Be stronger, improve my self-esteem, feel better . . . | 79% | 8.06 |
| 2 | Anxious symptoms | Feel less anxious, be less abrupt, control anger and irritability . . . | 76% | 8.32 |
| 3 | Difficulties in social integration and behavioral inhibition | Get to know more people, integrate, communicate my opinions and feelings better, manage my shyness . . . | 58.06% | 8.36 |
| 4 | Desire to progress | Learn a trade, do activities, find work, bring over my children, know myself . . . | 43.55% | 7.85 |
| 5 | Family relations | Improve the relationship with my children, make my mother trust me more. . . . | 24.19% | 7.4 |
| 6 | Difficulties in everyday life | Have place to live, work, get my papers, have a future. . . . | 22.58% | 9.07 |
| 7 | Health concerns | Reduce back pain, headaches, muscle pain, sleep better . . . | 16.13% | 8.3 |
| 8 | Confusional symptoms | Be less confused, order my life, not forget things, be able to concentrate . . . | 6.45% | 7.25 |
| 9 | Fear | Feel less afraid . . . | 1.6% | 8 |

The management and reduction of anxious-depressive symptoms, improvement of social relationships to achieve greater integration, and the desire for progress were the participants' most frequently identified goals. From a quantitative point of view, the difficulties to get ahead in daily life, acquire a home, find a job, obtain documentation, and so on, are what the participants perceived as posing a higher level of difficulty.

We used the RCI in a subject-to-subject analysis to determine clinically significant changes at the individual level in each of the participants who completed the 12-month follow up. Participants who showed recovery or improvement in the target behaviors and in the GSI of the SCL-90-R were considered improved. Participants who maintained the improvement between posttreatment and the twelve-month follow-up and did not present any worsening either in the GSI of the SCL-90-R or in the target behaviors were also considered improved.

## Table 7. Individual Evolution of the Participants

| Pre-Post | | | | | | | | | | | | Post-12-month follow-up | | | | | | | | | | | |
|---|---|---|---|---|---|---|---|---|---|---|---|---|---|---|---|---|---|---|---|---|---|---|---|
| PAR | Som | Ob | Sensi | Dep | Anx | Hos | Phob | Par | Psyc | GSI | Tar | Som | Ob | Sensi | Dep | Anx | Hos | Phob | Par | Psyc | GSI | Tar | PAR |
| 1 | I | S | I | I | I | S | S | S | I | I | R | I | R | R | I | R | W | R | R | R | I | I | 1 |
| 2 | R | R | R | R | R | S | S | I | I | R | R | S | S | S | S | S | W | S | S | S | S | W | 2 |
| 3 | S | W | S | S | S | W | S | S | S | S | R | I | I | R | S | I | W | S | R | R | I | W | 3 |
| 4 | S | S | S | I | I | I | S | W | S | S | R | S | I | I | R | I | I | S | R | I | R | I | 4 |
| 5 | R | R | R | R | I | R | I | R | R | R | R | S | S | S | S | W | S | S | S | S | W | S | 5 |
| 6 | S | I | I | R | I | S | S | S | I | I | R | R | I | S | R | I | S | S | I | I | R | I | 6 |
| 7 | S | S | S | I | I | S | S | I | I | I | R | S | I | I | I | S | S | I | S | R | I | S | 7 |
| 8 | I | S | S | I | I | I | S | S | I | S | R | S | S | I | W | I | R | W | R | S | I | S | 8 |
| 9 | S | I | I | I | S | S | S | S | I | I | R | S | W | S | S | I | S | W | S | S | S | W | 9 |
| 10 | S | S | S | I | S | S | I | I | S | I | I | R | S | W | S | S | W | S | W | S | W | S | 10 |
| 11 | R | I | R | I | I | I | I | I | S | R | R | I | S | I | S | S | S | S | S | I | I | S | 11 |
| 12 | I | I | S | I | R | S | R | R | I | R | R | S | I | I | R | S | S | W | S | I | I | I | 12 |
| 13 | W | S | S | S | S | S | S | S | S | S | R | I | S | S | S | S | S | S | S | S | S | S | 13 |
| 14 | S | S | W | I | S | S | W | I | S | S | I | R | S | R | R | I | S | S | I | I | I | R | 14 |
| 15 | S | S | S | I | S | S | S | S | S | R | S | S | S | S | I | S | S | S | S | S | S | S | 15 |
| 16 | R | R | R | R | R | S | R | I | R | R | R | S | I | S | S | S | S | S | I | S | S | S | 16 |
| 17 | I | I | I | R | R | R | S | I | I | R | I | W | W | S | W | S | S | S | S | S | S | R | 17 |
| 18 | S | I | S | R | S | S | S | S | I | I | I | R | R | I | I | R | S | S | W | S | I | I | 18 |
| 19 | S | S | W | S | S | S | W | S | W | R | I | R | I | I | S | S | S | S | S | I | W | W | 19 |
| 20 | S | S | S | I | S | S | S | S | S | R | S | S | S | I | S | S | S | S | I | S | S | S | 20 |
| 21 | S | W | S | S | S | S | S | W | S | S | R | W | S | W | I | W | W | S | I | S | W | I | 21 |

PAR: Participant; Som: Somatization disorder; Ob: Obsession-compulsion; Sensi: Interpersonal sensitivity; Dep: Depression; Anx: Anxiety; Hos: Hostility; Phob: Phobic anxiety; Par: Paranoid ideation; Psyc: Psychoticism; GSI: Global Severity Index; Tar: Target behaviors.
Recovered (R) > 1.96; Improved (I) 1 – 1.96; Same (S) 0.1 –1; Worse (W) < 0.

Thirteen participants (62 percent) improved or recovered between the pre- and posttreatment assessments. This means that the program helped them to normalize the situation they were undergoing, decrease their anxious-depressive symptoms and feelings of estrangement and alienation from others, their worries and level of somatization. Between posttreatment and the twelve-month follow-up, 71.43 percent of the participants maintained the improvement achieved at posttreatment. There was evidence of less therapeutic change in the subscales of hostility, phobic anxiety, and paranoid ideation.

## Discussion

The psychological support program applied helps immigrants to reduce psychological distress, decrease the perception of difficulty of the target behaviors that they propose, and raise their levels of self-esteem. The good results achieved at posttreatment were maintained at the twelve-month follow-up and confirm those obtained in a previous work of five cases (Salaberría, Sánchez, and Corral 2009). The implementation of preventive programs of psychological assistance for immigrants has proven to be an effective strategy to reduce migratory stress and facilitate the processes of adaptation in the first phase of settlement of the migratory process (Interian and Díaz Martínez 2007).

In relation to the different components of the program, these seem to affect mainly anxious-depressive-somatic symptoms and confusion, and, to a lesser extent, components of hostility. From a social and clinical point of view, this is an important fact because when hostile characteristics are not resolved, they tend to transcend and perpetuate in future generations and they can merge with other psychopathological elements, increasing the levels of conflict, especially in the second generation (Grant, Stinson, Hasin, Dawson, Choy, and Anderson 2004).

Therapy positively impacts the perception of the level of difficulty of the target behaviors, with similar results as other programs that have been applied with population suffering from chronic stressors (Crespo and López 2008; Pachankis, Hatzenbuehler, Rendine, Safran, and Parson 2015; Polo-López, Salaberría, and Echeburúa 2015). It is therefore essential to work with the goals that the patient wants to achieve so the help will be effective (Smith, Domenech, and Bernal 2010).

One of the difficulties of working with this population is the lack of therapeutic adherence and the high level of dropout (Gimeno, Lafuente, and Gonzalez 2014), an aspect that was also observed in this study. Participants who drop out do so primarily because they find work, the central aim of their immigration project. Thus, mental health strategies should address participants of low socioeconomic status with pressing economic needs (Kaltman, Hurtado de Mendoza, Serrano, and Gonzales 2016). Immigrants who do not finish the therapy have lower self-esteem and greater cultural alienation than those who complete it. These variables should be taken into account in order to adapt the treatment approaches, create culturally sensitive treatments, and identify risk and protective factors (Barrera, Castro, Strycker, and Toobert 2013; Kalibatseva and Leong 2014; Fathi, Renner, and Juen 2015; Leong, Park, and Kalibatseva 2013).

From a clinical point of view, throughout the therapy, themes emerged such as long-distance motherhood, guilt for leaving the children, the ambivalence produced by contact with the family that remains in the country of origin, the difficulty of achieving the migratory goals, and the need to rethink them, ruminative questioning of the type "Should I stay or should I go back?" These aspects are addressed and discussed during the sessions. In addition, we sometimes had to provide information on the processing of registration, health cards, approval processes of academic studies, access to housing, job hunting, financial aid, and so on. Immigrants had often received this information from the social services, but their anxiety had prevented them from processing it and they came to the sessions confused and with disorganized documentation.

During the therapeutic sessions, sayings, stories, and songs of the culture of origin emerged, which the immigrants connected with the work that was being carried out. These materials were registered in the workbook as a reminder and served as a bridge between everyday life and the psychological support sessions, and the culture of origin and the host country. It should be kept in mind that these cultural and identity aspects are important to work with immigrants (Antoniades, Mazza, and Brijnath 2014; Fleischmann and Verkuyten 2016).

Despite the fact that the psychological support program has helped participants, this study presents some limitations. On the one hand, the profile of the immigrant attended to is Latin American women, and therefore, it would be appropriate to observe what results were obtained with other migration profiles (for example, Arab, and sub-Saharan males, Asians, and so on). On the other hand, the therapy was provided in individual sessions; it could be interesting to compare it with the application in group format (Gimeno-Bayón 2007). From a methodological point of view, the present work is a controlled case study and, therefore, the lack of a control group implies that results should be taken with caution.

However, despite the limitations, this work has some strengths such as the launching of a program of psychological support structured for migratory stress and its evaluation at the short, medium, and long term, the differential study of participants who dropped out of therapy, as well as the analysis of the results from a group and individual point of view.

This therapy aimed to provide immigrants with a space for listening, reflection, acceptance, and containment; a place to rebuild themselves, reposition themselves, recover, regain strength, and incorporate skills and strategies to feel better and, thus, continue their migration process.

## Bibliography

Atxotegi, Joseba. *Como evaluar el estrés y el duelo migratorio. Escalas de evaluación de factores de riesgo en salud mental: aplicación al estrés y el duelo migratorio. Escala Ulises.* Llanca: Ediciones el Mundo de la Mente, 2009.

———. "Concordancia entre evaluadores en la detección de factores de riesgo en la salud mental de la inmigración: escala Ulises." *Norte de Salud Mental* 57 (2017): 13–23.

Antoniades, Josefine, Danielle Mazza, and Bianca Brijnath. "Efficacy of Depression Treatments for Immigrant Patients: Results from a Systematic Review." *BMC Psychiatry* 14 (2014): 176.

Aponte, Joseph F., Robin Young Rivers, and Julian Wohl. *Psychological Interventions and Cultural Diversity.* Boston: Ally and Bacon, 1995.

Barrera Jr, Manuel, Felipe G. Castro, Lisa A. Strycker, and Deborah J. Toobert. "Cultural Adaptations of Behavioral Health Interventions: A Progress Report." *Journal of Consulting and Clinical Psychology* 81 (2013): 196–205.

Bischoff, Alexander, and Philippe Wanner. "The Self-reported Health of Immigrant Groups in Switzerland." *Journal of Immigrant and Minority Health* 10 (2007): 325–35.

Bourque, François, Els van der Ven, Paulo Fusar-Poli, and Ashok Malla. "Immigration, Social Environment and Onset of Psychotic Disorders." *Current Pharmaceutical Design* 18 (2012): 518–26.

Bughra, Dinesh. "Migration and Mental Health." *Acta Psychiatrica Scandinavica* 109 (2004): 68–73.

Crespo, María, and Javier López. *El estrés en cuidadores de mayores dependientes.* Madrid: Pirámide, 2008.

De Pedro, R. "La diversidad como herramienta. Una experiencia multicultural en un grupo terapéutico." Paper presented at the World Psychiatric Association Conference, "Migration, Mental Health, and Multiculturalism in the 21st Century," Barcelona, October 30–November 1, 2010.

Derogatis, Leonard. *The SCL-90-R.* Baltimore: Clinical Psychometric Research, 1975.

Díaz Olalla, José Manuel. "Situación actual de la inmigración en España. Desigualdades en salud." In *Manual de atención al inmigrante,* edited by Joaquín Morera, Alberto Alonso, and Helena Huerga. Barcelona: Ergón, 2009.

Elgorriaga, Edurne. "Ajuste psicológico y salud mental de la población inmigrante. Influencia del género y la cultura." Ph.D. dissertation, University of the Basque Country, 2011.

Falicov, Celia. "Migración, pérdida ambigua y ritual." *Perspectivas sistémicas* 69 (2002): 1–9.

Fathi, Atefeh, Walter Renner, and Barbara Juen. "Group Based Cognitive Behavioral Therapy for Depressed Iranian Migrants in Austria." *International Journal of Psychological Studies* 7 (2015): 88–104.

Fleischmann, Fenella, and Maykel Verkuyten. "Dual Identity among Immigrants: Comparing Different Conceptualizations, their Measurements and Implications." *Cultural Diversity and Ethnic Minority Psychology* 22 (2016): 151–65.

Gimeno-Bayón, Ana. "Aprendizajes sobre psicoterapia transcultural obtenidos desde la asociación Oasis de ayuda psicológica al inmigrante." *Revista de Psicoterapia* 18 (2007): 27–64.

Gimeno, Adelina, María Josefa Lafuente, and Francisco González. "Análisis del proceso migratorio de las familias colombianas en España." *Escritos de Psicología* 7 (2014): 31–42.

Government of Canada. "Coping with Stress: It's your Health," 2008. At https://www.healthcanada.gc.ca/iyh.

González de Rivera, José Luis, C. De las Cuevas, Manuel Rodríguez-Abuín, and Francisco Rodríguez-Pulido. *El cuestionario de 90 síntomas. Adaptación española del SCL-90-R.* Madrid: TEA Ediciones, 2002.

Grant, Bridget F., Frederick S. Stinson, Deborah S. Hasin, Deborah A. Dawson, S. Patricia Chou, and Karyn Anderson. "Immigration and Lifetime Prevalence of DSM-IV Psychiatric Disorders among Mexican Americans and Non-Hispanic Whites in the United States." *Archives of General Psychiatry* 61 (2004): 1226–32.

Haasen, Christian, Cueneyt Demiralay, and Johannes Reimer. "Acculturation and Mental Distress among Russian and Iranian migrants in Germany." *European Psychiatry* 23 (2008): S10–S13.

Hatzenbuehler, Mark L. "How Does Sexual Minority Stigma "Get Under the Skin?" A Psychological Mediation Framework." *Psychological Bulletin* 135 (2009): 707–30.

Hoffmann, Stefan G., Anu Asnaani, Imke J. J. Vonk, Alice T. Sawyer, and Angela Fang. "The Efficacy of Cognitive Behavioral Therapy: A Review of Meta-analyses." *Cognitive Therapy Research* 36 (2012): 427–40.

Ingleby, David. *Forced Migration and Mental Health: Rethinking the Care of Refugees and Displaced Persons.* New York: Springer Publishing, 2005.

Interian, Alejandro, and Angelica M. Díaz-Martínez. "Considerations for Culturally Competent Cognitive-behavioral Therapy for Depression with Hispanic Patients." *Cognitive and Behavioral Practice* 14 (2007): 84–97.

Jacobson, Neil S., and Paula Truax. "Clinical Significance: A Statistical Approach to Refining

Meaningful Change in Psychotherapy Research." *Journal of Consulting and Clinical Psychology* 59 (1991): 12–19.

Kalibatseva, Zornitsa, and Frederick T. L. Leong. "A Critical Review of Culturally Sensitive Treatments for Depression: Recommendations for Intervention and Research." *Psychological Services* 11 (2014): 433–50.

Kaltman, Stacey I., Alejandra Hurtado de Mendoza, Adriana Serrano, and Felisa A. Gonzales. "A Mental Health Intervention Strategy for Low-income, Trauma-exposed Latino Immigrants in Primary Care: A Preliminary Study." *American Journal of Ortopsychiatry* 86 (2016): 345–54.

Leong, Frederick, Yong Sue Park, and Zornitsa Kalibatseva. "Disentangling Immigrant Status in Mental Health: Psychological Protective and Risk Factors among Latino and Asian American Immigrants." *American Journal of Ortopsychiatry* 83 (2013): 361–71.

Levecque, Katia, Ina Lodewiycks, and Jan Vranken. "Depression and Generalized Anxiety in the General Population in Belgium: A Comparison between Native an Immigrant Groups." *Journal of Affective Disorders* 97 (2007): 229–39.

Llop, Alba, Ingrid Vargas, Irene Garcia, Marta-Beatriz Aller, and María LuisaVazquez. "Immigrants' Access to Health Care in Spain: A Review." *Revista Española de Salud Pública* 88 (2014): 715–34.

Meyer, Ilan H. "Prejudice, Social Stress, and Mental Health in Lesbian, Gay and Bisexual Populations: Conceptual Issues and Research Evidence." *Psychological Bulletin* 129 (2003): 674–97.

Morgan, Craig, and Gerard Hutchinson. "The Social Determinants of Psychosis in Migrant and Ethnic Minority Population: A Public Health Tragedy." *Psychological Medicine* 40 (2010): 705–9.

Muiño, Luis. "Salud mental e inmigración." In *Manual de atención al inmigrante*, edited by Joaquin Morera, Alberto Alonso, and Helena Huerga. Barcelona: Ergón, 2009.

Ogles, Benjamin M., Kirk M. Lunnen, and Kyle Bonesteel. "Clinical Significance: History, Application and Current Practice." *Clinical Psychology Review* 21 (2001): 421–46.

Oppedal, Brit, Espen Røysamb, and David Lacklud. "The Effect of Acculturation and Social Support on Change in Mental Health among Young Immigrants." *International Journal of Behavioral Development* 28 (2004): 481–94.

Pachankis, John E., Mark L. Hatzenbuehler, H. Jonathon Rendine, Steven A. Safran, and Jeffrey T. Parsons. "LGB-Affirmative Cognitive-behavioral Therapy for Young Adult Gay and Bisexual Men: A Randomized Controlled Trial of a Transdiagnostic Minority Stress Approach." *Journal of Consulting and Clinical Psychology* 83 (2015): 875–89.

Pérez-Sales, Pau. "Patología psiquiátrica en población inmigrante." In *Manual de atención al inmigrante*, edited by Joaquín Morera, Alberto Alonso, and Helena Huerga. Madrid: Ergón, 2009.

Polo-López, Rocío, Karmele Salaberria, and Enrique Echeburúa. "Effectiveness of a Psychological Support Program for Relatives of People with Mental Disorders Compared to a Control Group: A Randomized Trial." *Behavior Research and Therapy* 68 (2015): 13–18.

Pumariega, Andrés J., Eugenio Quiroz Rothe, and JoAnne B. Pumariega. "Mental Health of Immigrants and Refugees." *Community Mental Health Journal* 41 (2005): 581–97.

Remor, Eduardo, Montserrat Amorós, and José Antonio Carrobles. "Eficacia de un programa manualizado de intervención en grupo para la potenciación de las fortalezas y recursos psicológicos." *Anales de Psicología* 26 (2010): 49–57.

Rosenberg, Morris. *Society and the Adolescent Self-image.* New Jersey: Princeton, 1965.

Ruben, J. Rubén, Gabriela López-Zenón, Melanie Domenech, Ana Rocío Escobar, Michael Whitehead, Cris Sullivan, and Guillermo Bernal. "A Balancing Act: Integrating Evidence-based

Knowledge and Cultural Relevance in a Program of Prevention Parenting Research with Latino/a Immigrants." *Family Process* 55 (2016): 321–37.

SAHMSA (Substance Abuse and Mental Health Services Administration). Racial/ethnic differences in mental health service use among adults. Publication No. SMA-15-4906. Rocville, MD: SAHMSA, 2015.

Salaberría, Karmele, Analia Sánchez, and Paz Corral. "Eficacia de un programa de apoyo psicológico a mujeres inmigrantes: un estudio de casos." *Revista de Psicopatología y Psicología Clínica* 14 (2009): 153–64.

Salaberría, Karmele, and Analia Sánchez. "Estrés migratorio y salud mental." *Psicología Conductual* 25 (2017): 419–32.

Salinero, Miguel, Rodrigo Jiménez-García, Carmen de Burgos, Rosa M. Chico, and Paloma Gómez-Campelo. "Common Mental Disorders in Primary Health Care: Differences between Latin American-born and Spanish-born residents in Madrid." *Social Psychiatry and Psychiatric Epidemiology* 50 (2015): 429–43.

Sanz, Luis Javier, Isabel Elustondo, Magdalena Valverde, José F. Montilla, and Marta Miralles. "Salud mental e inmigración: adhesión al tratamiento ambulatorio." *Revista de la Asociación Española de Neuropsiquiatría* 27 (2007): 281–91.

Sarria, Antonio, Ana Isabel Hijas, Rocío Carmona, and Luís Andrés Gimeno. "A Systematic Review of the Use of Health Services by Immigrants and Native Populations." *Public Health Review* 3 (2007): 28.

Sayed-Ahmad Beiruti, Nabil. "Experiencia de migración y salud mental. Hacia un nuevo modelo de salud." In *La persona más allá de la migración. Manual de intervención psicosocial con personas migrantes*, edited by Luisa Melero. Valencia: Fundación CeiMigra, 2010.

Smith, Timothy B., Melanie Domenech, and Guillermo Bernal. "Culture." *Journal of Clinical Psychology* 67 (2010): 166–75.

Strain, James J., Kim G. Klipstein, and Jeffrey H. Newcorn. "Adjustment Disorders." In *Essentials of Psychiatry*, edited by Robert E. Hales, Stuart C. Yudofsky, and Glen O. Gabbard. Arlington: American Psychiatric Publishing, 2010.

Valiente, Rosa María, Bonifacio Sandín, Paloma Chorot, Miguel Angel Santed, and José Luis González de Rivera. "Sucesos vitales mayores y estrés: efectos psicopatológicos asociados al cambio por migración." *Psiquis* 17 (1996): 211–30.

Ward, Russell A. "The Impact of Subjective Age and Stigma on Older Persons." *Journal of Gerontology* 32 (1997): 227–32.

Watters, Charles. "Migration and Mental Health Care in Europe: Report of a Preliminary Mapping Exercise." *Journal of Ethnic and Migration Studies* (2002): 153–72.

Wittig, Ulla, Jutta U. Lindert, Martin Merbach, and Elmar Brähler. "Mental Health of Patients from Different Cultures in Germany." *European Psychiatry* 23 (2008): s28–s35.

# 6

# Acculturation among Basques and Brazilians

## Looking in the Mirror

*Sonia De Luca, Nekane Basabe, and José J. Pizarro*

During the last couple of centuries, the Basque Country has been heavily marked by emigration, as well as being one of the main destinations for Latin American immigrants. In the Brazilian case, Basque immigration has also been noticeable. Even though on a smaller scale compared to Argentina, Venezuela, and Chile, Spanish and Basque emigration has been constant and it has increased since the beginning of the twenty-first century (Gives 2013).

Historically, Brazil has been considered a host country for immigrants since it was claimed for the Portuguese crown in the year 1500 (Girard 2009). In the twentieth century, and more specifically during the 1980s, it changed from being a receptor to a sender of migrants, a fact that has steadily grown in recent years. Mainly due to materialistic motivations, Brazilian immigration to Spain started to become important during the 1990s, while the reverse (that is, Spanish immigration to Brazil) has meaningfully increased since 2008, substantially motivated by the effects of the economic crisis (Masanet and Padilla 2010; Sallé 2009).

Among the countries with more than 100,000 Brazilian immigrants, Spain held the fifth position by the year 2013 (Itamaraty 2013). In 2014, there were 4,517 Brazilian immigrants living in the Basque Country without having dual citizenship (PERE 2014). The arrival of Brazilian immigrants in the Basque Country, and especially in Vitoria-Gasteiz, started to be considered important in the 1990s due to specific agreements among different companies from the technological sector. As time went by, these arrangements increased and allowed the reuniting of nuclear and extended families of those who came first. According to an estimate by PERE (Padrón de españoles residentes en el extranjero, Register of Spaniards living abroad) (PERE 2014) and Itamaraty (2013), there are approximately 119,000 Brazilian immigrants in Spain, and about 117,523 Spanish immigrants in Brazil.

This chapter reviews different studies on acculturation, sociocultural learning, and cultural shock among Basque immigrants in Brazil, and Brazilian ones in the Basque Country. With that aim, we describe different studies that have evaluated the dimensions of sociocultural adjustment among migrants, as well as differences in cultural values between Brazil, Spain, and the Basque Country. Additionally, these analyses are complemented with others from studies carried out in the Basque Country, and finally, one comparing cultural shock in a paired sample of Basque and Brazilian immigrants.

## Acculturation and Sociocultural Adaptation

Acculturation processes are deeply rooted and implicit in migrations all over the world. In these contexts, a great deal of intercultural contact takes place among different groups (for example, different ethnic groups and those from different cultures). All of this affects multiple social groups such as refugees, sojourners (that is, international students, expatriates, and so on), and immigrants, and generates significant changes for those who engage in these dynamics (Ward, Bochner, and Furnham 2001). Regarding migrating populations in particular, acculturation induces more changes for those who are part of the minority rather than the dominant or the majority in any given host society, although there may be long-term cultural changes for the latter (Berry 2008). According to John W. Berry (2008), contact and participation in a host society on the one side, and maintenance of the original culture and identity on the other, are the two key elements that migrant people combine in several ways or acculturation strategies (see also Chun, Organista, and Marín 2003). In his model, Berry proposes one of the most famous typologies of ethnic migrant strategies, which are *assimilation* (adopting the host culture and losing the original culture), *integration* (combining both), *separation* (from the host culture and maintenance of the original culture), and *marginalization* (exclusion from both cultural groups) (Berry 2001, 2008).

Sociocultural adjustment to a new culture not only involves an acculturation strategy to be adopted, but also several other issues, such as incorporating social skills that allow immigrants to cope with in the new culture, as well as developing behaviors to establish good relations with the people in the host society and learn behavior ways to solve social tasks (Moghaddam, Taylor, and Wright 1993). Even though psychological and sociocultural adjustments are related to each other, they have different patterns, temporal evolution, and psychosocial correlates (Chun, Organista, and Marín 2003). Sociocultural adjustment is related to social skills acquisition, and it is influenced by the length of residence in the new culture, cultural knowledge, cultural distance, interactions with host nationals, and language fluency (Ward and Kennedy 1999).

With regard to particular instances of competence acquisition, the study of culture shock has been described as having particular domains (Ward and Kennedy 1999). First, the domain of *cultural empathy* and *relatedness* refers to understanding the local perspective, its values and world views, and intercultural communication, such as making friends or making oneself understood. Second, *impersonal endeavors* and *perils* have to do with managing impersonal interactions, bureaucracy, authority, unsatisfactory services, and unpleasant people. In a study in the Basque Country (de Luca, Bobowik, and Basabe 2011), it was found that Brazilian immigrants reported difficulties relative to two areas. The first was cultural learning and communication and such difficulties related to understanding the local perspective, getting used to the rhythm of life, food, climate, religious rituals and practice, living away from the family, making oneself understood, making friends, and understanding jokes and humor. The second, social distance management, was connected to dealing with people in authority, with unpleasant people, with people staring at them, with unsatisfactory services, with bureaucracy, and members of the opposite sex (de Luca, Bobowik, and Basabe 2011).

On the other hand, the length of stay in a new culture is one of the stronger factors affecting sociocultural adjustment. Specifically, time evolution adaptation is especially low at the beginning and then improves in the earlier stages until it reaches a plateau (Ward, Bochner, and Furnham 2001). Another important factor is contacting with and relating to host national peoples because it provides opportunities for cultural learning and culture-specific skill acquisition, and it provides resources for gaining support from members of the host society (Zlobina, Basabe, and Páez 2008). Congruently, empirical data from the Basque Country corroborates the fact that sociocultural difficulties were greater at the beginning of the adaptation process, decreasing over the length of residence, and were associated with more socioeconomic difficulties, less social support, hedonic well-being, and perceived control (de Luca, Bobowik, and Basabe 2011).

Finally, the acculturation strategies adopted by Brazilians did indeed affect their sociocultural adjustment. In particular, behavioral separation was related to more sociocultural adaptation problems, while marginalization impeded cultural learning and communication. These data also support the bicultural strategy, which is associated with better sociocultural adjustment, as has been proved in several studies. As an example, one meta-analysis of 83 studies shows a strong

and positive association between biculturalism and adjustment, both psychological and sociocultural (Nguyen and Benet-Martínez 2013).

## Cultural Shock and Cultural Dimensions

Cultural dimensions refer to the cultural values that characterize societies. Geert
Hofstede's cultural *individualism* refers to the priority given to the person,
whereas *collectivism* refers to the group and more often to the extended family
(Hosftede 2001; Basabe and Ros 2005). Core aspects of individualist beliefs are
personal independence and uniqueness, the importance attributed to competition, personal achievement, and an emphasis on internal attributes; in contrast,
a sense of duty and obligation toward the group and an emphasis on maintenance in-group harmony are features of collectivist beliefs (Oyserman, Coon,
and Kemmelmeier 2002). Latin Americans report a greater agreement with
collectivist beliefs and less with those of an individualistic type, compared to
Europeans and Spaniards—although the differences are moderate and less pronounced in the case of individualist beliefs.

*Hierarchy values* or *power distance* (Hofstede 2001) refer to the degree of
acceptance that power is unequally distributed in society, the maintenance of
an emotional distance between subordinates from authorities, and the acceptance of social norms that prescribe respect and formal deference toward those
of higher status (Basabe and Ros 2005; Hofstede 2001). Comparing data values
(Hofstede 2001), Brazil scores relatively higher in this dimension than does
Spain, which in turn scores higher in individualism. Regarding competition,
success, and personal achievement values, they were characterized by socioeconomic development and are more prominent in hierarchical and developing
countries than in post-materialist, developed, or more egalitarian societies (Basabe
and Ros 2005). In this sense, results from immigrants in the Basque Country and
in the European Union showed that immigrants score higher in conformity to
social and group norms, in personal promotion and achievement, and in power
values than native pairs (Basabe, Páez, Basabe, Aierdi, and Jiménez 2009).

Another cultural dimension described in anthropological literature is the
difference between *tight* and *loose* cultures (Gelfand et al. 2011) or *indulgent* versus
*restraint* cultures (Hofstede, Hofstede, and Minkov 2010). An indulgent culture
allows people to freely search for the desires and gratifications of basic needs;
they are focused on individual happiness, freedom, and personal control, whereas
in a restraint-type culture, strict norms are imposed to regulate gratifications.
According to this, Brazil can be represented as an indulgent culture and is ranked
at 26, compared to Spain at 45, in the study by Gelfand et al. (2011).

## Familism

If we took a snapshot of how intensely immigrants living in the Basque Country manifest different values, it would show a hierarchy of values composed of self-transcendence (namely, universalism and benevolence), hierarchical and bonding familism, and conversation, security, and conformity (Basabe et al., 2009).

Familism, in particular, is a cultural motivation implying a strong identification and linkage of people with their nuclear and extended family, as well as strong feelings of loyalty, reciprocity, and solidarity among members of the same group. There is a high familial interconnectedness among members of the extended family, relatives, and close friends of the family (Marin and VanOss 1991). On the other hand, familist values have been associated with collectivism and hierarchy, and they are present in Latin, African, and Asian cultures (Páez et al. 2003). Acculturation studies have suggested that familism constitutes one of the main shared values among Hispanic populations (Marín and Gamba 2003).

## Brazilians and Basques Immigrants: A Quantitative Study on Cultural Shock

In the following section, we will present a series of studies that analyze how Brazilian and Basque immigrants respond to the process of acculturation.

The first used a case control study, with two paired groups of Brazilians living in the Basque Country and Basques living in Brazil (São Paulo). The sample is composed of 47 matched pairs—paired by the length of residence, age, sex, education, and civil status (de Luca and Telletxea 2018)—and participants responded to a measure of sociocultural adjustment (the Spence Children's Anxiety Scale, or SCAS) (de Luca et al. 2011; Furnham and Bochner 1982; Ward and Kennedy 1999).

The results showed that during the first year, the difficulties were of great importance among both groups and cultural contexts. These changes were related to the interpersonal relationships dimension. Specifically, the difficulty in managing the social distance among the Basque newcomers to Brazil was higher for the older people, compared to Brazilians in the Basque Country. In addition, Basques reported more difficulties in adjusting to the warm climate, while Brazilians reported more problems in dealing with bureaucracy. Having a minority status had a more negative impact for Brazilians than for Basques, reflecting more perceived discrimination among Brazilians immigrants than Basques in Brazil.

Further, Brazilian immigrants perceived more difficulties in interpersonal relatedness, making friends, making themselves understood, and understanding the local perspective (such as jokes and the sense of humor). In relation to personal values, both Brazilian and Basque immigrants were open to change and stimulation and valued personal autonomy. On the one hand, Brazilian immigrants reported more collectivist values than their Basque counterparts. Further, the results showed they were more familist, conformist, promoted family networks of mutual support, and agreed with the hierarchy and deference to older people. On the other hand, Basque immigrants shared more individualistic values, prioritized more personal promotion and power, and at the same time, they supported traditions and reported a stronger ethnic identity.

## Brazilian and Basque Immigrants: A Qualitative Study

We now present two studies that analyze cultural shock among the same groups and conditions (namely, Basques in Brazil and Brazilians in the Basque Country). A qualitative perspective and methodology was applied to contrast the experience of living in these two cultural settings: the Basque Country, in which individualist and postmodern values are prominent; and Brazil, in which collectivist and hierarchical values are more frequent (Basabe and Ros 2005).

*Method and procedure*

*S1: Brazilians living in the Basque Country.* Sixteen participants (aged from 21 to 64; $M = 0.56$ $SD = 13.71$) took part in this qualitative study and were separated into three discussion groups, each of which was paired by sex (50 percent). An expert psychologist in group dynamics directed each group and the sessions were one hour in length. All sessions were recorded and transcribed, and a codification system was elaborated composed of four macro-categories. These categories were then evaluated by two independent and expert judges, who classified 267 ideas, and the inter-coder reliability index was $K = .863$ (Krippendorff's alpha; Hayes and Krippendorff 2007). The software *Atlast-ti* was used to count the ideas and create the relations between categories (that is, networks). Most of the ideas dealt with an ethnic minority experience (69 percent), ethnic stereotypes, the perception of discrimination, and ways of coping with the minority status in the host society. The others were related to the perception of cultural differences (31 percent). For this chapter, we will only report the perception of cultural differences between countries, cultural shock, and sociocultural differences.

*S2: Basques living in Brazil.* In this study, four people (all living in São Paulo) took part in four in-depth interviews, lasting one hour proximally. The participants' ages ranged from 24 to 62 years old (24, 35, 43, and 62 respectively), and 50 percent were women. All the questions (that is, for S1 and S2) were the same and addressed the perception of cultural, familial, and economic differences, cultural shock experiences, motives for migration, and ethnic minority experiences. As in the case of *S1*, all the data was recorded and transcribed for *S2*.

### Qualitative results

In the following section, some of the narratives from S1 and S2 are presented, illustrating the perceived differences in both contexts.

### Individualism – Collectivism

Brazilian participants express their perception of cultural differences between their own and host culture in regard to familism. Therefore, they give great importance to a strong adherence to loyalty, reciprocity, and solidarity among their family members. Conversely, Basque participants express the importance of receiving family help in specific contexts (for example, a grandparent looking after the grandchildren, or the reception of family members due to economic difficulties or loss of their housing), emphasizing group independence, the ability to make do for oneself, and personal goals.

> My brother earns the dough [money] and supports me . . . In Brazil, my parents don't have a lot of money, my siblings help with the monthly expenses (S1 – A6).

> Our . . . son was a baby . . . we were worried about being a long way from the family, he'd help us . . . with him. . . . for me, it was a great possibility for growing and professional recognition . . . I . . . was about to lose my job . . . my wife and I couldn't bear the fact of receiving financial help from the family, that'd be shameful . . . our parents, siblings, and grandparents don't have any economic responsibility for us (S2 – 1).

> My parents lost their jobs . . . they couldn't pay rent . . . we were living with my grandparents. Their unemployment compensation was about to finish and they couldn't admit the possibility of depending on my grandparents . . . and also for feeding them . . . they were horrified . . . [by] not finding a job . . . not being able to support us (S2 – 3).

### Motivation and Culture: Collectivism, Familism, and Materialism

The following excerpts depict the collectivism and familism that appears with the materialistic motivation of immigration and family promotion (namely, economic security, improving the quality of life in the family, and work).

Here, I'm much better; my brother earns the dough [money] and supports me . . . and gives me money to go out. In Brazil, my parents don't have a lot of money, my siblings help with the monthly expenses. For you to understand, in Brazil, the maximum I could do with the money I received from my parents was to go to McDonald's once, or twice a month. During vacations, I would always go to the beach, to my grandparents' house. Here, I can go to McDonald's every day and go away wherever I want . . . (S1 – A6).

*Motivation and Culture: Individualism and Personal Promotion*
Basque immigrants report a more individualistic speech focused on personal goals and family independence. In addition, there is a noticeably greater motivation to reach individual economic goals (for example, an improvement in the quality of life and family planning) and social promotion (for example, power and achievement), as well as self-development (for example, travel and getting to know other countries).

. . . coming here . . . it was the opportunity of having a better position in the company, more prestige, and a better salary . . . the possibility of changing our lives completely, reaching financial independence . . . paying the mortgage . . . My wife . . . [would] stop working and concentrate on raising our son. . . having more children without depending on the grandparents. She and I'd always wanted to live in other countries . . . (S2 – 1).

*Uncertainty Avoidance*
This category identifies how threatened immigrants feel by ambiguous situations, which they try to solve by means of using different codes and strict beliefs. Brazilian immigrants emphasize the insecurity of their origin country compared to the security of the host one. On the other hand, the Basque participants stress the emotional insecurity and the fear of unemployment in their country of origin.

. . . the company I used to work in proposed an ERE [expediente de regulación de empleo, labor force adjustment plan], or coming to work in Brazil. My partner . . . was looking for a job. I . . . had completed my internship in this company and I got a job here. With the economic situation of Spain and the Basque Country, we were afraid that we wouldn't get any other job if we didn't accept this offer (S2 – 2).

*Motivation and Culture: Uncertainty Avoidance and Social Insecurity*

Insecurity avoidance, in the Brazilians' speech, is associated with a search for social security and as a facilitator:

> Financially here in Vitoria, we are the same; the difference is that here, my husband and I work together. In Brazil, we barely saw each other during the whole day. We are calmer here as well because our children can go out alone without any fear of something bad happening. Comparing our life in the two countries, I can conclude there isn't any financial difference, but the quality of life we have here is not comparable with the one we had there. In Brazil, we used to live very well, but we didn't have the tranquility we have here in Spain (S1 – B2).

*Motivation and Culture: Uncertainty Avoidance, Individual Mobility, and Personal Promotion*

Basque immigrants prioritize individual mobility and personal promotion in the possibility of experiencing social insecurity in the host society. Uncertainty avoidance could in turn be associated with emotional insecurity (namely, the fear of not getting a job), and thus be considered a facilitating factor, as can be seen below.

> . . . I was invited to come and work as a director of the industrial department . . . for me it was a great opportunity for growing and professional recognition . . . I have been intimidated [by coming here] . . . that Brazil was very insecure and dangerous . . . I was about to not come. But the offer was too good . . . it was the opportunity of having a better position in the company, more prestige, and better salary . . . the possibility of changing our lives completely, reaching financial independence . . . paying the mortgage. . .we could have more children . . . we always wanted to live in other countries . . . we decided to face the unknown, the fear . . . the insecurity of the country . . . we have been here twenty-four years (S2 – 1).

In the same sense, uncertainty avoidance, individual mobility, and social support can be seen in the speech of Basque immigrants as facilitating factors:

> . . . My parents . . . they were terrified by the idea they wouldn't be able to support us. In the company in which my father used to work, he met several Brazilians who went to work in Vitoria . . . my father spoke with them . . . they got him a job here . . . (S2 – 3).

*Short- versus Long-Term Orientation and Indulgent versus Restraint Culture*
This section refers to the perception of differences in the orientation of both cultures. That is, the short- or long-term orientation, how they perceive interpersonal and economic planning, and whether they are oriented to the future or to the present. This dimension has not been widely discussed. In the particular case of Brazilians, a more immediate tendency regarding planning is observed. Likewise, an indulgent culture gives greater importance to the satisfaction of basic needs and the search of happiness and freedom.

> . . . with our salary we can indulge ourselves such as going to the beach on vacation, or eating out twice or three times a week . . . Nevertheless, I'm constantly worried whether money would be sufficient to pay the bills, the rent, power, gas, telephone, etc. (S1 – A5).

> . . . saving . . . at the beginning, it was not traveling and not spending on unnecessary things and all of that was rewarded . . . with the money we saved . . . we bought a house . . . two cars . . . we have twins . . . we want them to study and grow up here (S2 – 2).

*Motivation and Culture: Uncertainty Avoidance, Individual Mobility, and Personal Promotion*
In the case of Basque immigrants, long-term orientation is related to individual mobility and personal self-promotion. In the case of Brazilian immigrants, there is a predominance of loyalty and family promotion.

> . . . before . . . correctly speaking Portuguese . . . I was already working in the same company I work in today . . . I started . . . as a draftswoman . . . now, I'm a team manager . . . I feel proud and satisfied . . . with my job and the position I have in the company . . . I got it with a lot of effort and dedication . . . I'm continuing my training . . . to move up . . . (S2 – 4).

> . . . but it was tough at the beginning . . . I wanted to leave so badly, to go back to Brazil. But, for my employees, children, and husband, I decided to stay . . . (S1 – B2).

*Being an Ethnic Minority: Collectivism—Familism—Phenotype*
Among Brazilians, being part of an ethnic minority stands out, due to the discrimination they face. The phenotype (for example, their skin color) is a salient element in their speech and is considered to be an element that facilitates

discrimination. On the other side, there is no ethnic discrimination among Basques; on the contrary, they highlight good reception in the host society.

> Yes, due to my color and physiognomy . . . but I impose myself again when I say that my brother is a soccer player . . . I highly agree with my colleagues who say the black, mulatto, Latin, and Brazilian [people] are discriminated against because of their skin color and their way of dressing (S1 – A6).

> . . . Brazilian people are concerned about helping others, and I, as an immigrant, I felt welcomed by them. Since I got here, they were super nice with me, they would offer themselves if I needed something, I was invited to go out, to their houses . . . I was almost never left alone and I looked for comfort in them to put up with the distance (S2 – 1).

### Openness to Change

It is common among immigrants—Brazilians, Basques, and others—to highlight the possibilities immigration offers, the openness to other cultures and ways of living.

> . . . we can travel to any Spanish city or European country . . . (S1 – B5).

> . . . we can travel to every place we think of . . . further . . . greater possibilities to learn languages, practice sports, acquire a better culture (S1 – B5).

> . . . We were excited . . . the possibility of getting to know another country (S2 – 2).

> . . . learning Portuguese, to get to know the way of life in Brazil, to see the city, learn new things, get to know people . . . (S2 – 4).

### Cultural Shock: Sociability, Gender, and Social Distance and Expressivity

Different ways of socializing, friendship relationships, emotional expression, religious life vary from one culture to another, and they can constitute a source of cultural shock. Some of these excerpts depict these differences. For Brazilians, the relationship with the Basque *kuadrilla* (that is, a tight-knit group of close friends usually formed during childhood and adolescence) and gender-related separation are unexpected. For Basques, conversely, the ease in making friends, emotional expressivity, and the importance of home as a meeting place in Brazil are different.

. . . I've been living here for many years . . . One of the things that stands out since I got here . . . is the way the Basques keep their friendships, and how they behave when they are in a group of friends, or a *kuadrilla* as they say here, and how they meet another acquaintance from another *kuadrilla* . . . those who know each other speak as if everyone else didn't exist . . . At the beginning, I thought it was rude, but later understood it's their way (S1 – B1).

. . . difficult . . . to understand . . . young people go out with men . . . they don't mix or meet [groups of women] . . . (S1 – A4).

. . . in the Basque Country people meet more in the street . . . they plan to meet in the bars . . . in the restaurants, here "you invite" people to your house . . . Brazilians' houses are always open to receive whoever arrives . . . everyone is welcome to eat and drink . . . Here, it's much easier to make friends . . . to get to know a person who introduces you to someone and someone else, and someone else, and at the end, many of them become your friends (S2 – 1).

. . . sometimes I think . . . about the amount of friends I have here . . . I'm shocked . . . in Vitoria I had so little acquaintances . . . I don't know how I got to meet so many people . . . I think it was because . . . the way in which Brazilians related . . . they are so happy . . . cheerful . . . they are open to getting to know people . . . they go out with people they don't know . . . they gather people. This is their natural way . . . it's part of their life . . . (S2 – 3).

### Cultural Shock: The Food

. . . the food . . . at the beginning was very hard . . . now, I got used to it so much that whenever I go there [to the Basque Country], I always ask for more salt . . . we got used to it . . . faster with the food from here . . . we adapted to the food from there so as to be tastier. We miss . . . the lack of meat *empanadillas*, and chicken thighs with cheese from here, when we go to the Basque Country (S2 – 1).

For me the most difficult thing was getting used to the way of eating here [in Brazil], at home, we continue eating as if we were in Euskadi [the Basque Country] (S2 – 2).

## Cultural Shock: The Weather

. . . when I got here . . . I'd die of cold . . . for me the weather was hor-
rible . . . I wanted to go back to Brazil . . . I didn't want to be here . . .
the weather was very different from now, it was colder and people were
colder back then than now . . . After twenty-five years, I got used to the
weather and the food . . . I don't miss it anymore (S1 – C5).

Here the tropical weather, you're more comfortable, you can walk with
fewer clothes and you don't think whether it's going to cool down
or rain, you don't need your jacket . . . the weather is warmer and
that makes people more happy, open, and receptive. In comparison to
Euskadi where it's colder and people retract more and are more close-
minded (S2 – 2).

## Cultural Shock: The Religion

My husband's family is Catholic and Spiritist; at the beginning, I was
shocked, how can you believe in contrary things at the same time?
One believes in reincarnation and the other doesn't, getting along with
both, I understand both and practice them . . . (S2 – 4).

. . . the way of practicing religion was shocking . . . I'm Evangelical,
when I got here there 1–2 percent of the people were Evangelical, now
it has increased quite a lot . . . Before, there was a lot of racism, people
didn't like Evangelicals . . . when we used to speak in the streets and
put up flyers . . . they took them down . . . didn't accept us . . . now,
many people have become Evangelical (S1 – C5).

## Conclusions

This chapter has reviewed the evidence on sociocultural adaptation and sources
of cultural shock resulting from intercultural contact and acculturation in migrations. In the same vein, different studies on cultural differences among nations (Basabe and Ros 2005; Hofstede 2001) have shown the differences and
similarities between values, which in this case, has been exemplified with data
from Brazilians in the Basque Country and Basques in Brazil, as a way of seeing
one reality from two different perspectives.

Specifically, it has been shown that sociocultural adjustment improves
by increasing the time of residency in the new culture, interactions with
host nationals, and linguistic fluency (Ward and Kennedy 1999). Studies

on cultural shock have described two domains of acquiring cultural competence (Ward and Kennedy 1999). Both dimensions—cultural learning and communication on the one hand, and social distance management on the other—have been described in the Basque Country (de Luca, Bobowik, and Basabe 2011).

Finally, data from quantitative and qualitative studies have been reported, and similar and differential patterns of cultural shock for Brazilians and Basques can be seen. In particular, they described cultural shock related to the specific forms of behaving and to different values. For instance, the differential pattern can be seen for Brazilians in short-term orientation, more collectivism, and a greater orientation to familism. In contrast, Basques were more oriented to self-promotion and individualism and more long-term oriented. Furthermore, both groups displayed different patterns of uncertainty avoidance and openness to change, emphasizing the positive outcomes that immigration produces.

## Acknowledgments

This study was supported by the Spanish Ministry of Economy and Competitiveness [under Grant PSI2017-84145-P] and the University of the Basque Country [under Grant IT-666-13, Grant US13/11].

## Bibliography

Basabe, Nekane, Dario Páez, Xabier Aierdi, and Amaia Jiménez. *Calidad de vida, Bienestar subjetivo y Salud: inmigrantes en la CAPV*. Bilbao: Ikuspegi; UPV/EHU, 2009. At http://www.ikuspegi.org/documentos/investigacion/es/3ikusgai_salud_inmigracion_ikuspegi.pdf.

Basabe, Nekane, and María Ros. "Cultural dimensions and social behavior correlates: Individualism-Collectivism and Power Distance." *International Review of Social Psychology* 18, no. 1 (2005): 189–225.

Berry, John W. "A Psychology of Immigration." *Journal of Social Studies* 57 (2001): 615–31.

———. "Globalization and Acculturation." *International Journal of Intercultural Relations* 32, no. 4 (2008): 328–36.

Chun, Kevin M., Pamela Balls Organista, and Gerardo Marín, eds. *Acculturation: Advances in Theory, Measurement, and Applied Research*. Washington, DC: APA, 2003.

De Luca, Sonia, Magdalena Bobowik, and Nekane Basabe. "Adaptación sociocultural de inmigrantes brasileños en el País Vasco: Bienestar y aculturación." *Revista de Psicología Social* 26, no. 2 (2011): 275–94.

De Luca, Sonia, and Saioa Telletxea. "Choque y adaptación sociocultural una visión en espejo: vascos y brasileños." *Universitas Psychologica*, 16, no. 5 (2018): 1–14.

Furnham, Adrian, and Stephen Bochner. "Social Difficulty in a Foreign Culture: An Empirical

Analysis." In *Cultures in Contact: Studies in Cross-cultural Interaction*, edited by Stephen Bochner. Oxford: Pergamon, 1982.

Gelfand, Michele J. et al. "Differences between Tight and Loose Cultures: A 33-nation Study." *Science* 332, no. 6033 (2011): 1100–1104.

Girard, L. L. *A inserção de imigrantes europeus na cidade de Brasília*, 2009. At http://www.urbanidades. unb.br/artigo_1_luana_girard.pdf.

Gives, M.. *Emigración española contemporánea. San Juan de Pasto*, 2013. At http://ceilat.udenar.edu.co/ wpcontent/uploads/2014/05/EMIGRACION_ESPA%C3%91OLA_CONTEMPORANEA.pdf.

Hayes, Andrew and Klaus Krippendorff. "Answering the Call for a Standard Reliability Measure for Coding Data" *Communication Methods and Measures*, 1(2007), 77–89

Hofstede, Geert. *Culture's Consequences: Comparing Values, Behaviors, Institutions and Organizations Across Nations*. 2nd Edition. Thousand Oaks, CA: Sage, 2001.

Hofstede, Geert, Gert Jan Hofstede, and Michael Minkov. *Cultures and Organizations: Software of the Mind*. Revised and expanded 3rd Edition. New York: McGraw-Hill, 2010.

Itamaraty. *Brasileiros no mundo*, 2013. At http://www.brasileirosnomundo.itamaraty.gov. br/a-comunidade/estimativas-populacionais-das-comunidades/.

Marín, Gerardo, and Raymond J. Gamba. "Acculturation and Changes in Cultural Values." In *Acculturation: Advances in Theory, Measurement*, and Applied Research, edited by Kevin M. Chun, Pamela Balls Organista, and Gerardo Marín. Washington, DC: APA, 2003.

Marín, Gerardo, and Barbara VanOss. *Research with Latino Populations*. Newbury Park, CA: Sage, 1991.

Masanet, Erika R, and Beatriz Padilla. "La inmigración brasileña en Portugal y España: ¿Sistema migratorio ibérico?" *OBETS: Revista de Ciencias Sociales* 5 (2010): 49–86.

Moghaddam, Fathali M., Don M. Taylor, and Stephen C. Wright. *Social Psychology: A Cross-cultural Perspective*. New York: W. H. Freeman, 1993.

Nguyen, Angela-MinhTu D., and Verónica Benet-Martínez. "Biculturalism and Adjustment: A Meta-analysis." *Journal of Cross-Cultural Psychology* 44, no. 1 (2013): 122–59.

Oyserman, Daphna, Heather M. Coon, and Markus Kemmelmeier. "Rethinking Individualism and Collectivism: Evaluation of Theoretical Assumptions and Meta-analyses." *Psychological Bulletin* 128 (2002): 3–72.

Páez, Dario, Itziar Fernández, Silvia Ubillos, and Elena Zubieta, eds.. *Psicología social, Cultura y Educación*. Madrid: Prentice-Hall, 2003.

PERE. *Estadística del Padrón de españoles residentes en el extranjero a 1 de enero de 2014*, 2014. At http:// www.ine.es/prensa/np833.pdf.

Sallé, Mª Angeles, ed. *La emigración española en América: historias y lecciones para el futuro*. Madrid: Gobierno de España, Ministerio de Trabajo y Migración, 2009.

Ward, Colleen, and Antony Kennedy. "The Measurement of Sociocultural Adaptation." *International Journal of Intercultural Relations* 23 (1999): 659–78.

Ward, Colleen, Stephen Bochner, and Adrian Furnham. *The Psychology of Culture Shock*. East Sussex: Routledge, 2001.

Zlobina, Anna, Nekane Basabe, and Dario Páez. "Las estrategias de aculturación de los inmigrantes: su significado psicológico." *Revista de Psicología Social* 23, no. 2 (2008): 143–50.

# 7

# Immigrant Women Who Work as *Internas* and Mothers Who Are Here and There

## A Critical Look from the Practice of Professional Intervention in Gipuzkoa

*Katia Reimberg, Castello-Branco, and Heldy Soraya Ronquillo Peña*

The arrival of globalization meant the acceleration of certain flows: money, information, goods, and services, driven by power relationships that emphasize the inequalities between rich and poor countries. The social and economic reorganization generated by globalization and liberal capitalism has influenced the increase in migratory movements, in addition to a substantial change in their constitutive characteristics (Gil 2005). This is the context in which the process of feminization of migrations takes place, leading thousands of women—who are considered solely responsible for the welfare of their families—to migrate to Europe.

That is why, in recent decades, the presence of women from Latin America has increased in some countries such as Spain. As a result of this new reality, there has been much scholarly production in a wide range of disciplines, confirming a growing interest in conducting studies on topics such as the causes of emigration; global care chains; the formation of transnational families; the jobs that women have access to and their working conditions; culture shock; and the psychological effects on immigrants.

In this context, the work process developed by the professionals of the Bidez Bide Association, mainly with women from Latin American countries, allows us to contribute to the reflection. Their stories and experiences will be taken as a reference point. These women work as *internas*[1] for the care of the elderly in their destination society and that has many effects on their lives, including on the transnational relationship they maintain with their families in their country of origin; the reencounters with their sons and daughters, after several years of being apart; culture shock; and also the various forms of agency and resistance developed by women in this context.

First, we introduce the global and local context in which our Bidez Bide Association conducts its line of work to implement the counseling and information services given for the homologation and/or validation of foreign studies to the equivalent Spanish degree. Second, we will address the implementation of the proposal that takes place in the premises of the Women's Building in Donostia-San Sebastian. In this section reflections and contributions are presented based on the realities of women and their working conditions as *internas* who take care of elderly people. Third, we will reflect on the experiences of women who are exercising a transnational motherhood and regrouping their sons and daughters in their destination society. Fourth, we will address the line of work related to the production of social audiovisual media, emphasizing that the objective is to portray the realities of women and their families who reside here as well as of those who live in their countries of origin. These audiovisual materials are used as pedagogical tools that contribute to the awareness of and critical reflection on these transnational realities. Finally, we offer some considerations, lessons, and proposals, based on our work over the years.

## The Context of the Work of the Bidez Bide Association: Our Points of View Do Matter

The context of globalization and liberal capitalism, driven by power relationships, that favor the free circulation of goods and capital, has contributed to social and economic restructuring at a global level. This has emphasized the inequalities between rich and poor countries and has influenced the increase in international migratory movements in recent decades.

This context generates a crisis of care, both in countries of the North and in countries of the South. In Spain, this crisis has been manifested in an aging population and increased life expectancy, which implies a greater need for care. The integration of women into the job market, an expansion of the neoliberal policies with large social cuts that limit public resources to cover the increase in care needs, and the lack of co-responsibility of markets on one end and of men in relation to jobs related to care on the other, are generating a social problem of great magnitude (Ezquerra 2011).

In southern countries from which these immigrant women residing in Spain come, this crisis is due to, among other things, the structural adjustment plans and the many neoliberal reforms that have had a disproportionate impact on women. This has led to the emigration of thousands of women, as they were considered solely responsible for ensuring sustainability of their homes in contexts of a social reproduction crisis (Gregorio 1998).

The abovementioned situation forced the feminization of migrations, which in qualitative terms refers to the arrival of pioneer women in the migratory process. They take the lead in migrating on their own, initiating the migratory chain, and maintaining responsibilities in their countries of origin. Therefore, emigration is a strategy for confronting the crisis of care reproduction in the countries of the South (Parella 2006).

In that regard, one of the strategies used to address this care crisis in Spain has been to partially outsource some of the tasks that were previously undertaken at home at home or to partially pay for care work in the domestic field by hiring immigrant women (Pérez 2006).

Thus, since the 1990s, the presence of (especially) Latin American women who have responded to the so-called pull effect has increased as a consequence of economic growth and the crisis of global care. Likewise, the increase of native women in the country's job market promotes the demand for an alternative workforce to fulfill these tasks in the reproductive field and they usually fall upon immigrant women. Therefore, an internalization, externalization, and commercialization of these tasks occur. This demonstrates the close relationship between capitalism and patriarchy and that the "liberation" of many women occurs at the expense of the "oppression" of others. This leads to the perpetuation of gender inequalities, which perpetuate the economic order of capitalism (Contreras 2016).

As a consequence of these transnational migrations, global care chains are developed:

These are chains of transnational dimensions created with the aim of supporting life on a daily basis, and through them households transfer care chores from one to the next based on axes of power, which include gender, ethnicity, social class, and place of origin (Pérez 2007, 4).

Therefore, these global care chains allow us to visualize from a macro-level the transfer of global care from some women to others. In this sense, immigrant women are involved in reproductive work in the destination society (taking care of minors and elderly people). At the same time, they must delegate their own family responsibilities in their countries of origin to other women in their families, such as their mothers and sisters.

These chains are redefining themselves in the migratory process. The form and extension of the migratory process will depend on the intra-family distribution of care and other factors such as the existence of public services, the weight of the organized business sector, migration policies, and regulation of domestic employment(Pérez 2007).

Note that the destination society demands this kind of labor, and these women were not trained to perform these specific chores. The idea that it is "natural" for them to carry them out is still maintained nowadays; it is a role designated and assumed by this society.

In the year the association was created (2009), in a context of economic crisis, there was a significant foreign population in Spain. Specifically, in the province of Gipuzkoa[2] there were a total of 49,416 foreign people, of whom 24,265 were women and 25,151 were men, according to the Ikuspegi[3] data.

The association decided to work with the immigrant population from Latin American countries because of the origins of the founding members and because they already knew women who were taking care of the elderly and working in domestic service. At that time, in Gipuzkoa there were women from Colombia, Ecuador, Nicaragua, Brazil, Bolivia, and Argentina.

Regarding the evolution of the population of foreign origin residing in this autonomous community, according to the Ikuspegi data, in the province of Gipuzkoa, as of September 2018, the number had risen to 35,894 women, with the greatest presence of women from Nicaragua, Colombia, Honduras, and Ecuador. This is the population with which the association has a close relationship with and on which its work focuses.

## "They Did Not Ask Her If She Had Training"

As background, it is worth mentioning that one of the founding members of the association, with training in social work, a master's degree in migration and family issues, and a decade of professional experience in her country of origin, discovered that to generate income in this destination society, there was a significant demand for labor in the care of the elderly and in domestic service. She went to a municipal agency to ask about job offers and the professional worker who was trying to help her did not ask anything about her studies and stated that there were more job offers for women to clean houses and take care of elderly people. The underlying message was that to perform these jobs it was not necessary to have specific training: being a woman in the process of searching a paid job was just enough.

At the same time, she was informed that in order to work in her professional field it was necessary to validate the studies she had completed in her country of origin (either at the high school or university level).[4] While she was working (by the hour) taking care of a minor and a dependent elderly person, she initiated the procedures for homologation of her foreign university studies to the equivalent Spanish degree. This process took three years, which included claiming the validation of a subject, as well as taking exams in two other subjects, until she finally obtained her degree in Madrid. As there were no indications of the delivery of the homologated title, she wrote to the Ararteko[5] of Gipuzkoa to investigate the delay in the delivery of the aforementioned official document, which would allow her to work as a social worker in this destination society.

It was this experience and the certainty that some immigrant women she knew had high school, technical, and/or university studies and were taking care of the elderly that led[6] her to the creation of the association.

The main objectives proposed were to contribute to the defense of the human rights of immigrant women and their families, to provide training and empowerment of this group of women, and also to collaborate with other countries, through development cooperation projects.

## The Project Is Carried Out at the Women's Building in Donostia-San Sebastián[7]

The professionals who were going to carry this project out came from Latin American countries, with experience in community work with women's organizations and training in popular education, migrations, and feminism.

The project was aimed mainly at women who worked in domestic service and in the care of the elderly, so that they could be informed about the processes of homologation and/or validation of foreign studies to the equivalent Spanish degree. Additionally, backing was offered to women who required it, especially those who did not speak Spanish well and others who did not feel capable of accomplishing these processes on their own.

As there was no physical space in which to carry this work out, the project was presented to the Equality Techniques Department of the City of Donostia-San Sebastián, which at that time was responsible for the management of the Women's Building premises. The team appreciated that the proposal of the Bidez Bide Association responded to the objectives of this space for women.

This service was performed once a week and has been maintained to date.[8] Each person is offered information on the requirements to carry this process out. In the same way, data is collected from the people advised[9] to serve as input for the reports and new proposals responding to these realities. It should be mentioned that men were also welcomed, although in a lesser proportion. The working guideline is that men should accompany a woman they know (a friend or relative).

Given the demand created, other activities were incorporated into the project, including informative talks held in different towns in the province of Gipuzkoa. These were addressed mainly to women who were *internas* and who could not go to the Women's Building in Donostia-San Sebastián because they did not have enough time todo so.

From 2009 to 2018, customized counseling[10] has been provided. Moreover, occasionally, this work has been carried out in other towns in the province of Gipuzkoa, such as Zarautz, Azpeitia, Oñati, and Irun. Decentralized talks continue as well.

Additionally, the work has been expanded and a wide range of possibilities are presented so that women can reach personal development and lifelong learning. In this regard, basic advice and accompaniment are given to women who have completed studies and have not been able to access technical and/or higher education and to those who wish to undertake other training and diverse modalities for learning, as well as economic ventures.

In order to carry this project out, social workers, immigrant departments of different city councils, immigrant organizations, and the Women's Building Association  implement a network and permanent coordination among themselves. Based on participants' reports and recorded data, we have obtained the following information: up until 2017, 1,059 women and 516 men were counseled, with 90 percent of them from countries in Latin America such as Nicaragua, Honduras, Colombia, Bolivia, and Ecuador.

## Breaking Stereotypes

Based on the work done over these years with counseling, information, and accompanying actions with the process of homologation and/or validation of foreign studies, as well as with the informative talks-workshops in different towns in Gipuzkoa, it was possible to verify that women have high school as well as university diplomas and degrees obtained in their country of origin.

Moreover, in the case of women with bachelor's degrees or technical studies, they have professional experience that is not being used in the destination country, since most of them work in domestic service, in the care of the elderly, and also in the restaurant/food industry. These situations generate feelings of frustration and helplessness due to the loss of status. This is described by Joseba Atxotegi (2018, p. 21) as mourning for social status.

This is the (target) group that decides to initiate the process of homologation or validation of their studies, since they want to try to relocate themselves in other labor niches more appropriate for their professional training. The same thing happens with women who have a baccalaureate: they expect to continue their professional training, for which they are asked to have at least a validated high school degree or the equivalent compulsory secondary education certificate.[II]

It has also been verified that women who have not completed their secondary education studies or baccalaureate decide to finish them in their limited spare time, and they request additional information to start this process. This is a group with which we have worked, with the purpose of helping to empower them and initiate a personal process aimed at achieving equal opportunities and enriching their personal project.

In the case of women with domestic jobs, they generally wish to take part in other activities linked to the training that they received in their country of origin or, at least, undertake a higher professional training course or continue their higher education, which would allow them to get out of this labor niche. Likewise, those who did not finish mandatory studies, such as the secondary education certificate or baccalaureate show interest in completing them.

The process of homologation of studies begins once the women have managed to solve their practical gender needs: accommodation, payment of the debts incurred in their country of origin, legalization of their administrative situation, acquiring a job, and being able to send money back regularly to fulfill their children's needs. It is not until those needs are met that they can decide to satisfy other needs linked to their strategic gender interests: empowerment, employment improvement, additional training to the one they bring from their country, and homologation of their studies so that they are valid in the Spanish system.

In relation to the information about the process, requirements for homologation, and/or validation of studies, most of these women obtain the information in the country of destination, which implies that they have to start the process requesting the necessary official documents in their countries of origin. However, there is a small group of women who bring some of the documents with them. This bureaucratic procedure presents obstacles in both the country of origin and the country of destination, which means that the process is slow, tedious, and extends over time, discouraging many to restart the process or leaving it halfway.

The foreign population is usually ignorant about its rights, as is made clear by the scarce and incomplete information that women have regarding the possibilities of homologating and validating the studies taken in the country of origin. Moreover, they often lack knowledge about the opportunities that the country of destination can offer in relation to training and qualification throughout life.

On the other hand, additional studies, reports, and documents show that there is a certain level of ignorance and lack of information on the part of the native population toward the reality of immigrants.[12] There are myths and prejudices regarding the levels of training and work experience that immigrants bring from their countries, reflected comments such as "immigrant women do not have studies, are ignorant, and illiterate."[13]

### I Have Only Been an Interna[14]

During all these years of work with immigrant women, we have had the opportunity to listen to their stories, their experiences as women, mothers, and workers, mainly from those who are *internas* in the care of the elderly. Based on our experiences counseling and listening to these women, reading the literature,[15] and conducting an in-depth interview with a woman who is an *interna*,[16] we will outline some characteristics of the realities facing these women.

Women who did not work in these labor niches in their countries of origin, because they had their careers (they have technical or university training), feel a loss of social status. This generates low self-esteem and feelings of impotence and inferiority, even though they know that all work is worthy.

It is quite clear that there are asymmetric relations of power and discrimination between the immigrant woman and the person who hires her.[17] Additionally, there is a different position between the two of them. In this regard, one of the important contributions was made by María Lugones (2011) who defined the coloniality of gender as "a conceptual device that goes beyond the binary and hegemonic categories that have sought to respond to the reality of women." In this sense, for this author, coloniality permeated all areas of social existence. Therefore, it must not only be applied to racial classification, but must also indicate how gender was structured according to the establishment of differences that inferiorized women from asymmetric power relations, which have lasted throughout history.

That is why it is necessary to decolonize knowledge, since the social sciences have contributed to configuring ways of understanding the social reality of others from a Eurocentric and ethnocentric perspective (Contreras 2016).

This contributes to the deterioration of self-esteem among these immigrant women, so they end up assuming they have little worth as human beings, as Ophelia points out: "Until now I have not valued myself, I believe I am insignificant. Complexes, traumas, and sufferings are the only feelings appearing inside of me. Then I say to myself: this has to be my job, I have only been an *interna*, from Peru until now."

This is the space in which negotiations about contracts and working conditions take place. These negotiations will depend on a number of factors: the offer made by the contracting family, the needs of the immigrant woman, and her administrative situation. In addition, the personal situation and the context of being without a social network come into play, together with the uncertainty of not having an indefinite contract. This is because in the case of women who care for the elderly, they know that the contract ends when the person dies or when the family takes this person to a retirement home. Therefore, there are several reasons that lead many women to not negotiate fair working conditions and that lead to situations of exploitation and relationships of subordination.

> All contracts are formal, but conditions are not complied with. It is not written anywhere that you have rest hours or vacations, not even in my current contract. That happens to us all, because we are afraid of losing our job. At that moment you are worried about not having a job. I wanted to immediately have another job where I could sleep, so I did not ask about my working conditions, I just accepted them.[18]

The fact of living and working full-time in the home of the elderly person they take care of contributes to the great dependency and subordination underlying these working conditions and to these women accepting working conditions not specified in the contract. Moreover, affections and feelings come into play, and they are mixed with the employment relationship that they have to maintain. Therefore, dependency is also established with the person they are looking after. This is confirmed by Ophelia's testimony:

> I went to work for a lady, here in Zurriola. That lady was of very high lineage. Her daughters were professors and pharmacists, and they all were very *pija*[19] and refined. I was there for the lady, I always slept with the lady. I mean, my bad luck was that they made me sleep with the lady and I could not say anything; they hired me for that. I slept with the lady.

This intense twenty-four-hour work does not allow immigrant women to set limits with the family that hires them in terms of maintaining their privacy; they do not even have their own space to rest and sleep. This gives families the right to make decisions that benefit only the well-being of the elderly person, without considering that these decisions are made at the expense of the physical and emotional health of the immigrant woman they have hired. This fact is confirmed by Ophelia, who in a previous job had to stop sleeping alone in her room in order to sleep in the same bed as the lady she was looking after.

I worked for a lady in Irun. Things were very good at the beginning. The lady was wonderful, until her daughters made me sleep with the lady and moved the husband to a different room. I was so overwhelmed by this lady, for almost six months. I could not sleep, because the lady would wake up at dawn two, three times. I had to carry her to the bathroom because she could not walk.

The testimony of another *interna*, who has a job taking care of an elderly person and who does not have any days off, illustrates this situation and its effect the mental health of the women who are doing this kind of work under these conditions: "I was assuming that the following month of November I would leave on Saturdays at 10 in the morning and I would go back in on Sundays at 9 o'clock at night. I told the lady that I was going to go crazy being an *interna* seven days a week."

As Sònia Parella (2006) discusses, other personal details come into play in the hiring of Latin American women to perform these care tasks. These features are linked to the worker's nature and personality more than to their training or preparation. These characteristics are associated with the performance commonly recognized as the "traditional role of women." In addition, attributes such as being "caring," "patient," and "docile" are valued, especially when taking care of elderly people. Basically you buy the trust, devotion, patience, and especially the time of "other" women. Therefore, the immigrant woman is preferred to perform certain tasks rather than the native woman, and this same immigrant worker is discouraged from performing other activities.

In this regard, Ophelia comments:

We [referring to Latin American women] are more humble, more docile. Whereas if they confront a Basque woman, they rise to the level of dialogue and discussion. But with us they always know that we are the "amen, amen." We are available full-time, we do hard work. Because they know that it is hard to take care of an elderly person. We do not have anyone, so we accept those twenty-four-hour conditions. Migrants accept this, natives don't, because they have all their families here and want to be with them.

Families that hire migrant women to perform care work and domestic service often display a coloniality of knowledge, which consists of "the positioning of Eurocentrism as the unique perspective of knowledge, which rules out the existence and viability of other epistemic rationalities and other knowledge that is not of European or Europeanized white men" (Walsh 2008, p. 137). This translates into affirmations or comments that native people have about the migrant people, which are based on ignorance, in general, about migratory realities and certain ideas about these people, reinforced by the mass media, in most cases. As Ophelia says:

> People here know that we are leaving our family behind, that many women live in a room with several people, they know by rumors, by the news. The lady I am taking care of, for example, would ask me: how are things over there? Do you know what they believe? That we still live with a feather in front and another feather behind. There is no way to remove that from their heads.

> It is true that we come from a lower middle class, but not all of us are so ignorant. We come with some basic knowledge on how to read and write and with the desire to work, don't we? In addition to that, they are very suspicious about hiring very young girls.

> That's what a woman told me: "I know my husband, I would not hire a Brazilian woman." That's what they think, that we only come to get drunk and have fun.

The stories of immigrant women show how they have internalized this difference between them (assuming themselves as the "others") and the people for whom they have worked. In this sense, we can speak of a coloniality of being, which is exercised through inferiorization, subalternization, and dehumanization. In this regard, Franz Fanon (1999) refers to the behavior of "nonexistence."[20] In addition, feeling "other" makes inclusion difficult in many cases, which in turn contributes to self-exclusion. In this respect Ophelia talks about the difficulty of belonging to this society of destiny with an eloquent story:

> The Basques can be very frank in a meeting, at a party, but in the street they say hello and pass by. They do not remember that they were in a meeting with you. You are not in their group. They do not integrate us. We want to enter but there is always a barrier. At least that is the way I have felt everywhere. They say no, we do not fit in, but there is a rejection, honey, I still feel that. They are standing on higher ground and I am still the employee.

Given this situation, one of the strategies that Ophelia has come to terms with, in order to feel like part of her surroundings and differentiate herself from the young Latin American girls that have just arrived, has been to dress with clothes and to color her hair to match those of the women she has taken care of over the years.

> If I have learned anything it's how to imitate, that's what they have taught me. The ladies I have worked for were very *pitucas*.[21] Everything in their look matched: earrings, necklace, shoes, scarf. And I was lucky that there was this lady who always bought stuff in the Chinese store for her and me. I have a dozen watches of all colors that the lady gave to me, I do not use them because the battery wears out and it gets expensive. See? I learned to dress up.

These situations of non-inclusion can help to foster relationships with other people from different backgrounds or from the same country. However, they allow the blooming of a number of strategies of resistance and agency. This translates into actions such as negotiating their free time to go to some association meetings, to the Women's Building, to church, and to meet with their friends. In Ophelia's case, she has been able to negotiate her free time to go to church, to her prayer group in a parish near the home in which she lives and works, and to meet with her friends.

> What I negotiated with the miss [the daughter of the lady she looks after] were Mondays when I pray to the image of Jesus in my church[22], on Thursdays I have my Bible readings, and every other Saturday I meet with a group of women in a parish of Gros. On Sundays I also get together with some Peruvian friends. I need those days for myself.

## Women Who Are Mothers: Their Experiences with Transnational Motherhood and Family Reunification

From our work in counseling and accompaniment to immigrant women who received services for the homologation of studies, we found that Latin American women who are mothers maintain a long-distance relationship with their children, who are basically brought up by other women, whether grandmothers, aunts, sisters, *comadres*, or neighbors. This form of organization of motherhood is a phenomenon known as "transnational" or "distant" maternity, or the "globalization of motherhood." It implies different ways, defined according to women's ethnic groups and social class, of managing child care and education (Parreñas 2001).

Solé and Parella (2005) show that Latin American women make up a heterogeneous and diverse group. However, we can mention some more or less common characteristics that have also been identified through the work carried out by professionals in the association: they are young women, with family responsibilities, with moderate or higher education. In some cases, it is they who initiate the migratory project, leaving their families in the country of origin. They are the main people responsible for economic sustenance, whether they have a partner or are single mothers.

The case of single mothers who exercise their maternal function from a distance has proven to take a much greater effort. This is especially true for those who do not have a work permit and have been waiting for years to become legal, hoping to visit their country and be reunited with their daughters and sons. These women live focused daily on work or in the search of sustenance for their family, working long and intense hours with low income and, in most cases, suffering from labor exploitation.[23]

For women who decide to regroup their sons and daughters, this process usually comes to fruition several years after the mother has arrived in the country of destination. In many cases it is done without any legal administrative procedure, because single women working in these labor niches (care and domestic service) find it very difficult to meet the requirements that the law establishes.[24] Faced with these requirements, which exceed the capabilities of a single mother, the wait is extended over time, generating large doses of suffering, stress, guilt, uncertainty, helplessness, and fear. These feelings significantly influence their daily lives.

Considering the realities described above, in 2012 a program called Zure Ondoan[25] was launched, in which the center of attention was the family and its members (parents, mothers, children, and adolescents). One of the projects was aimed mainly at mothers who take care of elderly people, as well as at those in domestic service.

The project was executed by a team of professionals from the fields of psychology and social work. A psychotherapeutic support service was offered, attended mainly by families whose responsible parent was only the mother as well as families with both parents. It is necessary to mention that women in this group worked all day and did not have a single opportunity to offer the necessary support and accompaniment for a minor and/or adolescent who would undergo the effects of the migratory process (mourning, cultural stress, alienation, poor social network, friendlessness). These families came from countries in Latin America (specifically Honduras, Nicaragua, Mexico, and Colombia) and some were beginning the process of reassembling their families after a period of separation.

The intervention was carried out by psychologists, offering one hour to an hour and a half sessions with the family members. This process had an average duration of twelve sessions, with a weekly or biweekly frequency, depending on the needs and the type of demand of the person or family concerned.

The social workers in the program stayed with the children, offering them fun activities. Meanwhile, the adult (mother, father) was in the session with the psychologists, who counseled the person or family, as needed. For example, they would accompany these mothers or fathers to town council premises to meet with the social workers of the local social services and help with the necessary steps to regulate their administrative situation (obtaining a health insurance card, getting financial aid, and registering with the Basque employment service, among others).

On a regular basis, team meetings were held to assess the progress and difficulties of the Zure Ondoan project; coordination and networking; analysis of each case; and, finally, planning the activities of the project. Likewise, these spaces served to assess the accompaniment and follow-up of the families and the coordination with tutors at the children's schools, with the social workers, and with professionals responsible for the referral/diversion of a person and/or family to the service.

In this process, the permanent coordination and the joint work with the professionals in the education centers, social services of the town councils, and social organizations involved in the intervention have been essential and necessary. This has helped to develop a comprehensive intervention for the people and/or families that the association helps. Moreover, it has allowed these people to obtain relevant information about these realities.

In the psychosocial intervention carried out,[26] the approach to the situation and family dynamics constituted one of the main demands of these families, both for those reunited in this country of destination or for those who had the structure and functioning of a transnational family, that is, with the parents here and the children there or with both parents distributed in the country of destination and the country of origin.

### Presence and Absence: Mothers and Fathers and the Process of Family Reunion

This section aims to highlight the main problems related to the performance of their roles as parents, after several years of separation from their children.

Parents had difficulties performing their parental duties. It could be extremely difficult to establish rules and limits with their offspring when such practices had been affected by migration, leading to an undefined role, weakening of authority, and affective disengagement. This situation is made worse if the relational functioning and the emotional climate in the family were not optimal in the country of origin.

On the other hand, the changes that occur during the separation period are difficult to accept, especially if the children are teenagers. For these families—in this moment of the life cycle—the reunion becomes more complex, both due to the changes generated by the migratory experience as well as the handling of the relationship and affective reconnection by parents and the adaptation to a new place with no peer network.

The expectations that parents have of their children are not in tune with what they are feeling; they find it difficult to empathize. Messages such as "If you do not improve school grades I'll send you to a boarding school" or "I will send you back if you do not behave yourself" are sent, ignoring the great emotional impact that the minor has when exposed to a new experience of separation, which could be perceived as abandonment.

Parents' abilities and competences were not adapted to the children's current needs, a situation that further impeded the rebuilding of the relationship and the forming of a new bond.

Moreover, parents did not have it easy, since they exercised a good deal of effort and contended with many limitations to their responsibility and the exercise of parental duties, while recognizing the wear and tear that the migratory project has entailed over the years. This reality shows that psychosocial intervention was necessary.

It is worth mentioning that immigrant families, due to their own condition and current circumstances, were often exposed to situations of social exclusion, and they lacked or had few social networks. Moreover, it needs to be shown that the lack of social protection toward these family nuclei was noticed.

There were cases in which parents were willing and able to attend, accompany, and educate their offspring. However, they were overwhelmed by trying to cover basic needs and also by the demands generated by administrative procedures they have to follow as immigrants.

## Minors and Teenagers:[27] Their Reality

We noticed that youth faced difficulties in the family reunion process and in forming a new bond with their parents: detachment; emotional problems: anger, rejection, resentment, night fears; depressive responses, anxiety; ambivalence; disruptive behaviors: attitudes of rebellion and transgression of norms; feelings of abandonment; apathy, withdrawal, and lack of interest in social relationships; difficulties in school integration: absenteeism, school mismatch, demotivation, poor performance; isolation; lack of adaptation to the new culture; and a desire to return to the country of origin.

## Women, Single Mothers

Throughout this process, women played an important role, since they constitute the affective and material support of a large number of the families dealt with. However, it is necessary to mention the number of obstacles they have to face, such as difficulties of integration in their destination, both in terms of work as well as the lack of a social network and administrative irregularity. The degree of vulnerability to which they were exposed was high.

They lived with a good deal suffering, feelings of impotence, enormous frustration, discouragement, and sadness. As expected, the physical and psychological exhaustion was visible in them and, in some cases, they suffered with depression, somatization, mood disorders, anxiety, and traumatic experiences due to having suffered violence and abuse.

## Making Transnational Realities Visible

From the work developed from 2009 to the present, a close relationship has been maintained with immigrant women of various origin and their families in Gipuzkoa. This process of counseling, accompaniment, active listening, and psychosocial intervention has allowed us to familiarize ourselves with their realities as women, as *internas* who take care of the elderly and work in domestic service, and as mothers who exercise their maternal role from a distance and in contexts of family reunification in this destination society.

In this sense, we assumed it was our ethical and professional responsibility to make known the impact of transnational migrations in the lives of these women residing in the Basque Country and their families in their countries of origin, framing these realities in the context of globalization.

That is why the production of social audiovisual media was proposed as a line of work, with the main objective of visualizing the invisible, breaking the prevailing prejudices and stereotypes in society. Moreover, such media allow a critical analysis of a certain reality, from a gendered, transcultural, and decolonial perspective. Likewise, it was necessary to circulate a different kind of presentation—new, alternative, and counterhegemonic—given by the protagonists themselves (women and their families), which the mass media do not offer.

From the first moment, it was interesting to show these transnational realities through images: realities here and there. Documentaries[28] were produced with grants from public organizations such as city/town councils, the

Provincial Council of Gipuzkoa, the Basque Government, and the Institute of Cinematography and Audiovisual Arts belonging to the Spanish Ministry of Education, Culture, and Sport.

It was considered important that this work be carried out by an interdisciplinary team, with professionals from the fields of communication, social sciences, and psychology. The professionals who daily accompany women and their families in their migratory trajectories also contributed—a priceless collaboration given the experience these professionals have working with this group of people, the training they had in the topics that were going to be addressed, and the perspective that they could provide, which needed to be imprinted on the abovementioned materials.

These materials are intended to contribute to awareness and social transformation in the destination society and in some countries of origin of the immigrant population in the Basque Autonomous Community. Therefore, they are used as pedagogical tools in formative and critical reflection processes with vocational training and university students, with women's organizations, and with the general population in this destination society.

## Final Considerations, Lessons, and Proposals

### Final Considerations

Immigrant women who have technical and/or university credentials and are working in Gipuzkoa as *internas* in the care of the elderly live in mourning for their loss of status. These situations generate feelings of frustration, anger, and impotence and diminish their self-esteem.

Placement of immigrant women as *internas* caring for elderly people requires almost full availability on their side. In addition, it responds to neocolonial stereotypes related to their countries of origin and personal features. In the specific case of women from Latin American countries, they are perceived as docile, delicate, respectful, and affectionate. This implies they are ideal for these jobs.

In the home space in which immigrant women work as *internas*, inequalities of gender, class, and ethnicity are evident. Asymmetric relations of power, discrimination, and a position of inferiority are reproduced between the working women and the hiring families, and it is all framed in a context of symbolic violence. This power increases dramatically when immigrant women are undocumented,[29] which hinders significantly their ability to negotiate their working conditions.

Women who are *internas* need to have almost total availability. The tasks they perform involve both physical and emotional/psychological support for the person they take care of. As for working conditions, after women's stories and studies were reviewed, those that stand out the most: they work more hours than legally allowed; there is an absence of personal space, and they put up with sexual harassment. All this has serious consequences on their physical and mental health.

Despite these migratory contexts that place women in situations of inequality and inferiority, they develop various strategies of resistance as forms of agency. Based on their stories, we see that they strengthen their skills and reinforce their confidence to overcome difficulties and negotiate the compliance of their rights as workers. In this process, they also search for other women with whom they establish a relationship of complicity and resistance.

Immigrant mothers who are responsible for the well-being of their families in their countries of origin live a long-distance maternity with feelings of guilt for having left their children under the care of other women. This gets worse when their countries of origin accuse them of being "unnatural and neglectful mothers."

*Internas* cannot fulfill the regrouping requirements that have to be met so that mothers can live with their children in this destination society. This prolongs these processes, generating large doses of suffering, stress, guilt, uncertainty, feelings of impotence, and fear; these negative feelings will significantly influence their daily lives.

Generally speaking, parents who decide to regroup after several years of separation by migration do not prepare themselves adequately for this process of reunion, and it becomes even more complex. In addition, it creates difficulties for them to raise their children, since there is a lack of definition of roles, weakening of authority, and affective disengagement.

There is a certain level of misinformation and ignorance about the reality of immigrants among the native citizens. In fact, there are a number of myths and prejudices that still persist in relation to the levels of training and work trajectory that the immigrants bring from their countries of origin.

### Lessons and Proposals

All people are holders of knowledge. To intervene professionally with anyone, it is essential to take as a reference point their personal trajectories and place them in a specific cultural, historical, political, and social context.

To intervene with the immigrant population it is necessary to carry out interdisciplinary work with a holistic view. This implies that the professionals have the ethical responsibility to carry out specialized and continuous training from a gender, cross-cultural, and decolonizing perspective.

The contributions of decolonizing feminism to our work with immigrant women have given us a sociohistorical view, which allows us to relate the subordination of immigrant women to historical power relations embodied in the notion of colonialism.

Networking (local and state/national) and the articulation of experiences, initiatives, and resources, both private and public, are essential. This will allow for policy proposals for a new model of care, as well as for inclusion processes for the immigrant population in this destination society.

It is necessary to raise awareness among the native population about these local migratory realities framed in a global context. From our experience, we value the strategic use of audiovisual media, when narrated by immigrants, to make these transnational migratory realities known.

It is necessary to contribute to the training of future professionals. We take as points of reference the different experiences and processes carried out by the Bidez Bide professionals: the University of the Basque Country provides a center of student practices for degrees in social anthropology, social work, and social education and provides workshops on local and global migratory realities, for professionals and university students.

## Bibliography

Atxotegi, Joseba. La inteligencia migratoria. Manual para inmigrantes en dificultades. Barcelona: Ned Ediciones, 2018.

Contreras, Paola. "Mujeres Latinoamericanas en Barcelona: Una aproximación en clave feminista." Paper presemted at the 12th Spanish Sociology Conference, GT 25, "Sociología 21 de las migraciones," Barcelona, May 13, 2016. At https://www.fes-sociologia.com/mujeres-latinoamericanas-en-barcelona-una-aproximacion-en-clave-femi/congress-papers/2065/ (last accessed October 7, 2018).

Contreras, Paola and Macarena Trujillo. "Desde las epistemologías feministas a los feminismos decoloniales: Aportes a los estudios sobre migraciones." Athenea Digital, no. 17 (2017):145-162.

Escudero, E (coord.); M. Díaz; R. García; M.J. Pérez. La realidad de las mujeres inmigrantes ante las intervenciones socio-sanitarias, educativas y laborales. EMAKUNDE. Vitoria-Gasteiz, 2011.

Ezquerra, Sandra. "Crisis de los cuidados y crisis sistémica: la reproducción como pilar de la economía llamada real." Investigaciones Feministas 2 (2011): 175–94. At https://core.ac.uk/download/pdf/38817053.pdf (last accessed October 20, 2018).

Fanon, Franz. Los condenados de la tierra. México D.F.: Fondo de Cultura Económica, 1999.

Gil, Sandra. "Cartografías migratorias: migraciones internacionales en el marco de las relaciones Norte-Sur." In La migración, un camino entre el desarrollo y la cooperación, edited by Nieves Zúñiga. Madrid: Centro de Investigación para la Paz, 2005.

Gregorio Gil, Carmen. Migración femenina. Su impacto en las relaciones de género. Madrid: Narcea Ediciones, 1998.

———. "Análisis de las migraciones transnacionales en el contexto español, revisitando la categoría de género desde una perspectiva etnográfica y feminista." Nueva Antropología 24, no. 74 (2011): 39–71. At http://www.scielo.org.mx/scielo.php?pid=S0185-06362011000100003&script=sci_abstract (last accessed Ocrober 24, 2018).

Lugones, María. "Hacia un feminismo decolonial." *Magazine La Manzana de la discordia,* Vol. 6, no. 2 (2011): 105-119.

Parella, Sònia. "Mujer, inmigrante y trabajadora: la triple discriminación. Barcelona." *Revista Papers* 79 (2006): 321-22. At https://papers.uab.cat/article/view/v79-martinez (last accessed October 20, 2018).

Parreñas, Rhacel Salazar. *Servants of Globalization: Women, Migration, and Domestic Work.* Stanford: Stanford University Press, 2001.

Pérez, Amaia. "Amenaza tormenta: la crisis de los cuidados y la reorganización del sistema económico." *Revista de Economía Crítica* 5 (March, 2006): 7-37. At http://revistaeconomiacritica.org/sites/default/files/revistas/n5/1_amenaza_tormenta.pdf (last accessed October 24, 2018).

————. "Cadenas globales de cuidados." In *Serie Género, Migración y Desarrollo. Cadenas globales de cuidado Instituto Internacional de Investigaciones y Capacitación de las Naciones Unidas para la Promoción de la Mujer (INSTRAW), República Dominicana.* Documento de trabajo 2 (2007): 1-9.

Pérez, M. D. Mujeres migrantes: realidades, estereotipos y perspectivas educativas. Revista Española de Educación Comparada (2008), 14.

Solé, Carlota, Sònia Parella. Negocios étnicos. Los comercios de los inmigrantes no comunitarios en Catalunya. Barcelona: Fundació CIDOB, 2005.

Walsh, Catherine. "Interculturalidad, plurinacionalidad y decolonialidad: las insurgencias político epistémicas de refundar el Estado." *Tábula Rasa* 9 (2008): 131-52. At http://www.scielo.org.co/pdf/tara/n9/n9a09.pdf (last accessed October 20, 2018).

## Notes

1   The word *interna* is used to describe the person who lives and works in the home of an elderly person she attends daily and takes care of. It is a job that is usually carried out by immigrant women. One should mention that those who actually get a contract have one as a "domestic employee."

2   Spain is divided into autonomous communities, which are themselves divided into provinces, and each province is, in turn, divided into city/town councils. An autonomous community is a Spanish administrative territorial entity that, within the constitutional legal system of the state, is provided with certain legislative autonomy with its own representatives and certain executive and administrative powers. Spain has seventeen autonomous communities and two autonomous cities (Ceuta and Melilla, located on the African continent). Two of those communities are archipelagoes: the Canary Islands and the Balearic Islands. The Basque Autonomous Community is formed by three provinces, also known as "historic territories": Araba (Álava), Bizkaia (Vizcaya), and Gipuzkoa (Guipúzcoa).

3   The Basque Immigration Observatory was created in 2004 "with a vocation to build a tool of public utility for the systematic knowledge of the phenomenon of foreign immigration in the Basque Country."

4   This information was obtained at the Sub-delegation of Education offices in Gipuzkoa, located in Donostia-San Sebastián.

5   The Ararteko is the Ombudsman's Office of the Basque Country. Its website indicates that its mission is to better represent all citizens in relation to the actions and public policies of the Basque administrations.

6   The board was formed with another local/native person and also an immigrant.

7   The Women's Building Association is the structure that guarantees that the Women's Building of Donostia is also managed by the women leading the empowerment processes developed here.

8   After eight years of having requested the City of Donostia-San Sebastián for the premises to carry out their activities, there is already a space to share with other associations. Services have been provided there since December 2018.

9   For each person helped, a data sheet is filled out on matters regarding their legal situation, working conditions, and family situation, among other aspects.

10  The team is made up of the person in charge of the project (with a degree in business administration and training in development cooperation) and two retired teachers, with experience in teaching vocational training students, who joined the team in 2017 and 2018, respectively.

11  In the Spanish educational system, this involves compulsory studies from first to fourth grade.

12  Parella, Sònia. "Woman, immigrant and worker: triple discrimination. Barcelona." Papers Magazine 79 (2006), 321-322. Contreras, Paola. "Latin American Women in Barcelona: A Feminist Approach." Report presented at the XII Spanish Congress of Sociology, Work Group 25, Sociology of Migrations, Barcelona, May 13, 2016.

13  Escudero, E (coord.); M. Díaz; R. García; M.J. Pérez: The reality of immigrant women when facing public health, educational and labor interventions. EMAKUNDE. Vitoria-Gasteiz, 2011. Pérez, M. D. Migrant women: realities, stereotypes and educational perspectives. Spanish Journal of Comparative Education (2008), 14.

14  Part of a testimony from a woman who is an *interna*.

15  The two professionals (a business administration graduate and a social worker) who work on the projects of the Bidez Bide Association participate in a reading group on topics related to feminism and decolonial studies.

16  A Peruvian woman (named Ophelia for this purpose) was interviewed. She has been an *interna* for fourteen years in Gipuzkoa.

17  Usually, a daughter of the older person hires the immigrant woman.

18  Ronquillo Peña, Heldy Soraya. *Trajectory of a Peruvian woman who works as an "interna" in San Sebastián. A look from decolonial feminism.* Research work for the subject Qualitative Methods and Techniques I, Degree in Social Anthropology, University of País Vasco, 2018.

19  *Pija* is a term that in Spain is used colloquially to designate a person who dresses and acts like a person of good social standing.

20  The author points out the relationship between reason-rationality and humanity: the most human are those that are part of formal rationality—Weber's means-end rationality, which is the rationality of modernity conceived from the "civilized" individual.

21  Peruvian term, which here would be a synonym of *pija*.

22  In the Catholic church Ophelia attends, they exhibit an image of Jesus every day. Any person is free to accompany this image in prayer, for as long as they wish. Ophelia performs this ritual every Monday.

23  Judging from the observed experiences, it can be stated that women who do not have work and residence permits usually work under conditions that violate their labor rights. The context of administrative irregularity in which they live contributes to their not feeling able to negotiate their rights as workers, so they are at the mercy of the decisions of the families that hire them.

24  The requirements that the law establishes include that the adult who regroups their sons or daughters must have a work contract with sufficient income to allow them to rent an apartment

in optimal conditions of habitability, besides guaranteeing the daily sustenance of the reunited family, among other requirements.

25   Report of the Program "Psychosocial Accompaniment and socio-educational actions with families and adolescents with migratory experiences", carried out by Bidez Bide in 2015.

26   During these four years, 74 families and a total of 113 people were assisted (mothers, fathers, minors, and adolescents).

27   Children and adolescents who had been regrouped by their mothers after several years of separation were attended to and accompanied (between four and eight years of living apart).

28   The trailers can be viewed on the association's blog: https://bidezbide.wordpress.com/material-audiovisual/.

29   To reside and work in this country you must have a work contract. Tourist visas expire after three months. If women with tourist visas wish to validate their legal status and obtain the first "rooting" permit, they must meet a number of requirements, such as being registered for three years in the local city council and having a contract, among other things. In addition to this, they are taking the risk of being caught while they are not documented, in which case the police would start a deportation procedure, as they do not have the required permit to reside and work legally in this country.

# 8

# The Migratory Process and Psychological Adjustment Among Recent Basque Immigrants in European Countries

*Edurne Elgorriaga, Ainara Arnoso, and Izaskun Ibabe*

As a result of the economic crisis of 2008, the most current migratory phenomenon concerning the Basque Country is emigration to other countries in the European Union (EU). The reasons for this include the desire to find job opportunities and greater professional and social recognition, despite the fact that mobility does not always guarantee that such expectations will be met. This wave of Basque migration and Spanish migration is not considered to be dramatic because the immigrants involved have higher levels of education and intercultural skills (Elgorriaga, Ibabe, and Arnoso 2019), and modern communication media facilitate their continued contact with family and friends (Alaminos and Santacreu 2010).

In cross-cultural psychology, migration is viewed as a transitory stage in which the emigrant moves from one society to another, with the consequent exposure to a new context. The changes that take place in this process and the contact with culturally dissimilar people, groups, and social influences have been defined as acculturation (Gibson 2001). According to Colleen Ward and Antony Kennedy (1999), acculturation requires sociocultural and psychological adaptation. Sociocultural (behavioral) adaptation is defined by behavioral competences and skills for interacting adequately in the host country in areas such as family, work, the educational system, and intergroup relationships (Ward and Kennedy 1999). This dimension is associated with financial solvency (De Luca, Bobowik, and Basabe 2011), cultural knowledge, language ability, low perception of discrimination, and low cultural distance (Ward and Kennedy 1999). In turn, psychological (emotional) adaptation is the degree of well-being felt by immigrants as a result of cultural contact and adjustment (Ward and Kennedy 1999), although it is evaluated through measures of stress, depression, anxiety, somatization, mental health, and life satisfaction (for example, Singh, McBride, and Kak 2015). This dimension is predicted by life changes (Ward and Kennedy 1999), social support (Singh et al. 2015), job conditions (Elgorriaga, Ibabe, and Arnoso 2016), and the emigrant's expectations (Mähönen, Leinonen, and Jasinskaja-Lahti 2013).

The difficulties experienced in social adaptation in a new society have implications for psychological adaptation and would justify the description of migration as stressful (Berry 1997) for different reasons, such as separation from family and friends in the country of origin (Atxotegi 2004), culture shock (Ward and Kennedy 1999), language barriers (Jasinskaja-Lahti, Liebkind, and Perhoniemi 2006), intergroup contacts (Berry 1997), the absence of social support (Singh et al. 2015), and unemployment (Singhammer and Bancila 2011). The effect of these factors on stress may vary from one cultural group to another and from one context to another (Berry 1997).

There are at least three theoretical models with which to investigate the mental health of immigrants: acculturation stress, the immigrant health paradox, and the salmon bias. During the migration process, if a person feels that the complexity of events experienced are undesirable, unpredictable, or uncontrollable, these are more likely to cause acculturative stress. A prolonged period of such perceived stress along with a lack of coping strategies lead to immigrants becoming vulnerable to developing mental health problems (Berry 1997; Singhammer and Bancila 2011). The relationship between acculturation stress and health has been defined as the *acculturation stress hypothesis* (Berry and Sam 1996). In line with this hypotheses, studies on European migration have shown that the immigrant population has worse mental health and less satisfaction than the native population (Singhammer and Bancila 2011; Wittig, Lindert, Merbach, and Brähler 2008).

Nevertheless, some researchers reject the acculturation stress hypothesis, showing the mental health of immigrants to be the same as or better than that of the native population (destination country) (Cuellar et al. 2004). These findings support the hypothesis of the *immigrant health paradox* (Markides and Coreil 1986), which posits that despite lower average socioeconomic status, the immigrant population has some physical and psychological health advantages compared to the native population. Studies based on the adult immigrant population in European countries have shown mental health and life satisfaction to be similar to the population of the country of origin (Elgorriaga et al. 2018; Erlinghagen 2011; Glaesmer et al. 2009). In general, these findings may be explained by the better political situation (Glaesmer et al. 2009) or better job situation (Elgorriaga et al. 2018) in place in the host country in comparison to the country of origin, as well as the existence of protective sociocultural factors, such as the actual social support of collectivist cultures or religious beliefs (Vega et al. 1998).

Another explanation is that migrants are selected by health status, which must be analyzed in two directions: the first hypothesis is that immigrants self-select from their native populations by having better physical and mental health, and the healthier people emigrate (Lu and Qin 2014). The second is the *salmon bias hypothesis* or *selective return migration*, which postulates that unhealthy migrants have a greater tendency to return to their origin communities in search of medical assistance and family support (Abraído-Lanza et al. 1999). This would explain why people with better health stay in the host country. The salmon bias was studied in relation to physical health but later studies showed that the hypothesis also occurred with mental health (Diaz, Koning, and Martínez-Conate 2017) and with perceived general health measures (Lu and Qin 2014). However, no study has yet found evidence in favor of the salmon bias hypothesis. The study of Emma Aguila, Jose Escarce, Mei Leng, and Leo Morales (2013), conducted with databases from the United States and Mexico and a sample of more than 10,000 people, could not confirm that the returnees had worse health than those who remained in the United States or those who had never emigrated. S. Heide Ullman, Noreen Goldman, and Douglas S. Massey (2011), Fernando Riosmena, César González-González, and Rebeca Wong (2012), and Georgiana Bostean (2013) confirm the salmon hypothesis with some health measures such as emotional disorders, perceived general health, and physical limitations but do not find any differences with other indicators. Moreover, Monica Sander (2007) finds that in Germany, while immigrant men with worse health returned to their country of origin, health was not a determinant for the return of immigrant women.

This diversity of results in the body of research regarding the mental health of immigrants may be due to the diversity of situations and conditions that occur in migratory processes and to methodological differences in the studies (for example, different measures of health and different comparison groups used in those studies: native population, refugees, other immigrants in the destination country, international students, non-immigrants in the origin country, or a mixture of people with different characteristics) (WHO 2010). In order to prevent these types of methodological problems, some authors have recommended a comparison between the mental health of immigrants and those who remain in the country of origin (Mirsky 1997), and the control of variables such as immigration status, gender, educational level, and employment status (Berry 1997).

In mental health, some gender differences have been found: women in general suffer more stress, depression, anxiety and somatization, while men have more substance abuse problems (WHO, 2010). The reasons for these gender disparities in mental health may be socioeconomic disadvantage, gender-based violence, low income and income inequality, low or subordinate social status and rank, and unremitting responsibility for the care of others (WHO 2010). In addition, the review carried out by Sarah Rosenfield and Dena Smith (2012) of gender and mental health indicates other explanations related to the processes of differential socialization of men and women, which mark what is "proper" or "appropriate" to express emotion, and these feelings condition the way they express their psychological troubles. Studies of immigrant populations confirm these results: in general, immigrant women suffer more from internalizing symptoms and stress-related disorders compared to immigrant men (Elgorriaga et al. 2018; Singh et al. 2015; Singhammer and Bancila 2011). It is known that constraints and opportunities differ for men and women in both the origin and the host society, and therefore, demands made on immigrants may be more or less salient for a particular gender (Aroian, Norris, Gonzalez de Chavez, Fernandez, and Averasturi 2008). Generally, immigrant women are exposed to more social and economic problems (Dion and Dion 2001), are more likely to suffer multiple discriminations (Haberfeld, Semyonor, and Cohen 2000), and have to face changes and/or an overload of roles and values (Aroian, Norris, and Chiang 2003). Nevertheless, the conclusion of a recent meta-analysis claims that there are no differences in life satisfaction between male and female immigrants (Bak-Klimek, Karatzias, Elliott, and Maclean 2015).

Previous studies with Spanish immigrants in Europe (Elgorriaga et al. 2016, 2018) show that their psychological adjustment is relatively good (the level of life satisfaction was moderate and stress levels and mental health symptoms were relatively low) and is similar to the population of origin. In addition, women present more stress and very slightly higher prevalence rates of somatization and anxiety/insomnia. However, there are no studies of the migratory process and the psychological adjustment of Basque immigrants in Europe.

## Goals and Hypotheses

The first objective of the present study was to examine the sociocultural adjustment of the Basque immigrant population in other European countries and to check whether there are differences between women and men in this process. Women are expected to have more social and economic difficulties in the host country than men (Aroain et al. 2008) (Hypothesis 1). The second purpose was to analyze whether the migration process is related to greater perceived stress, poorer mental health, and less life satisfaction, and whether there are gender differences in immigrant mental health. In this regard, we expected the psychological adjustment of Basque immigrants to be similar to that of the Basque population in the Basque Country (for example, Elgorriaga et al. 2018; Glaesmer et al. 2009) (Hypothesis 2). Furthermore, female immigrants were expected to display slightly higher levels of perceived stress and mental health symptoms than male immigrants (for example, Elgorriaga et al. 2018; Singh et al. 2015) but the same life satisfaction (Bak-Klimek et al. 2015) (Hypothesis 3). The third objective was to examine the predictive capacity of sociodemographic and migratory variables in relation to perceived stress, life satisfaction, and the mental health of Basque immigrants. The last objective was established to determine whether the psychological adjustment difficulties are related to the decision to return to Basque Country (Abraído-Lanza et al. 1999).

## Method

*Participants*

The sample was made up of a group of Basque immigrants in other European countries ($n$ = 86) and an equivalent control group of Basque non-immigrants ($n$ = 63). The total sample size is 149 Basques, aged between 20 and 55 ($M$ = 28.44 years; $SD$ = 5.56) and of both sexes (72.1 percent women and 27.9 percent men). University graduates made up 85 percent of the sample, 8.1 percent had completed vocational training, 4.7 percent are studying at university, and 1.2 percent secondary school education. The non-immigrant group was equivalent to the immigrant group in relation to sex, age, educational level, and employment situation because there are no statistically significant differences when comparing two groups: sex, ($X^2$(1, $N$ = 149) = .316, $p$ = .36), age ($t$(147) = .284, $p$ = .78), educational level ($X^2$(3, $N$ = 149) = 2.75, $p$ = .43), and employment situation ($X^2$(3, $N$ = 149) = 4.73, $p$ = .19).

*Procedure*

A questionnaire was designed in Spanish in a web survey format to allow completion online. A convenience sample was selected using the snowball technique (Taylor and Bodgan 1986). The first step involved obtaining data from the immigrant population. The chain began with 12 people living in Germany, the United Kingdom, Ireland, and France. The snowball technique is appropriate when access to the population is difficult and when there is no knowledge of their characteristics and real size (Heckathorn 2001). However, this technique has the drawbacks of low representativeness and similarity bias. To reduce this bias a call for participation was made on five Basque social networks and forums (Basques worldwide, Basques in Dublin, Basques in London, Basques in Germany, and Basques in Berlin). Inclusion criteria were being born in the Basque Country, having emigrated in the last 10 years, and being aged between 18 and 65. This procedure was followed by obtaining a sample of non-immigrant Basques, through 7 people. In all cases, information was provided on the objectives of the research, requesting permission to use the data as well as ensuring anonymity and confidentiality. The procedures were carried out in accordance with institutional, national, and international (APA) ethics guidelines.

*Variables and Instruments*

The immigrants completed all the questionnaires described below, while the non-immigrant population responded to all the questionnaires with the exception of the one on the characteristics of the migratory process.

*1. Sociodemographic characteristics:* An ad hoc questionnaire gathered information about some sociodemographic characteristics such as sex, age, educational level, and job status.

*2. Migratory characteristics.* The group of immigrants had to respond to questions related to the pre-migration and post-migration situation:

**Pre-migratory situation:**
- Pre-migratory job conditions (unemployment, time unemployed, and work experience).
- Previous migration experience (previously living in a foreign country, time of migration, and host country).
- Perception of their overall emotional health before emigration.
- Intention of staying in host country (permanent, provisional, or "not sure").

**Post-migratory situation:**
- The length of their stay abroad.
- The reason for having emigrated.
- Level of host country language.
- Residence.
- Perceived needs (improvement in job conditions, improvement in housing, improvement in host country language, social assistance, medical assistance, psychological assistance, and legal assistance).
- Post-migration job conditions (unemployment, workday, and job status).
- Social networks (contact and support with natives, endogroup and other immigrants; social network size emotional support).

- Family network (whether they have a partner, children, or other family members and where they live, intentions of family regrouping, family network size).
- Cultural identity (orientation to the host culture and culture of origin, strategies of acculturation, and perceived cultural distance).
- Evaluation of the situation in the host society (current situation compared to what was expected, achievement of migratory objectives, perception of their overall emotional health after emigration, and intention of settlement in the host country).

*Perceived Stress.* Perceived Stress Scale (PSS-14, Spanish version, Remor and Carrobles 2001). This scale was developed based on the transactional stress perspective defined by Lazarus and Folkman (1984) and measures the extent to which life events are undesirable, unpredictable, or uncontrollable. It is composed of fourteen items (for example, "In the last month, how often have you felt that you were unable to control the important things in your life?") with five response options (0 = Never, 4 = Very often). Cronbach's alpha of this study was .75.

*Life satisfaction.* Satisfaction with Life Scale (SWLS, Spanish version, Atienza, Pons, Balaguer, and García-Merita 2000). This scale is made up of five items with five response choices (1 = Totally disagree, 5 = Totally agree), and high scores indicate high levels of satisfaction or a positive assessment of one's accomplishments (for example, "I am satisfied with my life"). In this study the Cronbach's alpha was .87.

*Mental Health.* General Health Questionnaire (GHQ-28, Spanish version, Lobo, Pérez-Echevarría and Artal 1986). This consists of 28 items for detecting mental health problems suffered recently (for example, "Have you been getting scared or panicky for no good reason?"). The questionnaire is grouped into four sub-scales: somatic symptoms, anxiety/insomnia, severe depression, and social dysfunction. Each sub-scale consists of seven items with four progressively worsening response options with Likert scores (0, 1, 2, 3). The GHQ scores (0, 0, 1, 1) are used to identify the *prevalence of clinical symptoms*. A score of 0 is assigned to responses *0* and *1*, and 1 to responses *2* and *3*. The cut-off score is 5/6 (no case/case). According to results of the present study, internal consistency of this instrument as well as of its subscales was adequate. The Cronbach's alpha for the total scale was excellent ($\boxtimes$ = .90), and acceptable for all sub-scales (somatic symptoms $\boxtimes$ = .85, anxiety/insomnia $\boxtimes$ = .84, severe depression $\boxtimes$ = .74, and social dysfunction $\boxtimes$ = .78).

## Data Analysis

The SPSS program, version 23, was used for data analysis. First, the mean values and percentages of the sociodemographic and migratory characteristics of the group of immigrants were obtained. The student's $t$ test (quantitative variables) and chi-square test (qualitative variables) were applied to check for differences in the migratory processes between men and women. Analyses based on contingency tables with a full sample to establish any significant differences in the prevalence of clinical symptoms according to the immigrant condition or sex were also conducted.

Six multivariate analyses (MANOVA) were then conducted, with the immigrant and sex conditions as independent variables and the scores for perceived stress, life satisfaction, and mental health (somatic symptoms, anxiety/insomnia, social dysfunction, and severe depression) as dependent variables. Six multiple linear regression were used to determine the predictors of psychological adjustment (perceived stress, life satisfaction, somatic symptoms, anxiety/insomnia, social dysfunction, and severe depression). Finally, two logistic regression analyses with permanent settlement and provisional settlement as dependent variables were conducted. In both cases sociodemographic and mental health variables were independent variables.

## Results

### Pre-migratory Situation

**Job Status, Migration Experience, Perception of Their Overall Emotional Health, and Intention of Staying in the Host Country**

The analysis of the characteristics measured in relation to the socio-labor situation of Basques before they emigrated shows that there were no differences between men and women, except in their emotional health. Prior to emigrating, 20.34 percent were unemployed in the Basque Country with an average unemployment period of 8 months ($SD$ = 5.93 months). In addition, 64.7 percent had work experience before emigration. In relation to their previous migration experience, 36.5 percent had previously lived in another country for an average of 20.37 months ($SD$ = 16.58 months). But only 3.1 percent emigrated to the same country to which they had previously been.

Regarding the perception of their overall emotional health, there are statistically significant differences between men and women. It was found that men considered their health to be "poor-normal" and worse than that of women, who defined theirs as "normal-good" ($M$ = 2.83; $SD$ = 1.03) vs. $M$ = 3.55; $SD$ = 1.05) ($t$ = 2.85; $p$ = .006). Finally, when asked about their intention regarding settling in the new society before emigrating, 66.3 percent planned to return to Basque Country when they emigrated, 19.85 percent planned to stay permanently in the host country, and 14 percent were not sure what they would do.

*Post-migratory Situation*

**Social Integration and Basic Resources**

When a Basque migrant population establishes itself in Europe, the basic resources to start a new stage of life are covered, and this situation is similar for men and women. In this recent wave of migration, the average length of stay in Europe is 22.06 months ($SD$ = 14.44 months), with around 54.1 percent immigrating to Europe for less than one year, 27.1 percent between one and three years, 9.4 percent between three and five years, and 9.4 percent between five and ten years. The main reason for immigrating was jobs (38.8 percent), followed by learning the country's language (29.4 percent), seeking new experiences (8.2 percent), training (14.1 percent), and reuniting with their family (9.4 percent). Some 79 percent lived in a rental apartment, 7 percent in their own apartment, and 15.1 percent in other kinds of housing.

With regard to the host language, the Basque immigrant's mastery of the host country language is average ($M$ = 6.66; $SD$ = 2.02). Related to this data, Basque immigrants have moderate needs to improve the language ($M$ = 3.28; $SD$ = 1.37). However, other needs are almost not expressed: improvement in job conditions ($M$ = 2.27; $SD$ = 1.35), improvement in housing (M = 1.85; $SD$ = 1.24), legal assistance ($M$ = 1.96; $SD$ = 1.06), medical assistance ($M$ = 1.51; $SD$ = .78), psychological assistance ($M$ = 1.42; $SD$ = .83), and social assistance ($M$ = 1.16; $SD$ = .55).

*Job Conditions and Status*

The current job conditions of immigrant women were the same as immigrant men. In the host country, 75.6 percent of Basque immigrants have a job, 11.6 percent have an occupation that does not earn them a salary (student, internship, or housework), and 10.5 percent are unemployed. The majority (80 percent) work more than 35 hours per week, 15.4 percent between 20 and 34 hours, and 4.6 percent less than 19 hours (average of hours per week $M$ = 37.27, $SD$ = 8.08). Furthermore, 52.9 percent believe that their job status is better than their job status in the Basque Country, 35.7 percent that it is the same, and only 11.4 percent think that it is worse than in the Basque Country.

When the pre-migratory and post-migratory labor situation is compared, it can be observed that 72.6 percent currently had a job in the Basque Country,

7.1 percent had previously been employed and were now unemployed, 16.7 percent were previously unemployed in the Basque Country and found a job after migration, and 3.6 percent were unemployed both before and after migration.

## Family Network

The characteristics of family networks are also similar for Basque migrant men and women. People with a partner make up 60.5 percent of those surveyed, and in 72.5 percent of cases, the partner is in the country to which they have emigrated. Only 7.1 percent have children and in 66.67 percent of cases the children are with them. In addition, 4.7 percent have another person in their family in the host country, while 11.8 percent have thought about regrouping someone in their family. Finally, 45.9 percent have a family network, that is, they have at least a partner or an adult of their family in the host country.

## Social Network

Basque immigrants have less interaction with other Basque immigrants ($M$ = 2.64; $SD$ = 1.51) than with natives ($M$ = 3.17; $SD$ = .88) ($t$ = -7.66; $p$ > .000) or with immigrants from other countries ($M$ = 3.22; $SD$ = .79) ($t$ = -8.38; $p$ < .001). This contact is categorized as *moderate*.

Although the perception of contact is low when the size of the network in the host country analyzed is considered (the number of closest relationships), the average is 3.67 ($SD$ = 3.20). If people have more than two trusted contacts, the network is considered *good*. In addition, it is observed that they have substantial support. The level of perceived support from Basque immigrants is *medium* ($M$ = 3.75; $SD$ = 1.22), from other immigrants ($M$ = 3.11; $SD$ = .90), and from natives ($M$ = 3.02; $SD$ = 1.01), while emotional support is *medium-high* ($M$ = 4.08; $SD$ = .85).

## Cultural Identity

The orientation toward the maintenance of Basque culture ($M$ = 5.95; $SD$ = 1.82) is lower than the orientation to the host culture ($M$ = 7.84; $SD$ = 1.22), ($t$ = -8.13; $p$ < .001). In terms of acculturation strategies, the majority of Basque immigrants preferred integration (75.6 percent ) (desire to maintain the culture of origin and learn the culture of the host society), followed by assimilation (22.1 percent) (desire to adopt the new culture while rejecting their own culture), and only 2.3 percent adopt the separation strategy (trying to maintain the culture of origin while rejecting the new culture). Marginalization was not signaled by any person (rejecting both cultures). Regarding perceived cultural distance, there are statistically significant differences by sex ($t$ = 2.11, $p$ < .050), with Basque women immigrants perceiving less cultural distance to the host society ($M$ = 5.58; $SD$ = 1.66) than Basque men immigrants ($M$ = 6.17; $SD$ = 1.42). In both groups, the perception of cultural distance is *medium-high*.

*Evaluation of the Situation in the Host Society*
The Basque population assesses its immigrant situation in European countries as positive. For 60.5 percent, their current situation in the host society is better than they expected, while it is the same for 22.1 percent, and 17.4 percent confirm that is worse than they had imagined before emigrating. The perception of their overall emotional health in the host society is positive (*normal-good*) ($M$ = 3.64; $SD$ = .092), and there were no statistically significant differences between men and women: 12.9 percent stated that their emotional health is *poor*, 28.2 percent *normal*, 41.2 percent *good*, and 17.6 percent *very good*. Nobody reported it to be very bad. The perception of emotional health in the host society is better than they had in the Basque Country ($t$ = -1.99; $p$ >. 050).

Regarding the achievement of objectives, there are differences between women and men ($t$ = 2.11; $p$ >. 050): women achieved more migratory objectives ($M$ = 3.61, $SD$ =.66) than men ($M$ = 3.25, $SD$ =. 94).

Asked about their intention to settle after getting to know the host society, 54.7 percent said they would return to the Basque Country, 24.4 percent planned on staying permanently, and 20.9 percent were not sure. The differences between the intention before emigrating and at the moment asked are statistically significant ($X^2$ (1, $N$ = 86) = 31.34, $p$ >. 050). In general, once the host society's conditions are known, more people consider staying permanently and fewer provisionally.

*The Migration Process, Mental Health, and Gender Differences*
Table 1 presents the data on clinical symptoms prevalence (GHQ scores) as a function of the immigrant condition. No differences were found between immigrants and non-immigrants with regard to the prevalence of clinical symptoms, and there were also no differences in symptoms in either of these groups between men and women ($p$ > .050).

Furthermore, the overall effect of being an immigrant, or either male or female, on psychological adjustment was determined by performing six MANOVAS. The results showed significant effects for the variable female sex in *life satisfaction* ($F$ (1, 147) = 12.72; $p$ < a.001; $X^2$ = .081) and *severe depression* ($F$ (1, 149) = 6.31; $p$ = .013; $X^2$ = .042): women are more satisfied with life than men ($M$ = 3.83 vs. $M$ = 3.20) ($t$ = 3.66; $p$ < .001) and present less depression ($M$ = 1.41 vs. $M$ = 1.61) ($t$ = -2,53; $p$ = .013). Second, there are significant effects for the variable immigrant in *perceived stress* ($F$ (1, 141) = 4.92; $p$ = .028; $\eta_2$ = .035) and in *social dysfunction* ($F$ (1, 149) = 6.07; $p$ = .015; $\eta_2$ = .040): the Basque population in Europe perceives less stress ($M$ = 1.59) than Basques in the Basque Country ($M$ = 1.84) ($t$ = 2.37; $p$ =.019) and, furthermore, the immigrant population presents less social dysfunction ($M$ = 1.79) than people that did not emigrate ($M$ = 1.97) ($t$ = 2.43; $p$ = .016). Finally, in somatization and anxiety there are no statistically significant differences as a function of immigrant status or male/female.

**Table 1. Prevalence of mental health as a function of immigrant status**

|  | Basque population in the Basque Country | Basque immigrants in Europe | $\chi^2$ | $P$ |
|---|---|---|---|---|
| Somatization | 9.7% | 4.7% | 1.44 | .19 |
| Anxiety/Insomnia | 10.2% | 5.1% | 1.31 | .21 |
| Severe depression | 1.6% | 0% | 1.35 | .43 |
| Social dysfunction | 1.7% | 1.2% | .06 | .66 |

*Predictive Factors of the Psychological Adjustment of Immigrants*
The linear regression analyses shown in Table 2 reveal the predictive capacity of the sociodemographic and migratory variables in relation to perceived stress, life satisfaction, and mental health (somatization, anxiety/insomnia, social dysfunction, and severe depression).

The model associated with *perceived stress* predicted 26 percent, based on two variables: the need to improve job conditions and lack of achievement of migratory objectives ($R^2$ = .26, $F(2,77)$ = 14.43, $p$ < .001). The model referring to *life satisfaction* shows an explained variance of 32 percent and includes two significant predictors, achievement of migratory objectives and current situation compared to that expected ($R^2$ = .32, $F(2,84)$ = 21.10, $p$ < .001). The model of *somatization* is explained by four variables in the following order of importance: lack of family network, medical assistance needs, psychological assistance needs, and lack of contact with immigrants that predict 22 percent of variance, $R^2$ = .22, $F(4,841)$ = 6.74, $p$ < .001. The predictors of *anxiety/insomnia* were psychological assistance needs, lack of achievement of migratory objectives, and current situation is worse compared to that expected. This model explained 31 percent of variance, $R^2$ = .31, $F$ (3, 77) = 12.29, $p$ < .001. In the model of *depression,* there are four significant predictors: social assistance needs, being male, psychological assistance needs, and need to improve job conditions, predicting 24 percent of variance, $R^2$ = .24, $F$ (4, 84) = 5.75, $p$ < .001. Finally, the model of *social dysfunction* was predicted by not having a partner, the current situation being worse compared to the expected one, and the need to improve job conditions, explaining 26 percent of the variance, $R^2$ = .26, $F$ (3,80) = 10,26, $p$ < .001.

**Table 2. Multiple regression for variables of psychological adjustment**

| Variables | Model 1 Perceived stress | Model 2 Life satisfaction | Model 3 Somatization | Model 4 Anxiety | Model 5 Depression | Model 6 Social Dysfunction |
|---|---|---|---|---|---|---|
| 1. Current situation compared to the expected | - | .25** | - | -.25* | - | -.36 |
| 2. Improvement of job conditions | .31** | - | - | - | .24* | - |
| 3. Achievement of migratory objectives | -.30* | .41** | - | -.26* | - | -.25 |
| 4. Family network | *- | - | -.23** | - | - | - |
| 5. Contact with immigrants | - | - | -.24* | - | - | - |
| 6. Psychological assistance needs | - | - | .30* | .27* | .30** | - |
| 7. Medical assistance needs | - | - | .26** | - | - | - |
| 8. Being male | - | - | - | - | .24* | - |
| 9. Social assistance needs | - | - | - | - | .29* | - |
| 10. Having a partner | - | - | - | - | - | -.27 |
| Model F | 14.43*** | 21.10*** | 6.74*** | 12.29*** | 5.5*** | 10.26*** |
| $R^2$ | .26 | .32 | .22 | .31 | .24 | .26 |

$^*p$ ≤.5. $^{**}p$ ≤.01. $^{***}p$ ≤.001.

*Psychological Adjustment and Settlement*

Two logistic regression analyses were conducted, with permanent settlement and provisional settlement as dependent variables. Psychological adjustment variables did not predict permanent settlement or return to the Basque Country. The model referring to *permanent settlement* explained 32 percent of variance and included four significant predictors ($R^2$ = .32, $F$(4, 78) = 9.62; $p$ < .001). Permanent settlement was explained by a better current situation compared to the expected (⊠ = .32, $p$ < .01), lower educational level (⊠ = -.27, $p$ < .01), intentions of family regrouping (⊠ = .23, $p$ < .01), and higher level of host country language (⊠ = .22, $p$ < .01). Second, the model of *provisional settlement* or return to the Basque Country was predicted by a better emotional situation before immigration (⊠ = 39, $p$ < .001), lower orientation to learning the culture of host society (⊠ = -.32, $p$ < .001), and worse current situation compared to the expected (⊠ = -.32, $p$ < .001) ($R^2$ = .32, $F$(3, 83) = 15.10; $p$ < .001).

## Discussion

This study was performed with the goal of examining the sociocultural adjustment of the Basque immigrant population in European countries. The Basque immigrants in this sample are relatively young and emigrated less than three years ago. They have a high educational level and command the language spoken in the host country. In the Basque Country, before migration, the social and employment situation was similar for men and women. Some 20 percent were unemployed and 30 percent had experience of being an immigrant, but only 3 percent had returned to the country to which they had previously been. This means that in the present migration process, the knowledge of the host country is low. The intention of settling in European countries was provisional for 66 percent. Finally, the perception of their overall emotional health was "normal," but women considered that their health was better than men's health.

When Basque immigrants arrive in the country, the sociocultural situation is perceived as positive. First, basic resources are seen to be covered. Only 10 percent are unemployed, the majority work more than 35 hours a week, and they consider that their work status is equal to or better than that which they had in the Basque Country. It seems that working conditions in the host country are good. In addition, immigrants do not have a pressing need to improve work or housing conditions, and the needs for medical, psychological, legal, and social assistance are low. It is worth noting that the need to improve the host language is moderate. Second, family networks are of medium strength, with 45 percent of the Basque immigrant population having a partner or an adult in their family in the host country. The size of the network is considered good, although contact with Basque immigrants is low, and contact with the native population and other immigrants is moderate. Moreover, social support with all groups is medium and emotional support in general is medium-high. In relation to identity issues, immigrants, especially men, perceived a moderate-high culture distance to the host country but the orientation to learn the culture of new society was high.

Based on this situation, the assessment of their migration process is positive. Some 60 percent consider that their current situation is better than expected before migrating, and more than 20 percent feel better. Participants in the study state that their emotional health is good and that it is better than that perceived in the Basque Country. They consider that their migration expectations are being fulfilled, especially among women. In fact, they have changed their opinion about settling and after living in other European countries, and there are more people who decided not to return to the Basque Country, compared to the opinions before emigrating.

The results do not support Hypothesis 1, or previous studies (Aroain et al. 2008; Dion and Dion 2001) because Basque immigrant women do not have more social and economic difficulties in the host country in comparison to Basque immigrant men.

In line with the second hypothesis, life satisfaction and mental health (prevalence and scores of symptoms of somatization, anxiety/insomnia, and severe depression) were similar in Basque immigrants and Basques who remained in the Basque Country. However, the lower scores of perceived stress and social dysfunction of immigrants indicate that their psychological adjustment is better than those of Basque non-immigrants. These results are consistent with those obtained by previous studies in European countries comparing immigrants and people who remained at home in stress, mental health (Elgorriaga et al. 2016; Glaesmer et al. 2009), and life satisfaction (Erlinghagen 2011; Neto and Barros 2007). These results support the immigrant health paradox (Markides and Coreil 1986), which postulates that the mental health of the immigrants is similar to or better than that of the native population or their fellow citizens born in the host country. In the European context, Heide Glaesmer et al (2009). found that when migration is not associated with low socioeconomic status, immigrants and non-immigrants present a similar mental health level. This is explained by the fact that Basque people have a job in the host country and, in comparison to other immigrant groups, enjoy advantages such as legal status, relative similarities in terms of culture, and geographical proximity. These results are similar to those found among Spanish immigrants in European countries (Elgorriaga et al. 2018).

The hypothesis that women immigrants would show slightly higher levels of perceived stress and mental health symptoms than immigrant men but the same life satisfaction has been partially confirmed. In the present study, immigrant women and men presented similar rates of perceived stress and mental health (prevalence of four clinical symptoms and scores for somatization, anxiety/insomnia, and social dysfunction). However, in contrast to previous studies on mental health (for example, Singh et al. 2015) and life satisfaction (Bak-Klimek et al. 2015), women immigrants present more life satisfaction and less severe depression. These results in women's psychological adjustment could be explained by the positive conditions of Basque immigrant women in the host country. In comparison with other studies (Aroain eta al. 2008), the social and economic situation of Basque immigrant women and men are similar, and therefore, women would not have more stressors or would not be more vulnerable than men.

The third objective was performed with the goal of identifying the most important predictive factors of the psychological adjustment of Basque immigrants. We should note that the achievement of migratory objectives and a better current situation compared to the expected are stronger than other variables in their predictive capacity. It seems that psychological assistance needs could predict the psychological adjustment of Basque immigrants in European countries.

The most important predictors (current situation compared to the expected and achievement or migratory objectives) are related to expectations, and previous research has indicated the relevance of unrealistic expectations and the frustration of not fulfilling them (Berry 1997; Mähönen et al. 2013) in explaining immigrants' psychological adjustment. On the other hand, in line with other studies (Bak-Klimek et al. 2015), Basque immigrants' perceived stress, life satisfaction, and mental health are primarily related to subjective aspects of the conditions of the migratory process and not so much to objective sociodemographic migratory characteristics.

The final objective was to explore whether psychological adjustment difficulties predicted the decision to return to the Basque Country. The *salmon bias hypothesis* (Abraído-Lanza et al. 1999) postulates that immigrants with physical problems have a greater tendency to return to their society of origin. Other studies have shown that this phenomenon also occurred with mental health measures (Diaz et al. 2017) and with perceived general health measures (Lu and Qin 2014). The results of the present study do not confirm the salmon hypothesis. According to previous studies (Bostean 2013; Riosmena et al. 2012; Ullman et al. 2011), in the immigration of the Basque population to Europe, mental health (perceived stress, life satisfaction, and mental health symptoms) does not predict a return home. However, other factors have been found that explain the decision of Basque immigrants to stay in the host country or to return to the Basque Country. Permanence in the host countries is positively predicted by having a better situation than expected, by the intention to regroup the family, and by having a good level of the host country language, yet negatively by educational level. The predictive power of expectations (Duleep 1994) and family reunification (Contant and Massey 2012) had been demonstrated previously. On the other hand, three factors explain the return to the Basque Country: the fact that the emotional situation in the Basque Country before migrating was good, low orientation toward learning the culture of the host society, and the perception that the situation in the host country is worse than expected. Once again, the importance of expectations becomes evident (Duleep 1994), and new factors appear, such as the psychological link with host society (Constant and Massey 2012).

The factors explaining the settlement options indicate that when the Basque immigrant population has a good economic and social situation in the host society, the probability of remaining there is greater. However, when immigrants do not achieve their migratory objectives, when they do not establish links with the host society, and their emotional situation in Basque Country was positive, there is a greater likelihood that they will return. In this sense, migratory success would be related to permanent settlement, and failure with a return home, which is consonant with neoclassical economic theory (Sjastaad 1963 in Constant and Massey 2002). This theory views return migration as a cost-benefit decision, with immigrants deciding to stay or return in order to maximize expected net lifetime earnings.

While this study presents certain limitations, such as sample size, biases arising from the online gathering of information, and the problems inherent in transversal research, conclusions can be drawn that allow us to understand the characteristics of the migratory process of the Basque population to European countries in the last 10 years. In sum, the adjustment to the new society is positive: they do not have great difficulties or needs, they know the language of the host country, they have a job, and the social networks are good. The privileged migratory conditions tend to generate less perceived stress, fewer mental health problems, and high life satisfaction. The positive sociocultural adjustment makes many people decide to settle down definitively in the host society.

## Bibliography

Abraído-Lanza, Ana F., Bruce P. Dohrenwend, Daisy S. Ng-Mak, and Blake Turner. "The Latino Mortality Paradox: A Test of the "Salmon Bias" and Healthy Migrant Hypotheses." *American Journal of Public Health* 89, no.10 (1999): 1543–48.

Atxotegi, Joseba. "Emigrar en situación extrema: el Síndrome del inmigrante con estrés crónico y múltiple (Síndrome de Ulises)." *Norte de Salud Mental* 21 (2004): 39–52.

Aguila, Emma, Jose Escarce, Mei Leng, and Leo Morales. "Health Status and Behavioral Risk Factors in Older Adult Mexicans and Mexican Immigrants to the United States." *Journal of Aging and Health* 25, no. 1 (2013): 136–58.

Alaminos, Antonio, and Oscar Santacreu. "La emigración cualificada española en Francia y Alemania." *Papers. Revista de sociología* 95, no.1 (2010): 201–11.

Aroian, Karen J., Anne E. Norris, María Asunción González de Chávez, and Lourdes María García Averasturi.. "Gender Differences in Psychological Distress among Latin American Immigrants to the Canary Islands." *Sex Roles* 59 (2008): 107–18.

Atienza, Francisco L., Diana Pons, Isabel Balaguer, and Marisa García-Merita. "Propiedades psicométricas de la escala de satisfacción con la vida en adolescents." *Psicothema* 12, no. 2 (2000): 314–19

Bak-Klimek, Anna, Thanos Karatzias, Lawrie Elliott, and Rory Maclean. "The Determinants of Well-being among International Economic Immigrants: A Systematic Literature Review and Meta-analysis." *Applied Research in Quality of Life* 10, no. 1 (2015): 161–88.

Berry, John W. "Immigration, Acculturation, and Adaptation." *Applied Psychology: An International Review* 46 (1997): 5–68.

Berry, John W., and David L. Sam.. "Acculturation and Adaptation." In *Handbook of Cross-cultural Psychology: Social Behavior and Application*, edited by John .W. Berry, Marshall H. Senegall, and Cigdem Kagitçibasi. Boston: Allyn & Bacon, 1996.

Bostean, Georgiana. "Does Selective Migration Explain the Hispanic Paradox? A Comparative Analysis of Mexicans in the U.S. and Mexico." *Journal of Immigrant Minority Health* 15 (2013): 624–35.

Constant, Amelie, and Douglas S. Massey. "Return Migration by German Guest-workers: Neoclassical versus New Economic Theories." *International Migration* 40 (2002): 5–34.

Cuellar, Israel, Elena Bastida, and Sara M. Braccio. "Residency in the United States, Subjective Well-being, and Depression in an Older Mexican-origin Sample." *Journal of Aging and Health* 16, no. 4 (2004): 447–66.

De Luca, Sonia, Magdalena Bobowik, and Nekane Basabe. "Adaptación sociocultural de inmigrantes brasileños en el País Vasco: bienestar y aculturación." *Revista de Psicología Social* 26, no. 2 (2011): 275–94.

Díaz, Christina J., Stephanie M. Koning, and Ana P. Martínez-Donate. "Moving Beyond Salmon Bias: Mexican Return Migration and Health Selection." *Demography* 53, no 6 (2016): 2005–30.

Dion, Karen K., and Kenneth L. Dion. "Gender and Cultural Adaptation in Immigrant Families." *Journal of Social Issues* 57, no. 3 (2001): 511–21.

Duleep, Harriet O. "Social Security and the Emigration of Immigrants." *Social Security Bulletin* 57 (1994): 37–52.

Elgorriaga, Edurne, Izaskun Ibabe, and Ainara Arnoso. "Españoles que emigran a países de la Unión Europea: predictores de su ajuste psicológico." *Revista de Psicología Social* 3, no. 2 (2016): 332–51.

———. "Mental Health of Spanish Immigrants in Germany and the UK in Comparison to Non-immigrants and Migration Protective Factors." *Psychosocial Intervention* 28, no. 1 (2019): 19–27.

Erlinghagen, Marcel. "Nowhere Better than Here? The Subjective Well-being of German Emigrants and Remigrants." *Comparative Population Studies* 36, no. 4 (2011): 899–926.

Gibson, Margaret A. "Immigrant Adaptation and Patterns of Acculturation." *Human Development* 44 (2001): 19–23.

Glaesmer, Heide, Ulla Wittig, Elmar Brahler, Alexander Martin, Ricarda Mewes, and Winfred Rief. "Are migrants more susceptible to mental disorders?" *Psychiatrische Praxis* 36, no. 1 (2009): 16–22.

Haberfeld, Yitchak, Moshe Semyonov, and Yinon Cohen. "Ethnicity and Labour Market Performance among Recent Immigrants from the Former Soviet Union to Israel." *European Sociological Review* 16, no. 3 (2000): 287–99.

Jasinskaja-Lahti, Inga, Karmela Liebkind, and Riku Perhoniemi. "Perceived discrimination and well-being: a victim study of different immigrant groups." *Journal of Community and Applied Social Psychology* 16, no. 4 (2006): 267–84.

Lazarus and Folkman. *Stress, appraisal, and coping*. New York: Springer, 1984.

Lobo, Antonio, María Jesús Pérez-Echevarría, and Jesús Artal. "Validity of the Scaled Version of the

General Health Questionnaire (GHQ-28) in a Spanish Population." *Psychological Medicine* 16 (1986): 135–40.

Lu, Yao, and Lijian Qin. "Healthy Migrant and Salmon Bias Hypotheses: A Study of Health and Internal Migration in China." *Social Science and Medicine* 102 (2014): 41–48.

Mähönen, Tuuli A., Elina Leinonen, and Inga Jasinskaja-Lahti. "Met Expectations and the Wellbeing of Diaspora Immigrants: A Longitudinal Study." *International Journal of Psychology* 48, no. 3 (2013): 324–33.

Markides, Kyriakos S., and Jeannine Coreil. "The Health of Hispanics in the Southwestern United States: An Epidemiologic Paradox." *Public Health Reports* 101, no. 3 (1986): 253–65.

Mirsky, Julia. "Psychological Distress among Immigrant Adolescents: Culture-specific Factors in the Case of Immigrants from the Former Soviet Union." *International Journal of Psychology* 32, no. 4 (1997): 221–30.

Neto, Felix, and Jose Barros. "Satisfaction with Life among Adolescents from Portuguese Immigrant Families in Switzerland." *Swiss Journal of Psychology* 66 (2007): 215–23.

Remor, Eduardo, and José Antonio Carrobles. "Versión Española de la Escala de Estrés Percibido (PSS-14): Estudio psicométrico en una muestra VIH+." *Ansiedad y Estrés* 7. nos. 2–3 (2001): 195–201.

Rief, Winfried. "Are Migrants more Susceptible to Mental Disorders? An Evaluation of a Representative Sample of the German General Population." *Psychiatrische Praxis* 36, no. 1 (2009): 16–22.

Riosmena, Fernando, César González-González, and Rebeca Wong. "El retorno reciente de Estados Unidos: salud, bienestar y vulnerabilidad de los adultos mayors." *Coyuntura Demográfica* 2 (2012): 63–67.

Rosenfield, Sarah, and Dena Smith. "Gender and mental health: do men and women have different amounts or types of problems." In *A Handbook for the Study of Mental Health*, edited by Teresa L. Scheid and Tony N. Brown. 2nd edition. New York: Cambridge University Press, 2012.

Sander, Monica. "Return Migration and the 'Healthy immigrant effect'." *SOEPpapers on Multidisciplinary Panel Data Research* 60 (2007): 1–39.

Singh, Shipra, Kimberly McBride, and Vivek Kak. "Role of Social Support in Examining Acculturative Stress and Psychological Distress among Asian American Immigrants and Three sub-groups: Results from NLAAS." *Journal of Immigrant and Minority Health* 17, no. 6 (2015): 1597–1606.

Singhammer, John, and Delia Bancila. "Associations between Stressful Events and Self-reported Mental Health Problems among Non-western Immigrants in Denmark." *Journal of Immigrant Minority Health* 13, no. 3 (2011): 371–78.

Taylor, Steven J., and Robert Bogdan. *Introducción a los métodos cualitativos de investigación.* Buenos Aires: Paidos, 1996.

Ullman, S. Heide, Noreen Goldman, and Douglas S. Massey. "Healthier Before they Migrate, Less Healthy when they Return? The Health of Returned Migrants in Mexico." *Social Science and Medicine* 73, no. 3 (2011): 421–28.

Vega, William A., Bohadan Kolody, Sergio Aguilar-Gaxiola, Ethel Alderete, Ralph Catalano, and Jorge Caraveo-Anduaga. 1998. "Lifetime Prevalence of *DSM-III-R* Psychiatric Disorders among Urban and Rural Mexican Americans in California." *Archives of General Psychiatry* 55, no. 9: 771–78.

Ward, Colleen, and Antony Kennedy. "The Measurement of Sociocultural Adaptation." *International Journal of Intercultural Relations* 23 (1999): 659-77.

WHO. *How Health Systems can address Health Inequalities Linked to Migration and Ethnicity.* Copenhagen: WHO Regional Office for Europe, 2010. At http://www.euro.who.int/__data/assets/pdf_file/0005/127526/e94497.pdf

Wittig, Ulla, Jutta Lindert, Martin Merbach, and Elmar Brähler. "Mental Health of Patients from Different Cultures in Germany." *European Psychiatry* 23, no. 1 (2008): 28–35.

# 9

# Migrations and Psychosocial Acculturation

## The Case of the Basque Country

*Nekane Basabe, Xabier Aierdi, and José J. Pizarro*

Migration is an inherent part of being human. People have been moving across international borders and within countries throughout history. Recent data (Abubakar et al. 2018) shows that nearly one seventh of the world's population is now living in a location different from the one in which they were born, and it was estimated that in 2017, 3 percent of the world's population were international migrants. The largest numbers of migrants are those who go to Asia, Europe, and North America, and the major movements, those happening within countries—four times greater than international migrants—are principally due to migrations from rural to urban areas in Asia, Africa, and Latin America.

This chapter describes the psychosocial acculturation process in current Basque society. First, it historically contextualizes the Basque Country as a region of emigrants and immigrants. We particularly focus on data from the Southern Basque Country, that is, the Basque Autonomous Community (hereafter, BAC), which is an autonomous region in the Spanish state. Second, we describe the composition of new immigrants who have arrived and settled in the Basque Country, providing a brief portrait of migration in the Basque Country and Spain and of native attitudes toward immigration. Next, we report on psychosocial models with which to analyze the acculturative strategies for immigrant minority groups, and the psychosocial factors that affect health, psychological, and social well-being among immigrants. Finally, we present a critical view of the Basque model of immigration and the future challenges for the twenty-first century.

## The Basque Country: External and Internal Migrations

*Basque Diaspora and Emigration*

Throughout recent history, the Basque Country has been a place in which migrations have been commonplace, as in the case of other regions and European countries (for example, Galicia in Spain, as well as Italy, Ireland, and Greece). All of this has contributed to establishing permanent cultural exchanges between local and other populations. For example, descendants of natives who live outside the Basque Country are numerous. There are estimated to be around 2 to 4 million people of Basque descent living in the Americas. In particular, 5 and 6 percent of the Argentinian and Uruguayan population, respectively, are thought to be of Basque descent (Aranda 1998; Crespo 1999).

The third generation of the Basque diaspora was assimilated by host countries in American societies. Nevertheless, Basque emigrants kept a symbolic identity with their land of origin and some formal ethnic organizations, such as those known as Euskal Etxea (literally "Basque House," Basque cultural centers), but most of the second and third generation did not speak Basque (Crespo 1999). According to an Argentinian survey (Germani 1971), 51 percent of Spanish emigrants were more attached to their country of origin than to Argentina, 94 percent did not intend to go back, and most of their friends were Argentinian and immigrants in equal numbers (90 percent).

*The Southern Basque Country: Internal Immigration and Social Diversity*

Simultaneously, the BAC has experienced extra-continental and internal emigration. At the beginning of the twentieth century, 50 percent of Bilbao's inhabitants came from other regions. During the period 1951–1979, a major immigration process took place, and by the end of that period a third of the population had been born outside the Basque Country: 19.45 percent were from Castile-Leon, 4.24 percent from Extremadura, 3.6 percent from Galicia, and 2.96 percent from Andalusia. These four social groups constituted 30 percent of the population, while people from Asturias and Aragon made up around 5 percent. A 1991 survey found that 31 percent of residents in the BAC had been born outside the community, 29 percent inside and had at least one of their parents from outside, and 7 percent had both parents from the BAC and with at least one grandparent from outside. Finally, only 33 percent made up the native population—with both parents and grandparents from the BAC (Ruiz Olabuénaga and Blanco 1994).

Internal immigrants in the last century mainly had a low economic status and came to settle definitively in the Basque Country. Therefore, biculturalism and assimilation were the dominant acculturation patterns (Blanco 1990). As in other countries in which internal immigration had been strong, in the BAC immigrants have settled progressively, and the third generation responds as native residents. In 1980, as immigrants had spent more time in the BAC, so their own self-definition as Basque increased (Páez, Basabe, Herranz, and Zubieta 2001).

Biculturalism in the BAC can also be seen in terms of the linguistic reality, in which Basque (Euskara) and Castilian (Spanish) are the two official languages. In recent decades, the institutional presence of Euskara has increased constantly. According to the 2016 sociolinguistic survey carried out in the Basque government, 55.2 percent of the population of the Basque Country is monolingual Castilian, 28.4 percent is bilingual Basque-Castilian, and 16.4 percent are passive bilingual—that is, they understand the Basque language but do not use it. Meanwhile, 34 percent of the population are Basque speakers in the BAC, 13 percent in Navarre, and 20.5 percent in the North or French Basque Country. Their daily use of Basque is disparate, depending on localities and linguistic regions (Gobierno Vasco, Gobierno de Navarra, and Euskararen Erakunde Publikoa 2016). In addition, Francisco José Llera, José M. Mata, Carmelo Moreno, and Rafael Leonisio (2018) find that two out of three people interviewed reported a bicultural identity—Basque and Spanish, with prevalence for the Basque identity—while 22 percent see themselves as just Basque and 3 percent as exclusively Spanish.

## The New Migration to the Southern Basque Country: External Immigration in the Twenty-First Century

*Panoramic Data of Immigration in the Basque Country (BAC)*

According to 2017 data from Ikuspegi (2018a)—a public organization that studies immigration in the BAC—the foreign population living in the European Union (EU) stood at 11.2 percent that year. Accordingly, the BAC is situated at a medium-low position within the EU, with 9 percent of its population being foreign. As regards the evolution of immigration in Spain, there has been a decrease since 2012, largely due to the enormous impact of the 2008 economic crisis. In the case of the BAC, it has followed an upward linear pattern, having gone from 7.3 percent in 2009 to 9 percent in 2017. The principal immigrants groups are from Morocco (14.3 percent), Romania (12.5 percent), Nicaragua (4.8 percent), and Bolivia (4.7 percent).

As for an economic perspective, macroeconomic analysis on the effect of asylum seekers in Europe concludes that they have a positive effect on host countries' economies (Abubakar et al. 2018). Immigrants in high-income countries (hereafter, HIC), such as member countries of the EU, work in areas providing social and medical care services, teaching children, and caring for older people, in hospitals, nursing homes, child-care centers, and domestic and professional cleaning services.

Different sociological *portraits* reveal that both Spain and the BAC are in a transition phase characterized by the passage from a stage based on the reception and receipt of the migratory flows to another focused on the integration and the management of these groups (Godenau et al. 2014). The immigrant population is in a disadvantaged situation compared to locals, especially on quality-of-life indexes. In the BAC, while a high level of well-being prevails among nationals, there is a significantly lower one in the foreign population (Godenau et al. 2014). Compared to other Spanish regions, there is a greater disparity between these two groups in indexes based on economic conditions (difficulties in making ends meet), housing (a higher number of people per room), and health (having worse perceived health). Notwithstanding this, when addressing age in this analyses, only a small difference in the general state of health is found (see below).

Regarding attitudes toward immigration, there is a mainly positive or neutral posture in Spain and in the Basque Country (Godenau et al. 2014). The tolerance index (hereafter, TI) summarizes a combination of different instruments that measure attitudes toward immigration and is interpreted as a public opinion barometer (Ikuspegi 2018b). The TI was 56.51 in 2007, and fell to 53.62 in 2012—as an effect of the economic crisis. Since then, it has risen to 59.71, in 2018. Temporal series of the TI show a small but steady increase in 2018, coinciding with an expansive stage in the economic growth. This parallelism supports the idea that tolerance toward immigration is intrinsically related to a greater trust in and certainty about a positive future for Basque society (Ikuspegi 2018b). These results in the BAC are grouped in different clusters, creating thus a tolerant group (31 percent, TI = 72.41), an ambivalent one (42.5 percent, TI = 59.02), and a reluctant one (26.5 percent, TI = 45.93).

Turning to citizenship, these data depict a profile characterized by adequate access to civic citizenship, with a large proportion of people from abroad with a regular administrative situation. Conversely, when it comes to social citizenship indicators, results are ambivalent, considering for instance the scholar integration gap between immigrants and natives (Godenau et al. 2014).

*Acculturation, Social Identities, and Acculturation Stress*
International migration to HICs makes different ethnics groups relate more easily in contemporary multicultural societies. In these contexts, individuals and groups of different cultural backgrounds engage each other more frequently

and, then, a process of acculturation begins, leading to cultural and psychological changes in both parties (Berry 2008).

Overall, there are two frameworks or models that can be used to describe acculturation processes from social psychology studies. The first one is John W. Berry's (1997) model, which explains cultural maintenance and the adoption of new cultures—namely, sharing beliefs, values, attitudes, and social relationships—in the contact between dominant (natives) and non-dominant groups (immigrants from different ethnic groups). Here, four acculturation profiles emerge according to the interaction among these groups. The first, *assimilation*, results from a loss of the ethnic culture at origin and an orientation to adopt the host culture. Second, *integration* results in the maintenance of both the origin and the host cultures and behaviors, while people engage in day-to-day interactions. The third, *separation*, results in the cultural and psychological maintenance of the original patterns as a result of minimizing interaction as much as possible. Finally, *marginalization* results in cultural and psychological loss, particularly among non-dominant populations, along with their exclusion from full and equitable participation in the wider society (Berry 2008). This last profile has been defined as diffuse because this category describes an individualist pattern of adaptation that characterizes young people with their own individual migration project (Basabe, Páez, Aierdi, and Jiménez 2009).

On the other hand, the second profile postulates an interactive acculturation model, in which the integration of immigrants depends on the host society's acculturation orientations toward target groups (Bourhis, Moise, Perreault, and Senecal 1997). Therefore, the possibility of social integration will depend on the position of dominant groups and public policies on immigration. Combining the language and cultural identity from the immigrant groups and the host society, the authors identify five acculturative strategies: *integrationism, assimilationism, segregationism, exclusionism,* and *individualism* (Bourhis et al. 1997). This perspective highlights that the host majority influences the adoption of strategies of minority groups and individuals. As can be inferred, both perspectives are complementary and, depending on the context, one or the other could be more salient. For instance, in the *melting pot* context, *assimilations* are the most common orientation, while *biculturalism* is more probable for groups of high social status or perceived as more culturally close to the host society; *segregation* attitudes promote *separation* strategies, and *exclusion* targets minors, resulting in *marginalization* (Berry 2008; López-Rodríguez, Zagefka, Navas, and Cuadrado 2014; van Osch and Breugelmans 2012).

In general, the attitudes at natives and the host society toward immigrants are highly dependent on the target group. In Spain, the most common responses vary from *assimilation* and *integration* for Latin Americans and Europeans, to *segregation*, in the case of people from Morocco (Navas, López-Rodríguez, and Cuadrado 2013). Recent data from the Basque Country (Ikuspegi 2018b) supports the hierarchy in the degree of acceptance of immigrants based on their origin. In this case, likeability on the part of EU citizens is greater toward people from Argentina, followed by sub-Saharans and Latin Americans; likeability toward Chinese and Asians is at an intermediate level, while the least likeable are considered to be Romanians, Moroccans, and Algerians.

In terms of age, there is an important study of young immigrants who have settled in thirteen societies in Europe, North America, Australia, and New Zealand (Berry, Phinney, Sam, and Vedder 2006), with a sample composed by 7,997 national and immigrant adolescents. The profiles were *integration* (36.4 percent of immigrant youth), (ethnic) *separation* (22.5 percent), (national) *assimilation* (18.7 percent), and (diffuse) *marginalization* (22.4 percent). As Berry (2008) concludes, young immigrants do not necessarily adopt acculturative strategies that make them more like their natives peers. This preference for bicultural strategies is common in different countries (Berry 2008). In the Basque Country, bicultural strategies are also common, especially in private areas—among family and relatives, friends, and family socialization measures—and on the contrary in public, where the most frequent strategy was *assimilation*. This could be explained by the characteristics of the latter contexts (for example, political participation and access to educational life), which can be understood as an incorporation in terms of equality into civil society (Basabe et al. 2009).

Moreover, a 2007 survey (N = 3,100 immigrants from fifteen nationalities) showed heterogeneity patterns among the immigrants' acculturation strategies. Colombian immigrants showed a high perception of discrimination, strong collective identity, and high satisfaction with life. Among the Chinese, a strategy of reclusion in their own ethnic group was frequent, and they reported an average score in life satisfaction. At the other extreme, Romanians and Africans reported a high level of perceived discrimination and low life satisfaction. In addition, the acculturative strategies for each collective were as follows: for Argentines, *assimilation* and *individualistic* or diffuse strategies; for Brazilians, *biculturalism*; for Romanians, *segregation* and *separation*; for North Africans, a preference for public *assimilation* or *biculturalism* and private *separation*; for sub-Saharan Africans, between assimilation and *segregation/separation*; and for Chinese, *separation* (Basabe et al. 2009).

In terms of outcomes, the acculturation process produces both sociocultural and psychological adaptations. In the BCA, immigrants' sociocultural adaptation is related to cultural learning and communication, on the one side, and hierarchy and social distance management, on the other. As Sonia de Luca, Magdalena Bobowik, and Nekane Basabe (2011) find, there was a greater reported impact at the beginning of the adaptation process, and it decreased over the length of residence, in which a *separation* pattern was related to more sociocultural adaptation problems and *marginalization* to impeded cultural learning and communication. Despite the cultural distance between immigrants and natives, both groups shared the basic social values (Spearman's r = .86 for hierarchy values). Further, natives are more individualist and immigrants more collectivist, especially sharing more familism (Basabe et al. 2009).

*Migrants' Health and Subjective Well-being Reflects the Circumstances of Migration*
An international review on migration and health-related outcomes (Abubakar et al. 2018) highlights several main conclusions. First, migrants generally contribute more to the wealth of host societies than they cost. Second, international migrants in HICs have, on average, a lower mortality than the local population, but at the same time, an increased morbidity among certain subgroups of migrants (for example, increased rates of mental illness among victims of human trafficking and people fleeing conflicts).

In addition, the so-called the *healthy migrant effect*—lower rates of mortality compared to the natives—is supported empirically. Nevertheless, this point of view is inadequate to properly describe the fact that the health status of migrants changes during the course of their lives and tends to decline over time (Abubakar et al. 2018). In particular, in older people, the time since immigration took place is associated with increased risks of chronic diseases for immigrants in the EU (Ladin and Reinhold 2013). Specifically, a meta-analysis of 96 studies shows only evidence supporting the *mortality advantage* of international migrants in high-income settings (Aldridge, Nellums, Bartlett, et al. in press, quoted in Abubakar et al. 2018).

Furthermore, mental illness rates tend to be higher among first-generation international migrants (namely, for depression, anxiety, and post-traumatic stress disorder, or PTSD) than for the host population rates (Close et al. 2016). The risks of having psychosis and schizophrenia are also consistently higher among migrants, compared to the host population. This difference will be associated to several risk factors, such as violence, traumatic events, and perceived discrimination (Major, Dovidio, and Link 2018), even though it should be acknowledged that there are cultural difficulties in differential diagnosis in mental health. At the same time, according to a systematic review of meta-analysis, refugees and asylum seekers had approximately doubled the prevalence of depression and anxiety, compared with labor migrants (Lindert et al. 2009). In Europe, a prospective observational study shows that older migrants' self-reported morbidity was greater compared with that of older native people, as was their risk of depression (a random sample of 31,115 noninstitutionalized men and women aged 50 and older, living in Austria, Germany, France, Switzerland, Belgium, Sweden, Denmark, the Netherlands, Spain, Italy, and Greece) (Ladin and Reinhold 2013).

With the intention of analyzing the health status in the Basque Country, a retrospective study was conducted with two random samples of 1,250 immigrants. The first sample consisted of participants from Colombia, Bolivia, Romania, Morocco, and sub-Saharan Africa. The second, a matched one, consisted of 500 Basques, aged between 18 and 65, and all of them were evaluated using the health-related quality-of-life items (SF-12, Ware, Kosinski, and Keller 1996). The results showed that the self-selection hypothesis was plausible for the physical health of Colombian and sub-Saharan African men compared to natives. Immigrants had poorer mental health than locals, especially African men and Bolivian women, and finally, acculturation stress and discrimination could explain poorer mental health in immigrants compared to natives (Sevillano, Basabe, Bobowik, and Aierdi 2013).

The evidence on mental health in economic migrants is disparate, varying by migrant group and host country. There are different risk factors that could explain these discrepancies, such as exposure to violence in pre-migration settings factors and protective factors such as the support of family and friends and positive school experience (Abubakar et al. 2018). At the same time, there are some protective factors related to ethnic identity, such as ethnic vitality. This variable refers to demographic and institutional prestige that allows ethnic, linguistic, and religious groups to behave and survive as a collective in multiethnic societies (Bourhis et al. 1997), which has in turn been related to a better social adaptation (Ward, Bochner, and Furnham 2001). In the BAC for example, Colombians reported more vitality than other ethnic immigrant groups (Basabe et al. 2009). Among Latin Americans immigrants, familism has been described as strong family protection networks associated with better psychological adjustment (Chun, Organista, and Marín 2002).

In the Basque Country study (Sevillano et al. 2013), subjective well-being analyzed by hedonic, psychological, and social well-being measures were different. Importantly, after controlling the analysis for perceived friendship and support, marital status, income, sex, and age, immigrants (compared to nationals) reported especially higher eudaimonic well-being— social contribution and actualization, personal growth, self-acceptance, and purpose in life—and lower levels of well-being only in terms of positive relations with others and a negative effect. As a whole, these results highlight the fact that immigration will be appraised as a positive process. Specifically, it will positively influence immigrants' psychological well-being, interpreted in terms of personal and family growth, and that is perceived as a contribution to the social capital of the host country. At the same time, immigration involves stress, a negative effect, and difficulties related to social integration, especially when interacting with host society members. In conclusion, immigration involves a development of personal strengths because of the successful negotiation of challenges in life, discrimination, and prejudice (Bobowik, Basabe, and Páez 2015). Finally, and from a collective point of view, immigrants' well-being would undoubtedly reflect the degree of social integration and mental health of a society.

## An Evaluation of the Basque Model of Immigration in the Twenty-First Century

This section includes some critical reflections about the current Basque model of immigration, together with several suggestions aimed at public policies and lawmakers (Aierdi and Fouassier 2014; Moreno et al. 2018).

*Sociological Portrait of Immigration in the BAC*

The current situation of immigration in the BAC within the political context of the Spanish state and the EU can be summarized in the following points:

Compared to other regions in Spain, the migratory phenomenon has a slower but also more stable insertion, mainly due to its productive and feminized structure.

In 2012, and for the first time, the BAC lost some of its immigrant population. However, the first signs of recovery from the economic crisis have brought the rise of new immigration movements, mainly from Latin America. This particular immigration comes to cover the necessity of labor in the field of nursing and care. In the same vein, it is worth mentioning that by the end of 2010, the first post-crisis nationalization was taking place, such as that of immigrants from Nicaragua and Honduras, with the proportion of women higher than 80 percent (Aierdi and Fouassier 2014).

The sporadic instances of population loss or deceleration are accompanied by a regular level of growth. Counterintuitively, during times of greater

irregularity there usually come periods of economic improvement. This is because the greater the crisis is, the greater the regularity, and vice versa. Periods
of economic activation work to promote migrations, which, at least in the beginning, result in greater irregularity (Aierdi and Fouassier 2014).

It is mainly a settling immigration, based on transnational affective
chains, in which, in many cases, women lead the migration process. As a
result, they are able to regroup their families in some cases; in others, conversely, familiar networks become cross-national and new ways of relating
are generated.

The immigrant population has been crucial in maintaining the Basque
population, as is the case in many other countries (Abubakar et al. 2018). The
migratory model is highly centered on the Latin American female incorporation into the labor market in fields related to nursing and care, domestic work,
and the hotel industry. Among the Latin American population, six out of ten
immigrants are women.

Regarding the temporal evaluation, the immigration process experiences circumstantial vicissitudes, but is, as a whole, relatively stable. That is,
the number of unregistered people is almost nothing, and the percentage and
volume of people with residence permits has remained stable. Further, there are
more nationalization processes (mainly among Latin Americans) and fewer irregular workers. As previously stated, in Spain there is adequate access to civic
citizenship (Godenau et al. 2014).

As a rule, verbally agreed jobs through social networks substitute for formal
contracts. These dynamics compensate for institutional gaps in coverage or go
against political filters. In the BAC, only a 13.5 percent of immigrants have settled by means of a formal contract, and only 8.6 percent among women. To put
it another way, migrations take place under secure circumstances and, on many
occasions, different figures such as the contract are *a posteriori* rationalizations
rather than instigators (Aierdi and Fouassier 2014).

According to different experts, it is time to face the settling and permanence of the foreign population in the Basque Country. In the opinion of Gorka
Moreno (2011), it should be necessary to go from the bus (that is, reception) to
the elevator (that is, ascending mobility). Further, it is possible to foresee maintenance of the contribution of immigrants, and their composition will be in accordance with the needs of the Basque population (Aierdi and Fouassier 2014).
What is more, there is still general satisfaction and a desire for integration and
permanence among the immigrant population (Departamento de Empleo y
Asuntos Sociales 2011; Shershneva 2014).

**Future Challenges and a *Stricto Sensu* Vision of Social Innovation**
By way of conclusion, there are at least four challenges that must be faced in Basque society: the difficulty in the labor insertion of the African population, especially among African women; second-generation immigrants (the children of those who emigrated) who do not necessarily cover their own parents' immigration costs; preferential treatment according to their education this generation receives; and the disconnection or lack of interaction of specific groups with the host society.

The Basque model of immigration has been established mainly ad hoc rather than on the basis of any political or social foresight, as probably occurs with every migration. In the BAC, sustainability has principally come down to women, who are guarantors of reproducibility and social care. This situation can be characterized as a continuum, with one pole consisting of native women and the other of immigrant women—primarily, Latin Americans. We consider it prudent to ask whether not only whether these successions viable, but also what they imply in terms of justice and gender equality.

Due to all the above, it is thought that innovation is necessary, but under a new innovation logic. The novelty consists in making the social subsystem a central and key foundation that is able to affect the other subsystems (namely those involving technology and labor). Usually, however, the pattern is the opposite, in which it is the social subsystem that needs to implement measures according to what is determined by the others. Furthermore, this situation unquestionably generates discomfort among ample sectors of society, which is manifested as institutional helplessness, which in turn generates a high level of political indifference. In addition, we are living in times of deep and significant changes, such as those regarding climate change and natural resources, the increasing expendability of human labor, and the subsequent social changes. Taking all the above into account, we should stop and think about a central issue: How can we guarantee social inclusion in a post-labor society that does not offer the same opportunities older generations had? To put it differently, if nowadays societies can no longer sustain outcomes based on meritocracy, is social inclusion even feasible?

We live in times in which economic tsunamis do not undermine the capitalist economy, but rather democratic principles. In this scenario, it is highly plausible that a xenophobic legislature may emerge in the EU parliament, which will not solve important social problems (such as population aging, the dilemma of a globalized economy and politics, and the clear abandonment of ample social sectors). Rather, it will use a wanted-but-unwelcome policy, affirming the needs of immigrant populations without openly claiming it in our own societies due to the political cost it might entail—as has been seen in Germany, where Angela Merkel's party has lost a third of its support because of its backing of accepting Syrian war refugees. In this context, populist and xenophobic parties are reinforced, and democratic politics face difficult times, as happens in different countries in the EU and the Americas. Even though structurally imperative, it is not socially accepted, and, unfortunately, many societies do not always go along with sensible decisions, due to their political class.

For this reason, the Basque Country, its authorities, and its social agents must reach an agreement to install an immigration policy with a strong sense of familism. This frame of reference does not aim at solving the problem of integrating of immigrants, but rather at making the Basque Country think about its own future.

## Conclusion

This chapter has analyzed immigration and its relationship to acculturation. The Basque Country has historically been an immigrant nation and, likewise, its current society is made up the descendants of early immigrants who settled during the last century, coming from different regions of Spain. In recent years, new immigrants from different continents have joined, thus making the Basque Country the heterogeneous place it currently is. We know that immigrants wish to settle in this society by different means and acculturation strategies, but they share the desire of having an inclusive citizenship. There is an urgent need to agree upon a Basque political model of immigration that confronts these new challenges and includes the whole population, with innovative proposals in which social considerations lead their technological and labor counterparts.

## Acknowledgments

This study was supported by the Spanish Ministry of Economy and Competitiveness [under Grant PSI2017-84145-P], and the University of the Basque Country [under Grant IT-666-13, Grant US13/11].

## Bibliography

Abubakar, Ibrahim, et al. "The UCL–*Lancet* Commission on Migration and Health: The Health of a World on the Move." *The Lancet* 392, no. 10164 (December 15–21, 2018): 2606–2654. At http:// www.sciencedirect.com/science/article/pii/S0140673618321147.

Aierdi, Xabier, and Maite Fouassier. "Apuntes sobre inmigración, sostenibilidad de la vida y modelo vasco de inmigración." In *Inmigración e impacto de la crisis. Anuario de la inmigración en Euskadi*, edited by Gorka Moreno. Bilbao: UPV/EHU, 2014. At http://www.ikuspegi.eus/documentos/ anuarios/anuario_2013_cas_OK.pdf.

Aranda, José. "La mezcla demográfica del pueblo vasco." *Claves* 87 (1998): 11–15.

Basabe, Nekane, Dario Páez, Xabier Aierdi, and Amaia Jiménez. *Calidad de vida, Bienestar subjetivo y Salud: inmigrantes en la CAPV.* Bilbao: Ikuspegi; UPV/EHU, 2009. At http://www.ikuspegi. org/documentos/investigacion/es/3ikusgai_salud_inmigracion_ikuspegi.pdf.

Blanco, Mª Crisitina. *La integración de los inmigrantes en Bilbao.* Bilbao: Ayuntamiento de Bilbao, 1990.

Berry, John W. "Immigration, Acculturation, and Adaptation." *Applied Psychology* 46, no. 1 (1997): 5–34.

———. "Globalization and Acculturation." *International Journal of Intercultural Relations* 32, no. 4 (2008): 328–36.

Berry, John W., Jean S. Phinney, David L. Sam, and Paul Vedder, eds. *Immigrant Youth in Cultural Transition: Acculturation, Identity, and Adaptation across National Contexts.* Mahwah, NJ: Lawrence Erlbaum Associates, 2006.

Bourhis, Richard Y., Lena Celine Moise, Stephane Perreault, and Sacha Senecal. "Towards an Interactive Acculturation Model: A Social Psychological Approach." *International Journal of Psychology* 32, no. 6 (1997): 369–86.

Close, Ciara, Anne Kouvonen, Tania J. Bosqui, Kishan Patel, Dermot O'Reilly, and Michael Donnelly. "The Mental Health and Wellbeing of First Generation Migrants: A Systematic-narrative Review of Reviews." *Global Health* 12 (2016): 47.

Crespo, Txema. "W. Douglass: Para ser vasco en otro país hace falta tener voluntad." *El País/País Vasco,* October 31, 1999, 16.

Chun, Kevin M., Pamela Balls Organista, and Gerardo Marín, eds. *Acculturation: Advances in Theory, Measurement, and Applied Research.* Washington, DC, 2003: APA.

Bobowik, Magdalena, Nekane Basabe, and Dario Páez. "The Bright Side of Migration: Hedonic, Psychological, and Social well-being in Immigrants in Spain." *Social Science Research* 51 (2015): 189–204.

De Luca, Sonia, Magdalena Bobowik, and Nekane Basabe. "Adaptación sociocultural de inmigrantes brasileños en el País Vasco: Bienestar y aculturación." *Revista de Psicología Social* 26, no. 2 (2011): 275–94.

Departamento de Empleo y Asuntos Sociales. *Encuesta de la Población Inmigrante Extranjera residente en la Comunidad Autónoma de Euskadi, EPIE 2010* (2011). Vitoria-Gasteiz: Departamento de Empleo y Asuntos Sociales, GV/EJ. At http://www.gizartelan. ejgv.euskadi.net/r45-obpubinm/es/contenidos/ informacion/publicacion_observ_inmigracion/es_publica/adjuntos/EPIE_2010_es.pdf.

Germani, Gino. *Política y Sociedad en una Época de Transición.* Buenos Aires: Paidós, 1971.

Gobierno Vasco, Gobierno de Navarra, and Euskararen Erakunde Publikoa. *VI Encuesta Sociolingüística del conjunto del territorio del euskara.* Vitoria-Gasteiz: GV/EJ, 2016. At http:// www.euskara.euskadi.eus/contenidos/informacion/argitalpenak/es_6092/adjuntos/2016%20 VI%20INK%20SOZLG%20-%20Euskal%20Herria%20gaz.pdf.

Godenau, Dirk, Sebastian Rinken, Antidio Martínez, and Gorka Moreno. *La integración de los inmigrantes en España: una propuesta de medición a escala regional.* Madrid: Ministerio de Empleo y Seguridad Social, 2014.

Ikuspegi. "Población de origen extranjero en la Unión Europea." *Panorámica 70* (August 2018). At http://www.ikuspegi.eus/documentos/panoramicas/es/pan70casOK.pdf.

———. "Percepciones y actitudes hacia la población de origen extranjero." *Barómetro 2018.* At http:// www.ikuspegi.eus/documentos/barometros/2018/bar_CAE_2018_CAS_web.pdf.

Ladin, Keren, and Steffen Reinhold. "Mental Health of Aging Immigrants and Native-born Men across 11 European Countries." *Journals of Gerontology Series B: Psychological Sciences and Social Sciences* 68, no. 2 (2013): 298–309.

Lindert, Jutta, Ondine S. von Ehrenstein, Stefan Priebe, Andreas Mielck, and Elmar Brähler. "Depression and Anxiety in Labor Migrants and Refugees—A Systematic Review and Meta-analysis." *Social Science and Medicine* 69 (2009): 246–57.

Llera, Francisco José, José M. Mata, Carmelo Moreno, and Rafael Leonisio. *Eusko-Barometro* (May 2018). At https://www.ehu.eus/eu/web/euskobarometro/home.

López-Rodríguez, Lucía, Hannah Zagefka, Marisol Navas, and Isabel Cuadrado. "Explaining Majority Members' Acculturation Preferences for Minority Members: A Mediation Model." *International Journal of Intercultural Relations* 38 (2014): 36–46.

Major, Brenda, John F. Dovidio, and Bruce G. Link, eds. *The Oxford Handbook of Stigma, Discrimination, and Health.* Oxford: Oxford University Press, 2018.

Moreno, Gorka. *Inmigración e impacto de la crisis. Anuario de la Inmigración en el País Vasco 2013.* Bilbao: Ikuspegi, 2011. At http://www.ikuspegi.eus/documentos/anuarios/anuario_2013_cas_OK.pdf.

———., ed. El proceso de integración del colectivo inmigrante en Euskadi. Análisis de la encuesta de la población inmigrante extranjera en la CAE. EPIE 2014. Bilbao: Universidad del País Vasco/ Euskal Herriko Unibertsitatea, 2018. At https://addi.ehu.es/bitstream/handle/10810/26909/ USPDF188687.pdf?sequence=1&isAllowed=y.

Navas, María Soledad, Lucía López-Rodríguez, and Isabel Cuadrado. "Mantenimiento y adaptación cultural de diferentes grupos inmigrantes: variables predictoras." *Anales de Psicología* 29 (2013): 207–216.

Páez, Dario, Nekane Basabe, Karmele Herranz, and Elena Zubieta. Aspectos psicosociales del entorno familiar de los educandos de Álava en el contexto general de la Comunidad Autónoma Vasca (CAV): Identidad social, lenguaje e inmigración en el País Vasco. Hernán Urrutia & Teresa Fernández Ulloa (Ed.), *Plurilingüismo y Educación en España y América (pp.* 141-201). Madrid: Dykinson, 2001.

Ruiz Olabuénaga, J. Ignacio, and Mª Cristina Blanco. *La inmigración vasca.* Bilbao: Universidad de Deusto, 1994.

Sevillano, Verónica, Nekane Basabe, Magdalena Bobowik, and Xabier Aierdi. "Health Quality of Life and Perceived Discrimination among Latin, African, and Eastern European Immigrants and Natives in Spain." *Ethnicity & Health* 19, no. 2 (2013): 178–97.

Shershneva, Julia. "La evolución del proceso de integración del colectivo inmigrante en la Comunidad Autónoma del País Vasco." In *Inmigración e impacto de la crisis. Anuario de la inmigración en Euskadi,* edited by Gorka Moreno. Bilbao: UPV/EHU, 2014. At http://www.ikuspegi.eus/ documentos/anuarios/anuario_2013_cas_OK.pdf.

Van Osch, Yvette M. J., and Seger M. Breugelmans. "Perceived Intergroup Difference as an Organizing Principle of Intercultural Attitudes and Acculturation Attitudes." *Journal of Cross-Cultural Psychology* 43 (2012): 801–21.

Ward, Colleen, Stephen Bochner, and Adrian Furnham. *The Psychology of Culture Shock.* East Sussex: Routledge, 2001.

Ware, John E., Mark Kosinski, and Susan D. Keller. "A 12-Item Short-Form Health Survey: Construction of Scales and Preliminary Test of Reliability and Validity." *Medical Care* 34, no. 3 (1996): 220–33.

# 10

# A Psychological and Psychosocial Analysis of the Radicalization of Young People of Immigrant Origin

*Joseba Atxotegi*

In this chapter, I will address one of the most complex and dramatic problems that our societies face today: the radicalization of young people of immigrant origin. I am going to refer especially to the more publicized attacks, such as those in Paris and Brussels in 2015 and 2016 and the attacks in Barcelona in 2017, as well as the realities of radicalization in the Basque Country.

## The Concept of Radicalization

Laurent Bonelli and Fabien Carrié (2018), authors of one of the largest studies on jihadism in France, define radicalization as a transgression of acceptable subversion. That is to say, there are reasonable degrees of transgression in social life, especially in the case of young people, but what is problematic is its intensity. From this perspective, there is a continuum between what would be naturally rebellious youth, hooliganism, and clear antisocial forms of behavior, with radicalization being the most extreme expression of this transgressive tendency.

However, this definition has its limitations because it places the emphasis, above all, on one aspect of radicalization, which is the intensity of the transgression, but not on other aspects such as the subject of transgression, beyond exceeding the limits of what society considers correct. So there would be transgression among young people who take drugs, for example, or those who belong to gangs.

## Psychological and Psychosocial Profile of Jihadists

As an expression of the debate in the social sciences and in mental health sciences about the psychological characteristics of people, generally young people, immersed in processes of radicalization and terrorism, John Horgan (2006) and David Puaud (2018) question the fact that the so-called terrorists have the profile of people with mental disorders, following the standard criteria of psychiatric classifications.

Thus, for example, it is a classic statement that terrorists are psychopaths and narcissists, something popularized by the media as a source of interest for the audience, given the morbid nature of the information. This approach fits poorly considering the amount of information that is known about the members of classic terrorist organizations, among which one of the basic characteristics is a high enough self-control and discipline to go unnoticed for long periods of time, enduring innumerable hardships by living in hiding, and tolerating lengthy jail sentences. The psychopath is defined by his impulsiveness rather than discipline and self-control, which allows him to be carried away by the moment, and the narcissist seeks to attract the gaze of others, and this exhibitionism is the antithesis of the terrorist's secrecy.

It should be noted that the term *psychopath* is increasingly used as an insult in the media, even in colloquial language, rather than as a clinical categorization. The Diagnostic and Statistical Manual of Mental Disorders (DSM-V), the most used psychiatric classification, does not even include it.

In response to these approaches, there must be a differentiation between terrorism linked to structured, hierarchical organizations and individual terrorists who act in an impulsive, individual, and very unplanned way.

The bombings at the Bataclán nightclub in Paris, in the airport, in the Brussels Zaventen airport in the Brussels metro, and especially on La Rambla in Barcelona are closer to belonging to the first type of terrorism. These acts were, relatively speaking, organized and planned, although these actors were far from the classic terrorist groups, endowed with a strong structure and organization. On the other hand, it should be noted that other attacks in Europe have had a more individual and impulsive profile, not linked to organized groups, and these are referred to as attacks carried out by "lone wolves."

In my opinion, based on this structuring, there are three types of terrorist radicalization: organized, with strict discipline of the group, typical of the large, classic terrorist groups; individual, involving "lone wolves"; and an intermediate form between the two, as is the case of the attacks in Catalonia, Bataclán, and Brussels.

In this section I will mainly use data and references from studies carried out in France. However, other countries have also developed instruments of study such as the barometer of the behavior of the MRCPV (Center de prévention de la radicalisationment à la violence/ Centre for the prevention of radicalization to violence) in Canada, the radicalization pyramid of the German office for the protection of the constitution, and the scale of terrorism by American psychologist Athali M. Moghadam (2005).

France has also set in motion the CPRAF (Cells for the Prevention of Radicalization and the Accompaniment of Families), as well as sixty RLC programs (referring to secularism and citizenship) framed in MNVI (National Mission of Care and Protection on the Phenomena of Radicalization). As has been said, soon there will be more people earning a living fighting radicalization than radicals, given the profusion of programs and centers.

However, there are a few empirical works on this type of terrorism. Fortunately, we already have important research such as those of Bonelli and Carrié (2018), who have developed an extensive study of nine hundred young people. The data was from the PIJ (Judicial Protection of Youth) of France. These authors obtained data through four sources: criminal measures by association linked to terrorism: 175 cases; civil measures for the risk of radicalization of minors: 189 cases; measures of precaution against the risk of radicalization: 364 cases; and measures to protect minors with radicalized parents (who have gone to war in Syria, for example): 140 cases.

Based on the study carried out and the data collected, the authors state that there are four types of radicalization:

1.  Compensatory radicalization: comes from a more personal, more individual dynamic. Individuals try to protect themselves from their dysfunctional, violent, insecure families. Through the practice of Islam, they find a new stronger identity that increases their self-esteem.
2.  Rebellious radicalization: it is also individual and is part of a context of acute family conflict. It is related to classic adolescent conflicts.
3.  Agnostic radicalization: young people who fail at school, close to the area of gangs and petty crime, who know the judicial and social system well. For them to admire jihadism, using their language, allows them to face the system they feel oppresses them, and destabilize and frighten the professionals with whom they deal.
4.  Utopian radicalization: accompanied by an ideological project and a political alternative to the social order.

Bonelli and Carrié (2018) propose that utopian radicalization is different from the other three, as we will analyze later. Each of the four types of radicalization has a psychological and psychosocial profile with its own characteristics, and the authors cited develop the following scheme:

| Family Group | Weak Regulation/Adjustment | Strong Regulation/Adjustment |
|---|---|---|
| Weak Integration | Appeasing radicalization<br>• Opposition to the family for reasons related to sexuality<br>• 67% woman | Rebellious radicalization<br>• Opposition to the family structure<br>• 50% males and females |
| Strong Integration | Agnostic radicalization<br>• for problems with institutions<br>• 88% men | Utopian radicalization<br>• for ideological reasons<br>• 69% men |

With the exception of utopian radicalization, the other three radicalizations are a reaction to family and institutional problems and seek to provoke, impress, and intimidate relatives and educators (speaking of the power of jihadist terrorism, of the battles won against the infidels in Afghanistan, Syria and other countries). The cases come from environments of social exclusion, precariousness, serious housing problems, sensitive neighborhoods, school failure, and so on; in the face of the difficult future that lies ahead, they position themselves in immediacy and focus on the increased self-esteem that they feel through their connection to the jihadist movement.

However, utopian radicalization, although it may share some of the psychosocial characteristics that define the other three types of radicalization, has other elements differentiating it along the lines of fanaticism, which I mentioned above and which, in my opinion, has more to do with paranoia and megalomania with psychopathic traits, as is usually pointed out in the media.

That is to say, recapitulating, based on Bonelli and Carrié's (2018) approach, there are two types of radicalized people: those who react to social and personal situations and the utopians.

In another piece of fieldwork carried out by the anthropologist Puaud (2018), it is also suggested that there are several types of jihadists:

1.  Those with serious psychological problems. Puaud (2018) refers to an interview in the newspaper *Le Figaró* with a senior police officer who stated that around 10 percent of those radicalized were recognized schizophrenics; he related the wave of radicalization to the suppression of beds for people suffering from psychosis in French hospitals, as a result of the problems of psychiatric reform in France that emptied the insane asylums without creating services for the attention those suffering from psychosis, as well as of the welfare cuts after the economic crisis of 2008.

2. Initiatory radicalization: this is not about young people from marginal classes, but from rural sectors, the middle class, and those without any academic problems. In Vesoul, in eastern France, for example, a dozen young people marched to fight in Syria. One was the son of a soldier, another the son of a doctor, another the son of a pharmacist. These young people said they were going to help the Syrian people. The first one who left immolated himself in February 2015. To the author it seems that they want to experience an initiatory experience, out of the ordinary, a rite of passage. In Lunel and Strasbourg, similar cases were seen.

3. Metaphysical radicalization is a life project.

4. Political radicalization: for example, for many jihadists, the Arab-Israeli conflict or the situation in Bosnia are the origin of their interest in politics and their radicalization.

In relation to the first outlined scheme (Scheme 1, 5) we could say that variants 2, 3, and 4 belong to the type of utopian radicalization described by Bonelli and Carrié (2018).

In any case, in relation to Puaud's (2018) argument, it should be noted that the category of young people of native origin who become radical jihadists has very few members; they exist, but they are a minority and join ISIS in the war zones in Syria and Afghanistan. These young people do not participate in terrorist actions against their own fellow citizens in their own country.

In the case of the attacks in Catalonia, unlike those in France and Belgium, the young people did not come from marginal neighborhoods, criminal environments, or the middle classes. The terrorists all came from Ripoll, a town in inland Catalonia, similar to Markina or perhaps Gernika in the Basque Country. Ripoll is considered the crucible and the origin of the kingdom of Catalonia; it is not just another town. It should be noted that, like the towns of the Basque Country, Ripoll does not have immigrant ghettos or structural, radical social exclusion. For this reason, the motivations for the terrorist action in these towns are more complex, as we will discuss in the following section. Those radicalized in Ripoll, who carried out the attacks in Barcelona and Cambrils, should occupy an intermediate category between those who are radicalized utopians and the reactive radicalized.

## On the Causes of Jihadist Radicalization

What can lead a whole group of young men apparently integrated in their society, in many ways similar to young immigrants in the Basque Country, to commit these acts of indiscriminate violence against their own fellow citizens, as in the case of the bombings in Barcelona and Cambrils in 2017, which caused fourteen deaths and dozens of wounded?

In the case of the attacks carried out by French and Belgian jihadists, almost all had been in prison; they lived in conflict-ridden neighborhoods (the so-called sensitive areas, to use politically correct language).

Some of the answers to these very difficult questions come from psychology and social psychology. From this perspective we can talk about risk factors, rather than causes, which are the conditions that favor these violent behaviors and allow these behaviors to arise.

Below, I propose the significant risk factors for the radicalization of immigrant youth, from the perspective of mental health:

*1. These youth have a complex and unstable identity and are more easily manipulated.*

The children of immigrants have a complex identity combining the culture of their parents with that of the host society (Atxotegi 2017), with cultural models that in some cases are very different, sometimes even contradictory. Their identity development may be further complicated when other risk factors are added, as we will see next.

Given their unstable identity, it is easy for these young men to be victims of sectarian processes that give them a solid and firm identity and reassure them emotionally. However, it is important to bear in mind that this sectarian indoctrination is established on the terrain of social tensions as we have discussed.

*2. They feel they are part of a precarious youth, with an even more complicated future than that of native young people.*

If the native/local youth already suffer from precariousness, especially since the financial crisis of 2008, immigrants have higher dropout rates and less education, which leads to worse jobs and wages. Integration suffers in this context. They tell me in the consultation of the service of attention to immigrants (SAPPIR, Psychopathological and Psychosocial Care Service for Immigrants and Refugees): how many high positions of the government, directors of institutes, or directors of a company are Moroccan or Arab? Of course, none of the twelve children in the Barcelona cell was in college, even though a considerable percentage of local youths of their age go to university. If the children of immigrants perceive themselves at a disadvantage relative to their native peers, this generates a very problematic situation.

*3. Integration of Youth.*

The integration of these youths is more difficult in the context of a narcissistic social model, based on emotion and intuition, which are much more easily manipulated than reason.

These young men with an identity crisis are very sensitive to suggestions by the sectarian groups that as jihadists they will be superior to the other youths who live in a corrupt, vice-ridden, secular society.

*4. The Existence of Racism.*

In Spain, a third of immigrants say they have suffered racism (SOS Racismo 2010). In France, a recent study (Centre Minkowska 2014) shows that applicants sending the exact same resume for a job were discriminated against based on the name on the return address and city center location: if it was a native name, the person was invited for an interview seventy-five times; but if there was an Arab name and an address in an outlying neighborhood, that person was invited for an interview just fourteen times.

In many European countries, including the Basque Country, Muslims encounter obstacles to worshipping. For example, in the Basque Country there is no mosque or minaret, and so Muslims must find a way to practice their religion, in basements or garages, which often even lack the proper sanitation conditions, making them feel that their religion has secondary status.

On the other hand, the fact that, in countries such as Spain and France, Catholicism can be studied in school but Islam cannot means that the teaching of the latter is often carried out by radical imams, in a system over which there is no control and that is often financed by Saudi Arabia.

In this sense, too, we can ask ourselves why, for example, none of the twelve young men from the cell that carried out the attack in Barcelona had a local romantic partner, which constitutes one of the best indicators of integration.

*5. They Have a Lower Self-Esteem.*

In relation to these aspects, Paula D'Ardenne (1999) has shown that immigrants and minorities have lower self-esteem than the native population, a result of feeling frequently excluded and socially undervalued. This situation makes these groups more easily manipulated by sectarian processes that offer them a superior identity with a supremacist model.

*6. Western neocolonialism generates wars that give rise to great suffering in the countries from which the immigrants originally come.*
This situation has great emotional repercussions, especially among young people living through a complex process of cultural identity construction and who feel excluded. We have already pointed out that in utopian radicalization, this type of discourse is of great importance.

*7. These young people need strong parental role models in the face of devaluation of the real parents.*
In the case of the attacks in Catalonia, a charismatic imam had great influence as a strong father figure for young terrorists to imitate and to follow. In France, this process has been studied a lot in radicalized young people who describe their parents as not integrated into the host society; these youth see their parents as failures in their migratory project, prematurely aged, living with chronic migratory grief, and thus as poor models to follow. All this has been accentuated by the financial crisis of 2008, which has destroyed innumerable migratory projects.

*8. Guilt manipulation as a factor.*
We know that many of these boys had taken drugs, had behaved in a way that was incompatible with their religion, and were manipulated by the idea that they should redeem themselves and repair their sins. It is easy to manipulate guilty feelings; all power systems do so. As Melanie Klein (1957) brilliantly demonstrates, it is very important that the reparation for guilt is not grandiose and sadistic and does not end up generating more suffering than the problem itself.

*9. Grim employment prospects as a factor.*
These jihadists were young and had low-level qualifications; they worked in factories, like Younes Abouyaaqoub, the author of the van attack on the Ramblas, or in kitchens, like Youssef Aallaa, and underwent periods of unemployment. None of the entire group of twelve young people went to university, like many young local people of their age in their towns do. They suffer because of an ethnification of the labor market in which, not only newly arrived immigrants, but their children (which is especially serious and worrisome) continue to occupy, as a collective, the lowest stratum in the labor market, demonstrating that the social elevator does not function well.

In any case, it is complex to relate this problem to radicalization since other young immigrants are also socially excluded but not radicalized. Perhaps, for example, Latin gangs would fit within this classification, looking to create a new identity.

**10. Access to education and the labor market as factors.**
There is a need to rethink the school model so that there is a real equality of opportunity in training and subsequent access to the labor market. Immigrants have double the school dropout rate than the native population, according to data from this year, and they find themselves segregated in the educational model, without access to semi-private education (There are private educational centers but they received substantial public subsidies). In the case of Catalonia, only 12 percent have access to such opportunities (*Informe de la Fundació Bofill* 2016).

**11. Athletics as opportunities for integration.**
Despite shortcomings in the education system, school is a meeting place with teachers and classmates from other groups. When the school ends there is a big break in the link, and young immigrants tend to disconnect from the native environments and from other groups, to ghettoize. Sports remain a space for socialization, but immigrants hardly play sports, as our own data show from SAPPIR (Psychopathological and Psychosocial Care Service for Immigrants and Refugees). The difficulties of access, of becoming federated and so on, should be revised to make it easier for immigrants and their children to participate in sports.

I have indicated in a very schematic way some significant psychosocial aspects to be considered in the debate over how our society should confront jihadist terrorism. But it must be very clear that from a psychosocial perspective we cannot talk about causes, because in this case, many of these psychosocial problems are suffered by other groups of immigrants who do not engage in violent behavior. Instead, we are discussing risk factors and circumstances that increase the chances of behavior.

Regrettably, in Spain, unlike in France, there have been hardly any discussions, let alone in-depth studies, on the causes of the jihadist attacks in Barcelona or on the networks dismantled in Irun, Bilbao, and Vitoria-Gasteiz, in the Basque Country. Our society has a difficult time moving from gestures, however well intentioned, to the analysis of social realities. And few realities are more important to analyze than the discomforting feelings that can lead twelve young people to indiscriminately kill their fellow citizens.

## Societal Responses

As a society, the collective grief for violent deaths is very complicated. The grief must be for all citizens who have died, including terrorists, who are also citizens and who form a part of the same social fabric. This grief is very difficult because there is a mixture of feelings that are very difficult to manage and integrate:

1.  Feelings of anger at any violent death of human beings either by terrorism
    or counterterrorism, by neocolonial wars, by ethnic cleansing. As evolu-
    tionary psychology has shown, humans, like other animal species, have an
    innate sense of justice, and we are very sensitive to everything that has to
    do with morality.

2.  Sadness for the loss of loved ones, neighbors, or simply fellow citizens that
    initiates the attachment instinct that is very important not only in humans,
    but in all mammals.

3.  Despair about the proper functioning of our society and the possibilities
    of coexistence.

All these feelings are very difficult to handle and bring to awareness the
high degree of destructiveness that we humans can have. Humans share aggression with other animal species, but our great development of symbolic functions
makes aggressiveness join hatred, revenge, destructive envy, and other feelings
that are very difficult to manage and integrate. Thus, tigers or lions hunt to get
the food they need, but not due to their emotions or fantasies of destruction.

In the official responses after terrorist attacks throughout Europe there
has been active and passive talk of mourning for citizens killed by terrorists.
However, as is well known, terrorists who are also citizens of society, despite
their terrible behavior, have also died in the attacks.

In a situation as painful and complex as mourning for violent deaths, four
very basic defense mechanisms are commonly used, as shown by cognitive psychology and psychoanalysis:

1.  Dissociation (dividing into two parts): Radically separating the good from
    the bad, so that they do not touch and have no relation. In this way the
    terrorists, and those who defend them, are radically separated from soci-
    ety: they are absolute inhuman evil, something that can only be eradicated.
    But that is not the reality, because, however monstrous they may be, they
    remain citizens of our society and we become equally monstrous if our atti-
    tude is to eliminate them at any price. If justice is vengeful, it is not justice.

2.  Searching for some scapegoat: these young people have had to suffer some
    kind of brainwashing or radical manipulation, because in our society this
    type of behavior is unimaginable. Thus, in Catalonia, the blame was placed
    on the imam of the Mosque of Ripoll, who was described as treacherous

and perverse. The mayor of Ripoll even said that he was a diabolical man. What can we do, then, if we face something diabolical, from beyond?

3. Negation: refusal to acknowledge reality. In the case of the dead in the attacks in Catalonia, we have to talk about mourning for fourteen people and not twenty-two, denying the very existence of those eight people also killed in a violent way. Nor even talk about them, as if these people and the groups that support them do not exist. This way, no one can care what family members, friends of those people, may be feeling: it seems that "magically" they no longer exist by not thinking about them.

4. Displacement of the problematic toward sensationalism, as the media often engage in, stirs the feelings of the population, showing the suffering of the victims and their families, favoring a exhibition of pain, and eventually converting the areas of attacks in areas of tourist attraction. Obviously, a few days later, a new story emerges that monopolizes all the headlines and the theme of the radicalization of young people of immigrant origin and the pain of the victims of the attacks disappears completely from the public and social agenda.

These psychological mechanisms, especially if not used extensively, are not a good strategy to solve a problem. Something is failing in our society when these attitudes are repeated.

The question is: How much truth can our society admit?

Violence reveals fundamental problems in our society, problems that are difficult to understand and very complex to analyze because they are multifactorial, and in today's world there are easy, magical solutions, tweeting, and images. But if we do not analyze and address the causes of the problem, there is a great risk that it will become chronic.

Unfortunately, what remains missing is an analysis of the causes, the origin of the deep discomfort that can lead some young people in a society to indiscriminately massacre their own fellow citizens.

## The Challenge of Psychological and Psychosocial Intervention with the Jihadists and with the Victims: On the Psychological Management of Victims' Trauma

It is well known and debated not only in healthcare but also in a debate that transcends this field, that there is an over-diagnosis of mental disorders, especially depression, which today covers much of the area of stress and grief, as Horowitz and Wakefield masterfully point out in *The Loss of Sadness* (2005).

And in the case of immigrants, this situation is even clearer and greater. As I point out (Atxotegi 2010, 2012), for example, can a person who is fully prepared to go on foot, running if necessary, twenty kilometers to look for a job, be diagnosed as depressed? Well, it frequently happens. It is on this basis that I described the Ulysses Syndrome in 2002 as chronic and creating multiple stressors among immigrants, and not as a mental disorder.

Along the same lines, I think it is important to debate whether there is an overdiagnosis of post-traumatic stress disorder, a situation linked in many cases to victims of terrorism. This is a picture that is often discussed in the media with little evidence and that, as we will see, for many researchers is really overdiagnosed.

The history of how this diagnosis of post-traumatic stress disorder came to be in the DSM clarifies this, since it was introduced into the psychiatric classifications after the Vietnam War by the enormous pressure of the powerful associations of war veterans who sought to have more economic aid and social benefits from the government after they returned to the United States. Given that the mutilated and those affected by physical injuries were granted huge financial aid, why not raise a whole area of even wider subsidy: mental pain? Given that the war disabled receive a lot of financial aid, an equivalent at the psychiatric level was sought.

As Chris R. Brewin (2006) points out in *Posttraumatic Stress Disorder: Malady or Myth?* (2006), this diagnosis does not arise from the research; it is not a scientific discovery, but it is incorporated into the DSM as a result of the pressure of interest groups. This author considers post-traumatic stress disorder a cultural and political construct.

In addition, even from quarters opposed to the Vietnam War, the introduction of this new disorder was also supported for non-scientific reasons, given that, because of the unpopularity of the war, there were also professionals who used the diagnosis of this disorder as a means, with humanitarian purposes, to prevent soldiers from returning to the battlefield.

Thus, the disorder was included in DSM-III, in 1980, by pressures from social groups, without field studies to support it. As Brewin (2006) points out, calling the condition a mental disorder has become part of the standard media reaction to traumatic situations and that most people are capable of developing.

It should be noted that the overlap between trauma and mental disorders has been masterfully studied from a psychoanalytic and classical psychopathological perspective. In the United States itself, the psychological problems related to traumas have been described since the American Civil War, and in 1889 Herman Oppenheim introduced the concept of *traumatic neurosis*. In his

*Studies on Hysteria* (1895) and *Five Lectures on Psychoanalysis* (1910), Freud associates trauma-related psychopathology with the impulse of repetition, as pointed out by Jean Laplanche (1985). In field studies, in 1906 Edouard Stierlin investigated the accident victims in Messina and observed that in 25 percent of those affected there were psychologically altered.

Abraham Kardiner, an American psychoanalyst with much experience in dealing with soldiers in World War II also developed the Freudian approach, *The Traumatic Neurosis of War* (1941), which relates the disturbances produced by trauma to hypervigilance and somatization.

Currently following the DSM-V criteria (2015), post-traumatic stress disorder is considered to affect 8 percent of the general population, a percentage much higher than that of schizophrenia and similar to that of depression, so it is understood that this overdiagnosis would constitute an important market niche for the pharmaceutical industry.

This diagnosis of PTSD raises the following main problems:

*1. The modification of the rules of diagnosis with the introduction of PTSD.*
With the diagnostic criteria used for post-traumatic stress disorder, the DSM alters its golden rule of not diagnosing by etiology, but by symptoms. Here the writers of the DSM skip over their own rules, showing once again that psychiatric diagnoses unfortunately lack rigor and are adapted to circumstances, in this case bowing to the pressures of the powerful groups of war veterans in the United States. The prime example, so often mentioned, of that lack of rigor in the classification of the DSM-V is how gay and lesbian associations pressured the meeting of the DSM-III committee in Chicago, making it impossible to leave if they did not remove homosexuality as a mental disorder, so the members of the committee removed it and could go home quietly. Obviously being gay or lesbian should never have been considered a mental disorder, and the reason why they were considered disorders in the history of psychiatry was a result of the submission of psychiatry to the pressures of social power.

All this shows us that psychopathology is still far from having a kind of "Tables of Mendeliev" based on solid theoretical criteria to classify disorders—tables that in the case of chemistry have not changed since the nineteenth century: They come from the times of Tsarism and have remained immovable under Lenin and Stalin in communism and under Putinism; the DSM almost doubles the number of disorders from one edition to another, in just twenty years, adapting to pressures and fashions. Thus the DSM I drafted in 1952 had 109 disorders and the DSM-V drafted in 2014 now has 396 disorders.

But the DSM-V not only violates its golden rule of not diagnosing by etiology with post-traumatic stress disorder, but elevates it to the category of conceptual referent in its classification model, puts it at the center of its classification model. That is to say post-traumatic stress disorder is not in any way just one more disorder but it has been turned into one of its twenty-two major categories of classification, in equal standing to depressive disorders, anxiety disorders, dissociative disorders; it rises to the category of honor, despite all the problems posed by this diagnosis.

### 2. Clinical errors in the approach to PTSD.
Regarding the over-diagnosis of this disorder, the following objections can be raised:

1.  From the clinical point of view, it is an enormous simplification to consider that all trauma must give rise to a single disorder, in this case PTSD. We know very well that stress, grief, and traumas can lead to a great diversity of mental disorders. Thus, clinically it is common to see how, after a traumatic situation, depressive, obsessive, and paranoid disorder, addictions appear.

2.  The duration of the disturbance due to the traumatic situation must be longer than one month (DSM-V, p. 272). It is absolutely normal, even common sense, that a person who has lived through a traumatic situation needs more than a month to overcome the situation, without this meaning that they suffer nothing less than a mental disorder!

3.  Witnesses, even those who have only heard about the traumatic event and not experienced it, may suffer from this disorder. In the United States, there has been such a "diagnostic furor" in relation to post-traumatic stress disorder.

4.  Any past, even forgotten, trauma can result in post-traumatic stress disorder. As is well known, there has been a strong tendency to constantly search for childhood traumas and, since memory is not very objective, it is not difficult for vulnerable people to have unreliable memories.

5.  Besides, to suffer from post-traumatic stress disorder, any trauma or adversity is valid; there is no singularity.

That is to say, we can see that there is a tendency to confuse trauma with disorder and to confuse the risk factor (trauma) with cause. It must be taken into account that in the stress-diathesis model (person) a single factor never determines the appearance of a disorder.

The risk of this overdiagnosis would be to treat people who do not have any disorder, with all the costs and side effects that may involve, mainly the use of psychotropic drugs; and to victimize people who have experienced traumatic situations, making it difficult for them to react psychologically and to put into action their own coping skills.

### 3. Our experience in the SAPPIR in relation to PTSD.

In our experience in the SAPPIR (Service of Psychopathological and Psychosocial Care for Immigrants and Refugees) in the Hospital de Sant Pere Claver in Barcelona, since 1994 we have been serving the foreign population, which in many cases has experienced extreme situations. This experience shows us that post-traumatic stress disorder is not as frequent a pathology as has been indicated and that it is overdiagnosed, as shown in the following graph of one of our investigations, in this case with more than one thousand immigrants and refugees. In our data of more than 1,500 immigrants who have been attended, the percentage of PTSD barely reaches 1.5 percent.

### 4. The risk of the overdiagnosis of PTSD is socially problematic.

The result of these successful campaigns to promote this disorder by the veterans' associations has been successful in the United States in subsequent years so that the diagnosis of the disorder has grown almost exponentially, after impressive marketing and promotion campaigns, even in the press, among those to highlight is the *New York Times* (Brewin 2006). However, years after this huge promotion of the disorder, a great controversy exists in the United States and has resulted in great concern about the effects of these campaigns for enormous negative effects.

Because after all these campaigns, the situation of war veterans, who were massively diagnosed as suffering from post-traumatic stress disorder, is very negative, very problematic, and has generated a great debate.

As has been pointed out, why did the veterans of the World War II, who lived through all the atrocities of Nazism, recover with hardly any problems from the traumas of the war, integrated themselves without major difficulties into American society, and yet now the veterans of war are a collective, full of problems, and with serious difficulties to integrate?

For some authors the cause is the massive profusion of the diagnosis of post-traumatic stress disorder that has stigmatized those who return from the war, and they have become in the eyes of the population, sick, violent, "dangerous madmen." All this has led to their isolation. They do not find jobs because people are afraid of them, and logically this rejection increases their frustration, their anger, their maladaptation, and their non-integration. Perhaps one of the best examples is at the movie character Rambo, a green beret, an elite soldier in the Vietnam War who does not adapt to living in society after returning to the United States. They think that they have risked their lives, their physical integrity, and their health for their country, and that now they are rejected.

And this overdiagnosis occurs not only in the context of the growing psychiatrization of everyday life, but sometimes, by an attempt to emphasize the seriousness of the problems suffered by these people to seek help, to give them resources. What is certain is that this psychiatrization of refugee pain has very negative consequences.

As Joel Paris (2013) points out in his review of the topic of trauma and psychopathology, there are numerous meta-analyses that show that no more than 20 percent of people who experience traumatic situations develop mental disorders, including post-traumatic stress disorder.

All the same, the victims of terrorism mostly do not suffer this disorder, but this does not mean that they do not need support and containment because it is normal that someone who has experienced a trauma re-experiences it at some time for a period of time, while developing it and dispelling it, but that does not mean that they suffer from a mental disorder. The long evolutionary history and natural selection would have given the majority of the population the ability to cope well with traumatic situations well.

From the evolutionary perspective we know that humans descend from ancestors who have survived a lot of dangers and adversities so we have great resilience, a great natural ability to resist traumatic situations.

## Bibliography

Atxotegi, Joseba. Cómo evaluar el estrés y el duelo migratorio. Escalas de evaluación de factores de riesgo en la migración. Aplicación al estrés y el duelo migratorio. Escala Ulises. Llançá: Ediciones El Mundo de la mente, 2010.

———. Emigrar en el siglo XXI: estrés y duelo migratorio en el mundo de hoy. El Síndrome del inmigrante con estrés crónico y múltiple-Síndrome de Ulises. Llançá: Ediciones el mundo de la mente, 2012..

Bonelli, Laurent, and Fabien Carrié. La fabrique de la radicalité. Une sociologie des jeunes djihadistes françaises. Paris: Seuil, 2018.

Brewin, Chris. Posttraumatic Stress Disorder: Malady or Myth? New Haven: Yale University Press, 2006.

Centre Minkowska Bulletin. Santé Mental et migration. Paris: Centre Minkowska, 2014.

D'Ardenne, Paula. Transcultural Counseling in Action. London: Sage Publications, 1999.

Diagnostic and Statistical Manual of Mental Disorders, I. New York: American Psychiatric Association, 1952.

Diagnostic and Statistical Manual of Mental Disorders, III. 1980. New York: American Psychiatric Association, 1980.

*Diagnostic and Statistical Manual of Mental Disorder, V.* New York: American Psychiatric Association, 2015.

Freud, Sigmund. "Estudios sobre la histeria." In *Obras completas de Freud.* Volume 1. Madrid: Editorial Biblioteca Nueva Biblioteca Nueva, 1895; 1984.

———. "Cinco estudios de Psicoanálisis. In *Obras completas de Freud.* Volume 5. Madrid: Editorial Biblioteca Nueva, 1910; 1984.

Fundació Bofill. *Informe annual de la Fundació Bofill.* Barcelona: Fundació Bofill, 2016.

Horgan, John. *Psicología del terrorismo.* Barcelona: Gedisa, 2006.

Horowitz, Allan V., and Jerome C. Wakefield. *The Loss of Sadness: How Psychiatry Transformed Normal Sorrow Into Depressive Disorder.* New York: Oxford University Press, 2005.

Kardiner, Abraham. *The Traumatic Neuroses of War.* New York: National Academies, *1941.*

Klein, Melanie. *Envidia y gratitud.* Barcelona: Paidós, 1957.

Laplanche, Jean. *Dictionaire de Psychoanalysis.* Paris: PUF, 1985.

Moghaddam, Fathali M. "The staircase to terrorism: a psychological exploration." *The American psychologist* 60, 2 (2005): 161-9.

Oppenheim, Herman. "Der Krieg und die traumatischen Neurosen." *Berliner Klinische Wochenschrift* 52: 257–61.

Paris, Joel. *Fads and Fallacies in Psychiatry.* London: RCPsych Publications, 2013.

Puaud, David. Le espectre de la radicalisation. L' administration sociale en temps de menace terroriste. Rennes: Presses de l'Ehesp, 2018.

*SOS Racismo Informe anual.* Madrid: SOS Racismo, 2010.

*SOS Racismo Informe anual.* Madrid: SOS Racismo, 2010.

Vega, William. "Lifetime Prevalence of Psychiatric Disorder among Mexican Americans." *Archives of Psychiatry* 55, 9 (1998): 771–78.

# Index

Note: Photographs, tables and associated captions are indicated by f or t following the page number.

UNICEF, 67
United Kingdom
  Basque children in exile in, 1–12
  Basque immigrant study in, 143–144
  migratory policies and interventions in,
    65–66, 70, 72
United States
  Basque diaspora to, ix, 45–61
  Basque exile to, 17
  Basque immigrant health in, 141
  Basque sheepherders in, viii–ix, 6, 16, 25–39,
    59–60
  colonization of, 46–48
  immigration laws in, 26–27, 36
  immigration to, viii, viii–ix, 16, 17–18, 25–39,
    45–61, 141
  political situation in, 66
  radicalization response in, 175
  undocumented immigrants in, 30, 36, 49–50
University of the Basque Country, vii, ix–x, 89,
  135, 170
University of Nevada, Center for Basque
  Studies, vii, viii
Uruguay
  Basque emigration to, 45, 50, 55, 160
  Basque sheepherders' emigration via, 28
  colonization of, 47
  consulates of, 55
  European emigration to, 48
US Army, 39
US Forest Service, 37

**V**
Venezuela, Basque emigration to, 17, 101
Vinson, Julien, 51–52
Vizcay, Martín, 28, 35, 38

**W**
Ward, Colleen, 139
weariness, in Ulysses Syndrome, 3, 21, 22

weather and climate
  acculturation to, 113
  Basque diaspora and exposure to new, 59
  Basque sheepherders' experiences with,
    34–35, 39
Wilson, R., 37
women
  as Basque immigrants (*see* immigrant wom-
    en's experiences)
  Basque psychological characterization of,
    41–42
  feminization of migrations by, 117, 119
  gender differences in European immigra-
    tion experiences of, 141–143, 146, 149–150,
    152–153
  gender roles and personality of, 120, 126, 133
  health system devaluing symptoms of, 23
  mother role of, 41–42, 117–118, 119, 128–132,
    134
  social status changes for, 35–36, 122, 124, 133
  violence toward refugee women, 67–68
Women's Building Association, 122, 137n7
Wong, Rebeca, 141
work. *See* employment
worry. *See* anxiety

**X**
"Xalbadoren heriotzean," 40–41
xenophobia
  European migratory policies and interven-
    tions reflecting, 67, 72, 74, 78, 169–170
  grief for experiences of, 21, 36–38

**Y**
Yemen, refugees from, 65
Yoldy, María, 36
young people. *See* children and young people

**Z**
Zure Ondoan program, 129–130

# About the Authors

OSCAR ÁLVAREZ GILA has a PhD in history. He is currently professor of Medieval, Modern and American History at the University of the Basque Country. He has also been a visiting professor at the Universities of Oxford (2008-2009), Nevada-Reno (2010-2011), Columbus State (2013-2014), and Stockholm (2016-2017). He also held the Jon Bilbao Chair at the Center for Basque Studies, University of Nevada, Reno, in 2019. He specializes in the study of inter-Atlantic migratory processes, mainly from the Basque Country to the Americas, during the 19th-20th centuries. Among his fields of research interest he has focused on the links between religion and migration, the institutionalization of Basque migrant communities abroad, and the construction of Basque diasporic identities through culture and symbology. He has also dealt with other related questions linked to migration, such as climate change or the use of genetics for historical studies of population.

AINARA ARNOSO has a PhD in psychology and a Master's in group analysis. She is assistant professor in the Department of Social Psychology at the University of the Basque Country UPV/EHU and she is director of the Master's in the psychology of organizations and psychosocial intervention at the same university. She has conducted research on gender violence, social exclusion, and evaluation of psychosocial intervention programs with different populations. From an applied perspective, her other research work focuses on migration processes and mental health, child-to-parent violence, and group interventions. Recent work about immigrants explores their health and mental health, as well as Spanish emigrants' intention to return and associated psychosocial factors.

JOSEBA ATXOTEGI is former secretary of the transcultural section of the World Psychiatric Association, psychiatrist, tenured professor of the University of Barcelona, professor at the University of Berkeley from 2005 to 2019, and guest professor at other universities in places such as Stanford University, Tokyo, New York, Paris, Oxford, and King's College, London. He is director of a postgraduate online course "Mental Health and Psychological Interventions with Immigrants, Minorities and the Socially Excluded" at the University of Barcelona in collaboration with the Paris V University and UC Berkeley director of SAPPIR (Servicio de Atención Psicopatológica y Psicosocial a Inmigrantes y Refugiados) of Hospital

Sant Pere Claver in Barcelona. The year 2002 has described the Ulysses Syndrome as an immigrant syndrome with chronic and multiple stresses. He serves as coordinator of Athena Network, a global network for the psychosocial help for immigrants living in extreme situations. His blog is "Salud mental en tiempos difíciles" in Publico the Newspaper.

NEKANE BASABE, PhD, is a full professor of social psychology at the University of the Basque Country in Spain and a member of the Research Group "Culture, Cognition and Emotion" (http://www.ehu.es/es/web/psicologiasocialcce). The main topics of her research are: health social psychology, migration, cultural shock, acculturation, and ethnic identities, and collective processes of cognition and emotion and cross-cultural social psychology. Since 1991 she has taught several undergraduate and graduate courses: health social psychology, social psychology, group, and organizational social psychology, psychology, and communication. A summary of her CV can be found at: http://orcid.org/0000-0003-4753-4299.

EDURNE ELGORRIAGA obtained her bachelor's degree in psychology from the University of Salamanca in 2003 and a PhD in Psychology from the University of the Basque Country UPV/EHU in 2011. She has a Master's degree in group analysis (University of Deusto, 2007). Currently, she is an assistant professor in the Department of Social Psychology at the University of the Basque Country UPV/EHU. Her research work focuses on migration processes and mental health, on child-to-parent violence, and on groups. She has participated in the design of an intervention program, "Early Intervention Program in Situation of Child-to-Parent Violence," and she has experience in the evaluation of psychosocial intervention programs with different populations.

IZASKUN IBABE is an assistant professor in the Department of Social Psychology and Methodology in Behavioral Sciences at the University of the Basque Country UPV/EHU, where she has worked since 1992. She has taught research methods courses at university to undergraduate students and postgraduate students. She has written extensively for academic journals on a wide range of subjects, including research methodology. She has conducted research on the psychology of family violence. She is codeveloper of the Early Intervention Program in Situation of Child-to-Parent Violence and a coauthor of its curriculum. Her recent work about immigrants explores their health and mental health, as well as Spanish emigrants' intention to return and associated psychosocial factors.

XABIER IRUJO is the director of the Center for Basque Studies at the University of Nevada, Reno. He was the first guest research scholar of the Manuel Irujo Chair at the University of Liverpool and has taught seminars on genocide and cultural genocide at Boise State University and at the University of California, Santa Barbara. He holds three Master's degrees in linguistics, history, and philosophy and has two PhDs in history and philosophy. Dr. Irujo has lectured in various American and European universities on issues related to Basque history and politics, and has specialized throughout his career in genocide studies. He has mentored several graduate students and he is a member of the editorial board of four academic presses. Dr. Irujo has authored more than fifteen books and a number of articles in specialized journals and has received awards and distinctions at national and international level. His recent books include *Gernika: Genealogy of a Lie* (Sussex Academic Press, 2019) and

*Gernika 1937: The Market Day Massacre* (University of Nevada Press, 2015). A summary of his CV can be found at: http://basque.unr.edu/academics-people-irujo.html.

IÑAKI MARKEZ is a physician specializing in psychiatry and a doctor of neurosciences at the University of the Basque Country. He is a university specialist in legal and forensic psychiatry and a social investigator. He is a professor in the master's degree in addiction at the University of Deusto. He is or has been a member of the Addiction Advisory Council of the Basque Government, Mental Health Advisory Council of the Department of Health of the Basque Government (2009-2014), OME-AEN, Basque Association of Mental Health and Community Psychiatry (president of 2008-2014), and other professional and scientific associations of mental health and public health. He is also a member of the board of trustees of the Castilla del Pino Foundation. He serves on the editorial board of several specialized publications and is director of the *Norte de salud mental* journal and Ekimen Publishing promoter. His recent books include *José Guimón, historias de un arquitecto de la psiquiatría y psicología vascas* (Ekimen editorial, 2018) and *De la Sexualidad diversa a la terapia (in)necesaria* (In press, 2020).

SONIA G. PADOAN RIBEIRO DE LUCA, is a postdoctoral researcher of social psychology at the University of the Basque Country in Spain and a member of the research group "Culture, Cognition, and Emotion" http://www.ehu.es/es/web/psicologiasocialcce. She graduated with a degree in clinical psychology at UNITAU, University of Taubate in Brazil, and did her PhD at the UPV/EHU, University of the Basque Country in Spain in social psychology. The main topics of her research are migration, culture shock, acculturation, ethnic identities, and organizational psychology. She has also specialized in clinical psychology working with individual and group therapies.

SORAYA RONQUILLO is a Peruvian social worker, popular educator, and decolonial feminist activist. After graduating with a diploma in social work from the Pontifical Catholic University of Peru in 1987, she gained experience working with women in popular canteens in Lima until 1999. In 1999, she moved to Spain with the aim of working with migrated population and continued her professional training as well as her studies of equality, interculturality, and development cooperation. At the same time, she worked as a tutor in the practice of students of social work and social anthropology at the University of the Basque Country. She also worked on family intervention projects with children at risk. Since 2009, she has been a member of Bidez Bide association and has been helping Latin-American immigrant women. Currently, she is studying her fourth year of social anthropology at the University of the Basque Country.

KARMELE SALABERRIA is a doctor in clinical psychology. She is a professor in the Department of Psychology at the University of the Basque Country. Her research has focused on the study of efficacy of psychological treatments in various mental disorders (social anxiety, mixed anxiety and depression disorder, chronic schizophrenia, and chronic pain), as well as the development of a psychological support program for populations suffering from chronic stress as immigrants and relatives of patients with severe mental disorders. She has taught at the faculty of psychology in the subjects of psychological treatments and cognitive-behavioral therapy.

ANALIA SANCHEZ, a doctor of psychology, works in private clinical practice. She has researched psychosocial aspects of the immigrant population in Argentina and Venezuela and she has developed psychological support programs for immigrant and Basque children through plastic expression. She has taught at the faculty of psychology in the subjects of personality psychology, health psychology, and child and adolescent treatment.

Made in the USA
Monee, IL
30 March 2022

93560887R00125